THE AutoCAD 3D Book

SECOND EDITION

George O. Head

Charles A. Pietra

Kenneth J. L. Segal

VENTANA
PRESS

THE AUTOCAD 3D BOOK

Library of Congress Cataloging-in-Publication Data

Head, George O., 1945-
        The AutoCAD 3D book / George O. Head, Charles A.
Pietra, and Kenneth J. L. Segal. -- 2nd ed.
            p.   cm.
        Includes bibliographical references and index.
        ISBN 0-940087-67-7
        1. AutoCAD (Computer program) I. Pietra, Charles A.
        II. Segal, Kenneth J. L.   III. Title.
T385.H373 1991
620'.0042'02855369--dc20   91-387
                                    CIP

Book design: David M. Kidd, Oakland, CA
Cover design: Holly Russell, Durham, NC
Technical editor: Greg Malkin, Cleveland, OH
Editorial staff: Marion Laird, Linda Pickett, Jeff Qualls, Pam Richardson
Production staff: Rhonda Angel, Alex Taylor, Karen Wysocki

Second Edition, First Printing
Printed in the United States of America

Ventana Press, Inc.
P.O. Box 2468
Chapel Hill, NC 27515
919/942-0220
FAX 919/942-1140

^{THE} AutoCAD 3D Book

SECOND EDITION

Limits of Liability and Disclaimer of Warranty

Trademarks

Trademarked names appear throughout this book. Rather than list the names and entities that own the trademarks or insert a trademark symbol with each mention of the trademarked name, the publisher states that it is using the names only for editorial purposes and to the benefit of the trademark owner with no intention of infringing upon that trademark.

About the Authors

George O. Head is president of Associated Market Research, a business management consulting firm for architects and engineers. He is the developer of A/E Solutions, a project management and financial accounting software package for architects and engineers. He is also author of *AutoLISP in Plain English* and co-author of *1000 AutoCAD Tips and Tricks* and *The AutoCAD Productivity Book* (all published by Ventana Press).

Charles A. Pietra is owner of MicroCAD Managers, an educational computer consulting company in Syracuse, NY, which specializes in CAD/CAE training services. A veteran AutoCAD trainer and curriculum developer, he has conducted workshops and lectures on AutoCAD and computer graphics. He may be reached at

MicroCAD Managers, Inc.
100 Elwood Davis Rd.
North Syracuse, NY 13212
(315) 451-4810

Kenneth J. L. Segal is research analyst for CADapult Ltd., a Wilmington, Delaware-based Authorized AutoCAD Dealer and Developer, which integrates systems for architectural design and facilities management. A longtime contributor to *CADence* magazine, he has reviewed and developed solutions for 3D modeling, animation and scene simulation.

Acknowledgments

The authors and publisher wish to express appreciation to the following individuals:

Bill Kramer
Bob Bradlee
Sidney and Norma Segal
Bob Mader
Cecelia Robinson
Ann Elizabeth Luoma
Jennie Pietra
Clare Pietra
Mary Votta
Brenda Williams

Illustration Credits for Chapter 11:

Figures 11-1, 11-2, 11-3 and 11-7 courtesy of Dinet Associates, Syracuse, NY.

Figures 11-4 and 11-5 courtesy of Environmental Design and Research, Syracuse, NY.

Figures 11-6 courtesy of MicroCAD Managers, Syracuse, NY.

Figure 11-8 courtesy of Environmental Design and Research, Syracuse, NY.

Figure 11-9 courtesy of Autodesk, Inc., Sausalito, CA.

Contents

CONTENTS

CONTENTS

CONTENTS

CONTENTS

List Of Figures

CONTENTS

CHAPTER THREE

CONTENTS

CHAPTER SIX

CHAPTER NINE

CONTENTS

Introduction

WHO NEEDS 3D?

With AutoCAD's Releases 10 and 11, you'll never draw the same way again. Why? Because everything you draw will be in 3D. Therefore, entities now have a Z coordinate in addition to the usual X and Y. Your drawings may look the same as before; but in reality, your entities have been created in 3D space, opening up vast new opportunities for managing almost any design or project more productively.

The 3D capabilities in Releases 10 and 11 enhance efficiency and productivity by giving you the tools you need to produce multiple views, elevations, perspectives, surfaces, meshes and renderings. But it goes beyond efficiency and productivity. Just as using CAD instead of a drawing board created a new world of opportunities, drawing—indeed *thinking*—in 3D has implications for nearly every AutoCAD professional, whether for 2D or 3D applications. And the possibilities are just beginning to be tapped.

Each AutoCAD user will discover which 3D tools fit his or her needs. Engineers can build computer-generated models as prototypes, to check tolerances and fits, thus avoiding time-consuming, expensive production of real prototypes. Architects can create realistic models, to avoid the cost of building miniatures. With an AutoCAD drawing, they can show how a structure might look from the street, or quickly "walk" a client through the building. And all AutoCAD professionals will appreciate the many new vistas Releases 10 and 11 offer in terms of multiple windows, dynamic viewing and the new User Coordinate System.

Anyone who's ever drawn more than one view of the same object can benefit from the increase in efficiency and productivity provided by AutoCAD's new 3D tools. And, with some practice and patience, drawing in 3D will become even easier than drawing in 2D.

WHAT IS 3D?

3D isn't a feature, like OBJECT SNAP or ZOOM. Rather, it's a series of tools that let you draw entities in 3D space, view them from any angle, manipulate them in entirely new ways and produce realistic computer models of objects quickly and inexpensively.

In normal 2D drafting, you were forced to draw an object as many as five times to create a representation of various views. With Releases 10 and 11, instead of drawing five different views of the same object, you draw it once, then rotate the object or viewpoint to access the desired view.

Look beyond the traditional ideas of 3D to the enhancements of AutoCAD for the purpose of 3D design. A few examples:

AutoCAD's User Coordinate System lets anyone who needs to work with more than one coordinate system at a time—civil and structural engineers, surveyors—define an unlimited set of coordinates. Even if you're drawing in PLAN view, you can set a variety of coordinate systems for entities and groups of entities. These coordinate systems can be rotated—even in PLAN view. This means you can maintain the original coordinates while the entire coordinate system is shifted. You can also translate coordinates between coordinate systems.

DYNAMIC VIEW (DVIEW) was developed for 3D to let you view an object from any angle and plane. But it has other outstanding features. The ZOOM is what might be considered a hardware zoom. By moving the cursor, you dynamically increase or decrease the magnification. A new dynamic PAN lets you "drag" the object rather than point to displacements. Even in PLAN view, an object can be rotated in any direction and viewed from any angle.

One of the most alluring aspects of 3D is its ability to maintain multiple windows on the same drawing—useful for 2D as well as 3D applications. With Releases 10 and 11 multiple viewports, you can switch between windows effortlessly. You can draw and edit in any window and the others are updated immediately. In addition to saving and restoring views and windows, you can even plot from each window individually.

These are only a few of the things you can do with the powerful 3D tools provided in Releases 10 and 11. The purpose of this book is to make learning and using these tools as easy and painless as possible. It will take a little effort, but you took the first step when you bought AutoCAD in the first place!

WHAT'S INSIDE?

The AutoCAD 3D Book teaches you how to use the powerful tools now available with AutoCAD's Releases 10 and 11. Chapters 1 through 6 take you step by step through the creation of a wire frame 3D drawing, then through the process of adding surfaces and meshes.

Veteran users will appreciate Chapter 7, "New Twists to Old Commands," which discusses numerous new and creative ways to adapt commands you've been using for years. And Chapter 8, "Tips and Tricks," gives everyone a head start with dozens of hands-on techniques and shortcuts for using 3D most effectively.

Chapter 9 introduces you to Solid Modeling and its applications. Chapter 10 is a tutorial for creating a solid model with AutoCAD Release 11 Advanced Modeling Extension. Chapter 11 focuses on presentation CAD, including shading, rendering, paint and animation software. This chapter shows you how to use your 3D models in presentations or as data to be manipulated in presentation software.

Finally, "The AutoCAD 3D Library" is a set of 30 AutoLISP routines that help smooth out the rough edges of Autodesk's ambitious releases. All users can benefit from the simpler programs; more advanced users will be able to revise many of the AutoLISP programs for additional power and performance. An optional diskette, containing all the programs found in the book, can save you the considerable time it takes to type them all in.

HOW WELL SHOULD YOU KNOW AUTOCAD?

This book assumes you understand the basics of CAD or AutoCAD, including commands such as LINE, ARC, CIRCLE, OBJECT SNAP and LAYER. You need not be an expert AutoCAD user, nor is any AutoLISP programming experience required. You'll learn new concepts to help you draw smarter and faster and work effectively with AutoCAD's new dimension.

HOW TO USE THIS BOOK

The AutoCAD 3D Book was written as a hands-on reference, based on the concept of learning by doing, to get you "thinking in 3D" as quickly as possible. Of course, you'll also find the book invaluable as a lasting reference; it will be the first book you turn to for information on the 3D features of Releases 10 and 11.

Beginning AutoCAD users should carefully read Chapters 1 through 8, taking the time to keyboard the drawings and examples.

If you're a veteran AutoCAD user, you'll probably find *The AutoCAD 3D Book* gives you all the information you need to become acquainted with Releases 10 and 11 without additional book purchases.

While you're learning 3D, work on your computer with the program in front of you. You can receive the most from the tutorial by working through the examples.

Read each explanation as it's presented. Then type, pick and draw as requested. Compare your screen with the illustrations given, then read the final explanation and tips that follow. Experiment with the different and new constructions relating to each concept.

SOFTWARE AND HARDWARE REQUIREMENTS

1. AutoCAD Releases 10 or 11. (However, to do the exercise in Chapter 10, you will need AutoCAD Release 11 and the Advanced Modeling Extension.)
2. A computer and operating system that can run AutoCAD. (If you have an MS-DOS computer, then 640K RAM memory is the minimum recommendation.)
3. A graphics board and monitor that can run AutoCAD.
4. A plotter or printer-plotter is valuable, but optional.
5. AME is required for Chapter 10.

RULES OF THE ROAD

As you know from working with AutoCAD, there are many ways to choose the same command:

Type it from the keyboard,
Pick it from a screen menu,
Pick it from the pull-down menus or dialog boxes, or
Pick it from the tablet menu.

It's too cumbersome to explain each method for every command each time it's used in this book. Instead, we do the following:

When a new command is first introduced, all the possibilities for choosing the command are given. After that, the command is shown between angle brackets (< >). Nested or multipart commands are separated by commas.

For example, a ZOOM ALL is later presented as <ZOOM, A>. A CIRCLE drawn as a center radius is <CIRCLE, CEN-RAD>.

<OS-ENDPOINT> means that you're to set OBJECT SNAP to Endpoint or the requested setting.

"Pick" refers to the pick button on your cursor. This is generally button 1, but it may differ from computer to computer.

"Confirm" refers to several commands that require confirmation. Any time you're asked to select objects, the objects selected are highlighted. You then confirm your selection by pressing <RETURN> or, in many cases, the second button on your cursor.

CROSSING or WINDOW refers to a method of selecting objects. When you're asked to select objects, you can type C or W, which lets you encircle the object with a box.

If you're manually typing AutoLISP programs featured in "The Auto-CAD Reference Library," distinguish between a 1, an l and an i, as well as a 0 and an O. If you find the AutoLISP programs useful, an optional diskette can get you using these programs immediately and without tedious error-checking. Finally,

Type: means to type the designated data in from the keyboard. <RETURN> indicates that you're to press the RETURN or ENTER key. Except with text, you can also press the space bar.

YOU'RE ON YOUR WAY . . .

With Releases 10 and 11, you can greatly improve the efficiency and quality of your drawings—whether 2D or 3D. AutoCAD's new approach to drawing won't go away with future releases, and you'll come face to face with these new commands at some point down the ever-changing CAD road. Learning something new is best done in increments—so let's take the first step.

Section I

WORKING IN AUTOCAD'S
NEW DIMENSION

1 **Basic Features**

OVERVIEW

Until Release 10, AutoCAD was based on a 2D coordinate system.

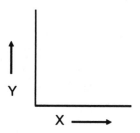

That is, the positive **Y** coordinates go up and the positive **X** coordinates go to the right. But now, AutoCAD's Release 10 provides features for drawing in 3D, which adds the **Z** coordinate. So where is **Z**?

We explain the 3D coordinate system by using what we call the *right-hand rule.* If you point the thumb of your right hand toward positive **X** and point your forefinger toward positive **Y**, then the remaining fingers, held away from your hand, point toward positive **Z**.

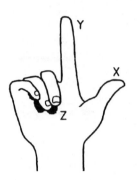

In Figure 1-1, note the direction of the arrows indicating the direction of the **X** and **Y** coordinates. The heavy lines around the square indicate the original 2D plan view. Assuming the square is one unit, the coordinates beginning at the point of origin are **0,0,0**; the top left, **0,1,0**; the upper right, **1,1,0**; and the lower right, **1,0,0**.

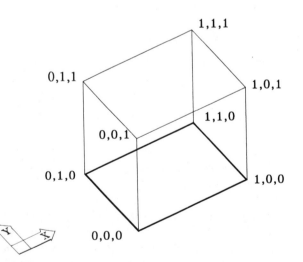

Figure 1-1: The World Coordinate System.

In each case the third coordinate is 0. This is the **Z** coordinate. Therefore, the point in space one unit above the point of origin is **0,0,1** (and so forth) around the points, one unit above each corner.

OUT WITH THE OLD, IN WITH THE NEW

To understand the features available with Releases 10 and 11, you need to understand some of the features that became available when AutoCAD first attempted 3D with Version 2.5. At that time, **ELEVATION** and **THICKNESS** were introduced. **ELEVATION** created the default value for the **Z** coordinate, drawing an entity at the default elevation above the **X, Y** plane. This provided a limited way to produce the **Z** coordinate for some entities.

THICKNESS gives you a shortcut for drawing 3D objects. By providing an **ELEVATION** of **0** and a **THICKNESS** of **4**, you could draw a square that would *extrude* four units into the **Z** axis. By choosing a 3D **VIEWPOINT**, you could examine wire frame views of the cube from different angles.

Version 2.6 and Release 9 provided three major improvements to this modest beginning: **3DLINE**, **3DFACE** and **3D FILTERS**.

3DLINE has been eliminated and replaced with **LINE**, with full 3D capabilities.

You can think of **3D FILTERS** as the "Gimme a Z" concept. In order to draw a 3D line, you had to pick a point on the **X, Y** plane. AutoCAD then asked for the value of the **Z** coordinate.

3D FACE provided a way to produce the illusion of a solid object and also let you produce hidden lines.

These limited beginnings quickly earned AutoCAD the nickname of "2 1/2 D" by its users. But as rudimentary a beginning as this was, these tools still play an important part in the procedures of the new releases.

But it's not just the addition of a few commands that have changed AutoCAD from its 2 1/2 D beginnings to a full 3D program; the entire structure of the program and its underlying precepts have changed. Let's briefly examine the new 3D tools you'll be using with Releases 10 and 11.

AUTOCAD'S USER COORDINATE SYSTEM

The basic problem with any 3D CAD system is that you're using a 2D input and a 2D output device. In other words, the only way you can select all coordinates at one time is through keyboard input. Of course, this is extremely difficult and cumbersome. The more natural way would be to use features such as **SNAP** and **OBJECT SNAP** and point to where you need to draw.

In AutoCAD's 2D world before Release 10, there was only one coordinate system, the **X, Y** system described previously. We now call this original system the **World Coordinate System (WCS)**.

Unfortunately, you can pick only two coordinates at a time using a mouse or digitizer. Therefore, you need a simpler way to pick all three coordinates: we call this method the **User Coordinate System (UCS)**.

Because an input device can select only two coordinates at once, a method was devised to choose which two coordinates would be input. By reassigning the directions of **X** and **Y** to reflect only one side of the object, the **Z** is held constant. As a result, you're drawing on only one 2D plane at any one time.

Every side you draw on will require its own **UCS**. Each User Coordinate System can be named, saved and recalled. As a result, you'll always be working with two dimensions somewhere in the drawing.

A NEW WAY TO VIEW

The most frustrating feature of AutoCAD's older 3D views was the **VIEWPOINT**. This "bulls-eye" approach to choosing the angle of view never let you know what was going to be drawn on your screen. The new method, dynamic view or **DVIEW**, is far superior.

DVIEW lets you rotate the object dynamically on the screen so that you can see exactly the angle of view and what you're looking at. Only part of the image is drawn on the screen until the cursor stops moving. You may also rotate only part of a complicated object. When the view is finally selected, the rest of the object rotates into view.

MANY POINTS OF VIEW

One of the most valuable and essential features of Releases 10 and 11 is the ability to split screens into multiple views (**VPORTS**). When you're drawing dynamically in 3D, it's vital to divide the screen into at least two different angles on the same object. As you begin to draw, you may have your **UCS** incorrectly set and not realize it; your drawing might look perfectly correct on the screen. Splitting the screen between different angles lets you confirm the accuracy of what you're drawing. You can also see when you've made a mistake and are drawing a line out into "deep space," rather than on the object.

But the real reason for multiple viewports is to let you work on the drawing from several views at once. That way, you can toggle from one view to another without rotating the drawing.

WHICH WAY IS UP?

When you first start working with 3D, it's often difficult to visualize where you are. In fact, while working with a wire frame drawing, two people may actually see the object from different vantage points.

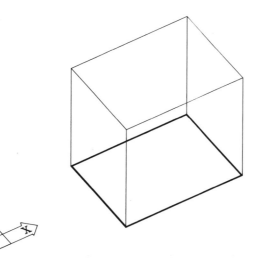

Figure 1-2: Are you on the top or the bottom?

For example, many people may see Figure 1-2 from the top of the box looking down. The heavy lines form the bottom of the box as you look into it. Others may see the box from the bottom, with the heavy lines forming the bottom of the box from underneath. See if you can adjust your eyes to see the box from both angles. As you do, the box will seem to move as your eyes adjust.

As a result, you must develop techniques to create faces and hide selected lines so that you know for sure which side you're actually drawing on.

Now look at Figure 1-3. This is how it would appear if you were looking at it from the bottom with the lines hidden.

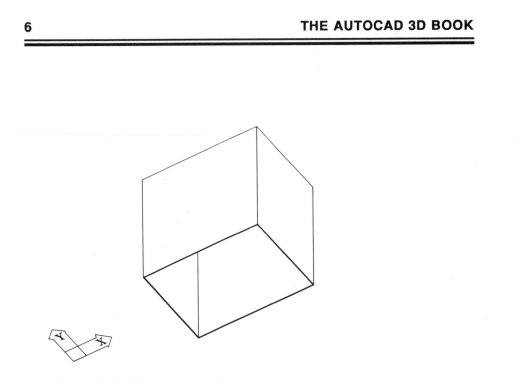

Figure 1-3: From the bottom.

Now look at Figure 1-4. This is how it would appear if you were looking at it from the top with the lines hidden.

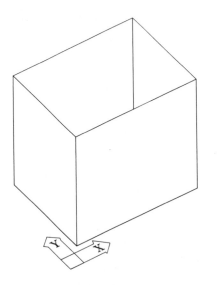

Figure 1-4: From the top.

GIVING SHAPE TO A DRAWING

One of the most powerful and valuable 3D tools is *surface modeling*—models created with Releases 10 and 11 can be transferred over to AutoSHADE or another shading program for shading and rendering. But for AutoSHADE to properly do its work, it must know the shape of an object. This is where meshes come in.

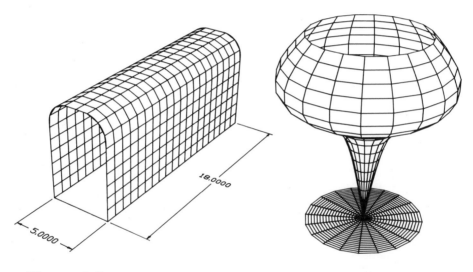

Figure 1-5   **Figure 1-6**

3D meshes are really a series of multiple **3DFACES** applied around the curvature or shape of the object. The density of the meshes is controlled by two system variables, **SURFTAB1** and **SURFTAB2**.

There are four special-purpose meshes and one general-purpose mesh available to you in Releases 10 and 11.

- **RULESURF** creates a surface mesh between two objects.

- **TABSURF** uses only one entity and extends the surface mesh out from the entity, using its general shape.

- **REVSURF** creates a circular mesh around a central axis.

- **EDGESURF** is used with a figure with exactly four sides or edges. Each side may be a polyline or a 3D polyline.

The **3DMESH** command creates a general-purpose mesh that requires you to assign each vertex to it. This command is more applicable through AutoLISP.

By using each of these commands correctly, you have the tools necessary to shape your models and then use them, with realistic renderings, through AutoSHADE.

MOVING ON

We've given you an idea of some of the powerful new tools available to you with Releases 10 and 11. The next chapter gets you drawing in 3D right away and gives you a good idea of how to use these important new tools.

So, let's get started.

2 Learning the Ropes

To begin your adjustment to the world of 3D, let's start with a simple exercise. You'll draw a cube with faces added to each side, and each side hatched with a different pattern. By rotating the cube and hiding the lines, you'll learn to visualize the effect of **DVIEW** and other 3D drawing tools.

STARTING YOUR DRAWING

So that you're drawing using the same units, make the following selections. Enter a new drawing (using item number **1** from the main AutoCAD menu). Name it whatever you like.
Once you're in the AutoCAD drawing, type in the following:

Type: UNITS <RETURN>

Response: Enter Choice, 1-5.

Type: 2 <RETURN>

This is decimal units.

Response: Number of digits to right of decimal point (0 to 8).

Type: 2 <RETURN>

Response: Choice, 1 to 5 (Angle measurement).

Type: 1 <RETURN>

This is decimal angles.

Response: Number of fractional places for display of angles (0 to 8).

Type: 2 <RETURN>

Response: Enter direction for angle 0.00.

Type: 0 <RETURN>

Response: Do you want angles measured clockwise?

Type: N <RETURN>

Now set your limits.

Type: LIMITS <RETURN>

Response: ON/OFF <Lower left corner.>

Type: 0,0 <RETURN>

Response: Upper right corner.

Type: 10,8 <RETURN>

Type: ZOOM A <RETURN>

Type: GRID 1 <RETURN>

Type: SNAP 1 <RETURN>

ZOOM ALL will ensure that you have a full grid on your screen.

DRAWING THE CUBE

You're now ready to draw the cube. Set **ELEVATION** and **THICKNESS**, then draw a square.

Type: ELEV <RETURN>

Response: New current elevation.

Type: 0 <RETURN>

Response: New current thickness.

Type: 4 <RETURN>

You can also set elevation and thickness from the screen menu by picking **SETTINGS** and then **ELEVATION**, or you can choose elevation and thickness from the pull-down menus. Move your cursor to the top of the pull-down menus and pick **SETTINGS**. Then select a submenu box called **ENTITY CREATION**. This will bring down a dialog box of entity creation modes.

At the bottom of the dialog box is **ELEVATION** and **THICKNESS**. You can change these by pointing to **ELEVATION** or **THICKNESS** and changing the number. Remember, when you change a feature in a dialog box, **CONFIRM** by choosing **OK** or **<RETURN>**.

Now that **ELEVATION** is set to **0** and **THICKNESS** is set to **4**, draw a 4 x 4 square using the **LINE** command (see Figure 2-1). Note the arrows pointing to the **X** and **Y** axes. In all Release 10 drawings, the **UCS** icon will appear in the lower left-hand portion of the screen to indicate where **X** and **Y** are in relation to the User Coordinate System. If the **UCS** and the World Coordinate System (**WCS**) are the same, an additional **W** will appear under the **Y**. If the **UCS** icon doesn't appear on your screen:

Type: UCSICON <RETURN>

Response: ON/OFF/All/Noorigin/ORigin.

Type: ON <RETURN>

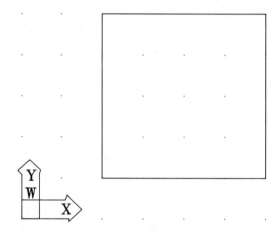

Figure 2-1: Draw object.

Now, in the same manner as before, set **ELEVATION** and **THICK-NESS** back to **0**.

Type: ELEV <RETURN>

Response: New current elevation.

Type: 0 <RETURN>

Response: New current thickness.

Type: 0 <RETURN>

USING DVIEW

You're now ready to examine your first view of the cube, using a new Release 10 feature called **DVIEW**. Select **DVIEW** from the screen menu under **DISPLAY**, from the pull-down menus under **DISPLAY**, or type **d v i e w** from the keyboard.

   When you're asked to **SELECT OBJECT**, do so by putting a **<CROSSING>** around the entire square. Confirm your selection with **<RETURN>**. Let's try it.

>   **Type:**   DVIEW <RETURN>

>   **Response:**   Select Objects:

> <CROSSING> Select entire object and <RETURN> to confirm.

   At the command line you'll now see several options:

CAmera/TArget/Distance/POints/PAn/Zoom/TWist/CLip/Hide/Off/Undo/eXit

   To choose these from the screen menu, select **DVIEW OPTIONS**. These options now appear and may be chosen from your screen menu.

   <CAmera>

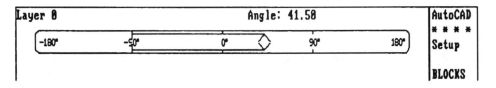

   Slide bar in DVIEW.

LIGHTS! CAMERA! ACTION!

Pick the **CAMERA** option. AutoCAD now wants to know the angle from which to view your drawing. On the right-hand side of the screen is a vertical slide bar beginning with **0** in the middle and advancing upward to a maximum of **90** degrees, and descending downward to a minimum of **-90** degrees. This is the angle of inclination from which you'll view the object. You can move your cursor up and down the slide bar to see this inclination dynamically. Make sure your **SNAP** is **OFF**.

When you've reached the desired inclination, pick to stop the rotation. For consistency in this exercise, enter the angles from the keyboard.

Type: 35 <RETURN>

At the top of the screen, you now see a horizontal slide bar that begins with 0 in the middle to a maximum of **180** degrees to the right and a minimum of **-180** degrees to the left. This is the left-right rotation of the object. Move your cursor left and right and watch the cube as it begins to rotate. When you have the desired left-right angle from which to view the object, you can pick and the rotation will stop.

Type: 50 <RETURN>

USING PAN

Chances are the cube may be slightly high on your screen, so let's get the feel of the dynamic **PAN**.

<PAn>

Position your cursor in the middle of the cube and pick to move it downward. Notice how the cube dynamically moves with you. When it's positioned in the center of your screen, then pick.

While you're in **DVIEW** you may continue to choose any of the options listed. When you're ready for the cube to be permanently positioned at the current view, confirm with **<RETURN>**.

Your screen should now look like Figure 2-2. If it doesn't, go back and begin again.

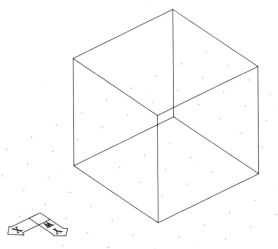

Figure 2-2: DVIEW of square.

WORKING WITH VPORTS

You're now ready to split your screen using the **VPORTS** command. You can choose **VPORTS** from the screen menu with **SETTINGS**. Because the **SETTINGS** command gives a multiple-screen menu, choose **NEXT**.

<VPORTS>

You're now asked to select how many views you want.

    Type: 2 <RETURN>

Response: Horizontal/Vertical.

    Type: V <RETURN>

Two views of the cube will now be displayed on your screen, as shown in Figure 2-3.

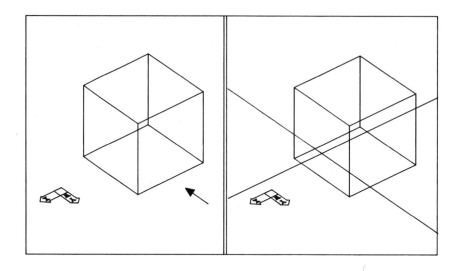

Figure 2-3: You are active in the right window.

By using the pull-down menus and the dialog box you get a much more visual effect. From the pull-down menus, pick **DISPLAY**. At the bottom is the **VPORTS** option, which is called **SET VIEWPORTS**. You now get an actual picture of how your viewports are going to look. Pick the two vertical windows if you haven't already done so. If you pick **VPORTS** from the screen or type it in a second time, the current screen will be further subdivided. This isn't true with the pull-down options. If this happens, simply pick **VPORTS SINGLE** and begin again.

You may be active in only one window at a time. To choose between one window or the other, move your cursor first to the left window. Pick. Crosshairs will now appear. Now move your cursor to the right window, where you'll see an arrow. This indicates that window isn't active. To choose the right window, move your cursor to the right window and pick. The crosshairs are now in your right window, with the arrow in your left.

Pick and make active the left window. Let's rotate the cube in the left window.

Type: DVIEW <RETURN>

Response: Select Objects:

<CROSSING> Select entire object and <RETURN> to confirm.

> **Type:** CAMERA <RETURN>

> **Response:** Enter angle from X-Y plane.

> **Type:** 35 <RETURN>

> **Response:** Enter angle in X-Y plane from X-axis.

> **Type:** 30 <RETURN>

> **Type:** <RETURN>

The second **<RETURN>** confirms the view. You should now have two slightly different views of the same object, as shown in Figure 2-4. Notice how you can tell the two different views or angles of the same entity by the different directions of the **X Y UCS** icon. The **W** is still visible, indicating that the **UCS** and the **WCS** are the same.

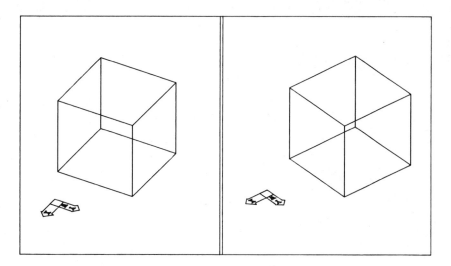

Figure 2-4: Two views of a cube.

Make sure you're active in the left screen. Next, let's put a **3DFACE** on the left side of the cube. When working in 3D, you'll be better off if each face or hatching pattern created is on a different layer.

Type: `LAYER <RETURN>`

Response: `?/Make/Set/New/ON/OFF/Color/Ltype/Freeze/Thaw.`

Type: `M <RETURN>`

Response: `New current layer.`

Type: `FACE1 <RETURN>`

Response: `?/Make/Set/New/ON/OFF/Color/Ltype/Freeze/Thaw.`

Type: `C <RETURN>`

Response: `Color`

Type: `1 <RETURN>`

Response: `Layer name(s) for color 1 (red) <FACE1>.`

Type: `<RETURN>`

Response: `?/Make/Set/New/ON/OFF/Color/Ltype/Freeze/Thaw.`

Type: `<RETURN>`

USING UCS

This "makes" and "sets" you to a layer called **FACE1** with **COLOR 1**. You're now ready to create your first **UCS**.

Type: UCS <RETURN>

Response: Origin/ZAxis/3point/Entity/View/X/Y/Z/Prev/
Restore/Save/Del/?

A variety of options that will be explained later are listed at the command line. For now, the one you want is **3POINT**.

Type: 3POINT <RETURN>

This lets you indicate a beginning origin and direction of the positive **X** and the positive **Y** (see Figure 2-5).

<OS-Intersection>

Pick the point indicated at **X1**. AutoCAD now wants to know the positive direction for the new **X** axis.

<OS-Intersection>

Pick the point indicated at **X2**. Finally you're asked for a positive direction for the **Y** axis.

<OS-Intersection>

Pick the point indicated at **Y3**. At that point the new **UCS** is displayed by the **UCS** icon.
You now need to save this **UCS**:

Type: UCS <RETURN>

Response: Origin/ZAxis/3point/Entity/View/X/Y/Z/Prev/
Restore/Save/Del/?

Type: S <RETURN>

Response: ?/Name of UCS.

Type: SIDE1 <RETURN>

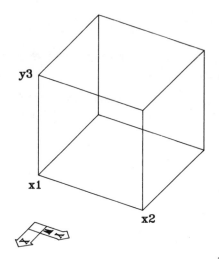

Figure 2-5: UCS 3POINT.

If you'll be picking your **UCS** from the pull-down menu (which is much more convenient), pick **SETTINGS**, then **UCS DIALOGUE**. Then pick **DEFINE NEW CURRENT UCS**. Pick **NAME**. Type **SIDE1** and **<RE-TURN>**. Then pick **ORIGIN, X AXIS, PLANE**.

This is slightly confusing in that the screen menu and the AutoCAD manual both call this **3POINT**, but the dialog box calls it **ORIGIN, X AXIS, PLANE**. You then pick the same points as before.

Note also that if you return to the dialog box, it's much easier to choose which **UCS** you want active at any one time by simply picking the current box beside the name of each **UCS** available to you. Note that the **UCS** icon has been changed.

ABOUT 3DFACE

Now that the **UCS** is set, let's add a **3DFACE**.

      Type: 3DFACE <RETURN>

The easiest place to pick **3DFACE** is from **3D** on the main AutoCAD screen menu, or to type it from the keyboard. You can get to **3DFACE** through the **DRAW** option of the pull-down menus in a roundabout way. Pick **3D CONSTRUCTION**. Pick one of the surfaces such as **Surface**

of REVOLUTION. Cancel the command with **CTRL-C**. Now the right screen menu with **3DFACE** is available. This is a lot of trouble, so the pull-down menu isn't viable for this command.

Refer to Figure 2-6.

<OS-Intersection>

Pick points **1**, **2**, **3** and **4**.

Type: <RETURN>

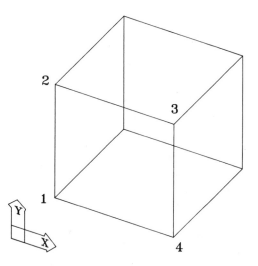

Figure 2-6: Apply 3DFACE.

A **3DFACE** is now in place on that side of your object.

Note how in Screen 2 the face is also outlined, but at a different angle. One reason you need a minimum of two screens is that if a mistake were made at this point, the **3DFACE** or entity drawn might look correct in one screen but be somewhere in outer space on the other! If the two screens both look correct, then you can be reasonably certain that your drawing is accurate.

Now let's see what happens if you hatch this. Make a new layer called **HATCH1** as **COLOR 1**.

<Layer, m, hatch1, c, 1, hatch1>

>   **Type:** LAYER <RETURN>

> **Response:** ?/Make/Set/New/ON/OFF/Color/Ltype/Freeze/Thaw.

>   **Type:** M <RETURN>

> **Response:** New current layer.

>   **Type:** HATCH1 <RETURN>

> **Response:** ?/Make/Set/New/ON/OFF/Color/Ltype/Freeze/Thaw.

>   **Type:** C <RETURN>

> **Response:** Color.

>   **Type:** 1 <RETURN>

> **Response:** Layer name(s) for color 1 (red)   <HATCH1>.

>   **Type:** <RETURN>

> **Response:** ?/Make/Set/New/ON/OFF/Color/Ltype/Freeze/Thaw.

>   **Type:** <RETURN>
>   <Hatch, u, 0, .5, N, L>

>   **Type:** HATCH <RETURN>

> **Response:** Pattern (? or name/U, style).

Type: U <RETURN>

Response: Angle for crosshatch lines.

Type: 0 <RETURN>

Response: Spacing between lines.

Type: .5 <RETURN>

Response: Double hatch area?

Type: N <RETURN>

Response: Select Objects:

Type: L <RETURN>

Your **3DFACE** should highlight at this point.

Type: <RETURN>

You should have a hatching pattern in both screens. Your left screen should look like Figure 2-7.

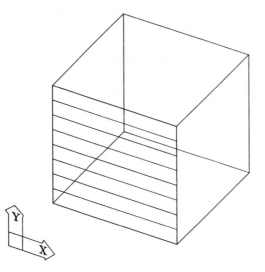

Figure 2-7: Hatch 3DFACE.

If the hatching pattern doesn't occur, it's because you didn't properly set the **UCS**. Go back and make sure the correct points were picked as in Figure 2-5.

You really don't need a **3DFACE** on each side to hide the lines, since **THICKNESS** creates the extrusion. But it's necessary if you want to hatch it, since you're really hatching the **3DFACE** and not the extrusion.

```
<HIDE>
```

HIDE your lines at this point and you'll see the effect in Figure 2-8.

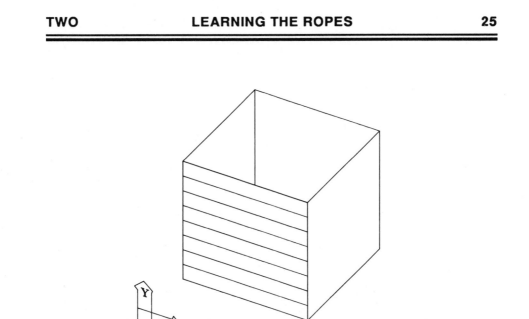

Figure 2-8: Hatch with hidden lines.

Now create a new **LAYER** called **FACE2** as **COLOR 2**.

Type: LAYER <RETURN>

Response: ?/Make/Set/New/ON/OFF/Color/Ltype/Freeze/Thaw.

Type: M <RETURN>

Response: New current layer.

Type: FACE2 <RETURN>

Response: ?/Make/Set/New/ON/OFF/Color/Ltype/Freeze/Thaw.

Type: C <RETURN>

Response: Color.

Type: 2 <RETURN>

Response: Layer name(s) for color 2 (yellow)   <FACE2>.

Type: <RETURN>

Response: ?/Make/Set/New/ON/OFF/Color/Ltype/Freeze/Thaw.

Type: <RETURN>

To learn the importance of the **UCS**, let's do a little experiment. Draw a line from point **1** to point **2** in as Figure 2-9. Don't use **OBJECT SNAP**, but try to draw the line as closely along the points indicated as possible. (If **OBJECT SNAP** is used, then you'll correctly **SNAP** to the intersections of two known points in 3D space.) However, let's see what can happen when using a **UCS** that isn't aligned correctly.

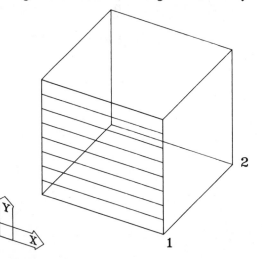

Figure 2-9: Draw a line.

Note Figure 2-10. Even though the line appears to be correctly drawn in Screen 1, it's off sharply in Screen 2. Therefore, you must create a new UCS for each side upon which you wish to draw.

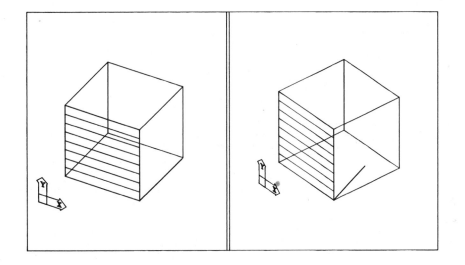

Figure 2-10: Things aren't what they appear to be.

Cancel and erase the line you just drew. Select a new **UCS** and choose **3POINT** or **ORIGIN, X AXIS, PLANE** and name or save it as **SIDE2**.

Type: UCS <RETURN>

Response: Origin/ZAxis/3point/Entity/View/X/Y/Z/Prev/
               Restore/Save/Del/?

Type: 3POINT <RETURN>

Response: Origin point.

Look at Figure 2-11. The origin will be the **<OS-Intersection>** of **X1**. The positive portion of the **X** axis will be the **<OS-Intersection>** of **X2**. The positive **X** portion of the **X, Y** plane will be the **<OS-Intersection>** of **Y3**.

<OS-Intersection>

Pick point **X1**.

Response: Point on positive portion of the X-axis.
                <OS-Intersection>

Pick point **X2**.

Response: Point on positive Y portion of the UCS X-Y plane.
                <OS-Intersection>

Pick point **Y3**.

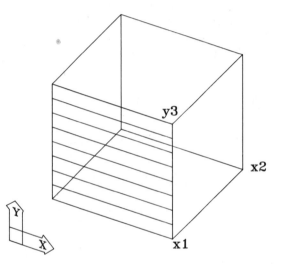

Figure 2-11: UCS 3POINT.

Note how the **UCS** icon has now shifted, with the **Y** pointing upward.

<3dface>

Refer to Figure 2-12. Using **<OS-Intersection>**, pick points **1**, **2**, **3** and **4**.

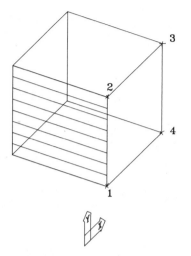

Figure 2-12: Apply 3DFACE.

In order to keep the hatched layers separate from your faces, make a new layer called **HATCH2** as **COLOR 2**.

```
<Layer, m, hatch2, c, 2>
```

Type:　LAYER <RETURN>

Response:　?/Make/Set/New/ON/OFF/Color/Ltype/Freeze/Thaw.

Type:　M <RETURN>

Response:　New current layer.

Type:　HATCH2 <RETURN>

Response:　?/Make/Set/New/ON/OFF/Color/Ltype/Freeze/Thaw.

Type:　C <RETURN>

Response: Color.

   Type: 2 <RETURN>

Response: Layer name(s) for color 2 (yellow) <HATCH2>.

   Type: <RETURN>

Response: ?/Make/Set/New/ON/OFF/Color/Ltype/Freeze/Thaw.

   Type: <RETURN>

You should now be on layer **HATCH2**. Let's **HATCH** side **2**.

```
<Hatch, hex, 2, 0, L>
Pattern for hatch is HEX
Scale for pattern is 2.
Angle is 0.
SELECT OBJECTS is LAST and CONFIRM.
```

   Type: HATCH <RETURN>

Response: Pattern (? or name/U, style).

   Type: HEX <RETURN>

Response: Scale for pattern.

   Type: 2 <RETURN>

Response: Angle for pattern.

   Type: 0 <RETURN>

Response: Select Objects:

Type: L <RETURN>

Type: <RETURN>

Note how neatly the pattern is hatched on the correct side. If you
HIDE your lines at this point, the cube begins to develop a nice visual
effect (see Figure 2-13).

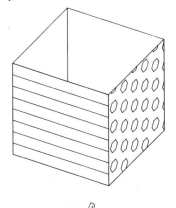

Figure 2-13: Hex hatch 3DFACE.

<Layer, m, face3, c, 3>

Make a new **LAYER** as **FACE3**, **COLOR 3**.

Type: LAYER <RETURN>

Response: ?/Make/Set/New/ON/OFF/Color/Ltype/Freeze/Thaw.

Type: M <RETURN>

Response: New current layer.

Type: FACE3 <RETURN>

Response: ?/Make/Set/New/ON/OFF/Color/Ltype/Freeze/Thaw.

Type: C <RETURN>

Response: Color.

Type: 3 <RETURN>

Response: Layer name(s) for color 3 (green) <FACE3>.

Type: <RETURN>

Response: ?/Make/Set/New/ON/OFF/Color/Ltype/Freeze/Thaw.

Type: <RETURN> <Layer, f, h*>

While you're using the **LAYER** command, **FREEZE** all hatching layers. In the exercises these always begin with the letter **H**. You need to do this so that the hatching pattern won't interfere with **<OS-Intersection>**, as it often does; this is one reason to put faces and hatching patterns on separate layers.

Type: LAYER <RETURN>

Response: ?/Make/Set/New/ON/OFF/Color/Ltype/Freeze/Thaw.

Type: F <RETURN>

Response: Layer name(s) to Freeze.

Type: H* <RETURN>

Response: ?/Make/Set/New/ON/OFF/Color/Ltype/Freeze/Thaw.

Type: <RETURN>

Now rotate your object.

Type: DVIEW <RETURN>

Response: Select Objects:

<CROSSING> Select entire object and <RETURN> to confirm.

Type: CAMERA <RETURN>

Response: Enter angle from X-Y plane.

Type: 35 <RETURN>

Response: Enter angle in X-Y plane from X axis.

Type: 160 <RETURN>

Type: <RETURN>

The second **<RETURN>** confirms the view. This has the effect of rotating the cube to where the straight-line hatch is in front of you and the hex pattern is to your left.

Now let's define a new **UCS**, called **SIDE3**. Using **3POINT** or **ORIGIN, X AXIS, PLANE**, pick the points as indicated in Figure 2-14.

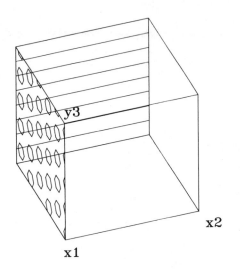

Figure 2-14: UCS 3POINT.

Use **<OS-Intersection>**. The origin point should be **X1**. The positive portion of the **X** axis is **X2** and the positive **Y** portion on the **X,Y** plane is **Y3**.

Now add the **3DFACE**, as illustrated in Figure 2-15.

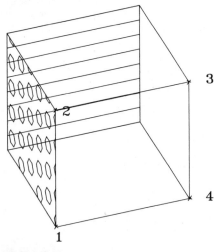

Figure 2-15: Apply 3DFACE.

`<3DFACE>`

Use **\<OS-Intersection\>**. Pick points **1**, **2**, **3** and **4**, then **CONFIRM**.

`<Layer, t, *>`

Enter the **LAYER** command and **THAW** all layers. You can do this with the * wild card.

`<Layer, m, hatch3, c, 3>`

While using the **LAYER** command, make a new layer called **HATCH3** as **COLOR 3**. You should now be on the **HATCH3** layer.

```
<Hatch, angle, 2, 0, L>
To HATCH the side:
Pattern is ANGLE.
The scale is 2.
The angle is 0.
SELECT OBJECTS is LAST and CONFIRM.
```

When the hatching is complete and the lines hidden, your screen should look like Figure 2-16.

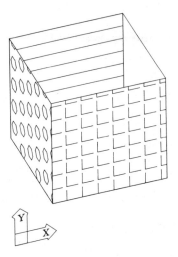

Figure 2-16: Angle hatch 3DFACE.

Rotate your cube one more time.

Type: DVIEW <RETURN>

Response: Select Objects:

<CROSSING> Select entire object and <RETURN> to confirm.

Type: CAMERA <RETURN>

Response: Enter angle from X-Y plane.

Type: 35 <RETURN>

Response: Enter angle in X-Y plane from X axis.

Type: -70 <RETURN>

Type: <RETURN>

The second **<RETURN>** confirms the view.

At this point it's hard to tell which side is which. The optical illusion is at its greatest. **HIDE** your lines to get some idea as to exactly where you are in space.

As you can see, you've simply rotated the view around to the blank side of the cube.

<Layer, m, face4, c, 4>

Make a **LAYER** called **FACE4** as **COLOR 4**.

<Layer, f, h*>
Freeze all HATCH layers by using the H*.
Define a new UCS called SIDE4.
Use 3POINT or ORIGIN, X AXIS, PLANE. Pick the points (Figure 2-17).

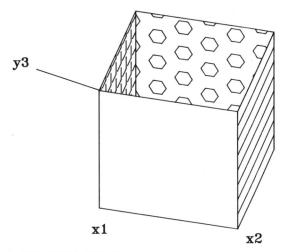

Figure 2-17: UCS 3Point.

Use **<OS-Intersection>**. The origin point should be **X1**. The positive portion of the **X** axis is **X2** and the positive **Y** portion on the **X,Y** plane is **Y3**.

Add the 3DFACE (as in Figure 2-18).

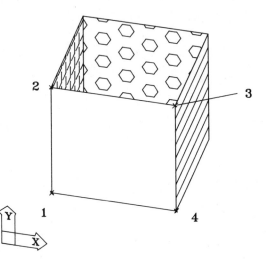

Figure 2-18: Apply 3DFACE.

```
<3DFACE>
```

Use **<OS-Intersection>**. Pick points **1**, **2**, **3** and **4**, then **CONFIRM**.

```
<Layer, t, *>
```

Enter the **LAYER** command and **THAW** all layers. This may be done with the * wild card.

```
<Layer, m, hatch4, c, 4>
```

Make a new **LAYER** called **HATCH4** as **COLOR 4**.

```
<Hatch, brick, 3, 0, L>
To HATCH the side:
Pattern is BRICK.
```

```
The scale is 3.
The angle is 0.
SELECT OBJECTS is LAST and CONFIRM.
```

Once the lines are hidden, the drawing should look like Figure 2-19.

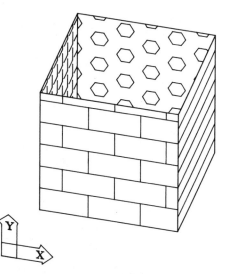

Figure 2-19: Brick hatch 3DFACE.

So far, you've gone around all four sides of the cube. You can insert the top and bottom of the cube the same way by simply rotating the vertical bar and increasing the angle of inclination from **35** degrees to **75** degrees relative to the **WCS**. The left-right rotation angle should be **-75** degrees.

You should produce the illustration found in Figure 2-20. As you can see, after the lines are hidden, you're looking at the top of the box.

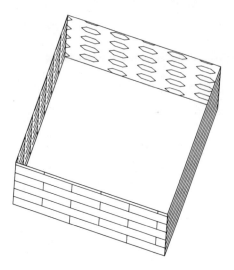

Figure 2-20: View from the top.

The box can be rotated to the bottom by using a negative angle of inclination.

MOVING ON

Through this exercise you've had the opportunity to use several commands that are described in detail in the next chapters. You've used **ELEVATION** and **THICKNESS** to draw the initial cube. The object was rotated into view with **DVIEW**. You learned to use **CAMERA** and **PAN**, only two of many options for viewing the object. You created one type of **UCS** and saved it for each side of the cube by using **3POINT**. You temporarily changed back to **UCS World** and then restored the previous **UCS**. Finally, you added **3DFACES** and hatched the cube's sides.

You should have a basic understanding of a few of the concepts and commands that help you draw in 3D. Now you're ready to learn the details of the most dramatic visual effects in AutoCAD.

3 Dynamic View

One of the most exciting aspects of Releases 10 and 11 is the dynamic view **(DVIEW)** feature. Unlike the older "bulls-eye" method of viewing a drawing in 3D space, **DVIEW** lets you actually see the object and *dynamically* rotate it in 3D space.

DVIEW's many options let you rotate the drawing precisely to the angle or view that you want to work with and place the target and camera at precisely the correct angles. To maintain a constant reference and relationship to an object in 3D space, you'll need to learn how to use the tools available under **DVIEW**. To understand **DVIEW**'s various options, let's create a simple floor plan and view it from different angles.

SETTING UP YOUR DRAWING

So that you have the same reference point as the illustrations in this chapter, use the following set-up procedure. Create a new drawing using the name you want. Use the following units and limits:

Architectural	4	16th inch
Degrees/minutes/seconds	2	Four units of precision
East	0 degrees	
Angles measured clockwise	No	
Limits are set to lower left-hand corner	0,0	
Upper right-hand corner	144', 96'	

In order to do this:

Type: UNITS <RETURN>

Response: Enter choice, 1 to 5.

Type: 4 <RETURN>

Response: Denominator of smallest fraction to display.

Type: 16 <RETURN>

Response: Systems of angle measure.

Type: 2 <RETURN>

Response: Number of fractional places for display of angles (0 to 8).

Type: 4 <RETURN>

Response: Enter direction for angle 0d0'0".

Type: 0 <RETURN>

Response: Do you want angles measured clockwise?

Type: N <RETURN>

You've now returned to the command line.

Type: LIMITS <RETURN>

Response: ON/OFF/<Lower left corner>.

Type: 0,0 <RETURN>

Response: Upper right corner.

Type: 144', 96' <RETURN>

You've now returned to the command line.

```
<ZOOM, A>
<GRID, 3'>
<SNAP, 3'>
```

You should now have **GRID** set to 3' apart with **SNAP** at 3'. Now set **ELEVATION** and **THICKNESS**.

Type: ELEV <RETURN>

Response: New current elevation.

Type: 0 <RETURN>

Response: New current thickness.

Type: 12' <RETURN>

Draw a 45' X 60' rectangle as illustrated in Figure 3-1, using the ordinary **LINE** command. Next, using the **LINE** command, draw three offices, as illustrated in Figure 3-2.

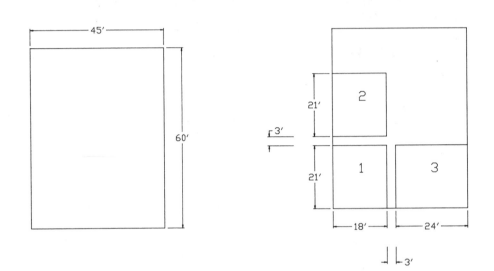

Figure 3-1: Draw office area.   **Figure 3-2: Add offices.**

Office #1   21' X 18'
Office #2   21' X 18'
Office #3   21' X 24'

Each office is separated by a 3' hallway. Don't include dimensions or office numbers in either of these illustrations.

Next, break each room and hallway as illustrated in Figure 3-3, at points **1, 2, 3, 4** and **5**. At points **1** and **2**, when you issue the **BREAK** command, you must first pick the entire line, then type **f** for **first point**. Then pick two points that are 3' apart. If **GRID** and **SNAP** are still set to **3'**, then you'll snap right to the break points. For points **3, 4** and **5**, the beginning break point is 3' inward from the door, then **1** grid point (**3'**) away. Thus, each door opening to the hallway and to each of the three rooms is **3'**.

Remember, do not include the numbers in your drawing. Your drawing should look the same as Figure 3-4.

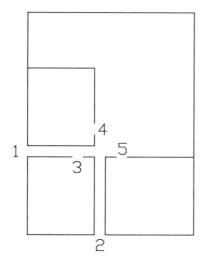

Figure 3-3: Break doors.

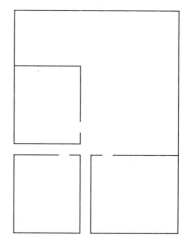

Figure 3-4: Plan view.

LOOKING AT YOUR DRAWING THROUGH DYNAMIC VIEW (DVIEW)

You can enter **DVIEW** three ways. First, you can:

Type: DVIEW <RETURN>

Response: Select Objects:

<CROSSING> Select entire object and <RETURN> to confirm.

If at this point you simply **<RETURN>** instead of selecting objects, AutoCAD will select its own object. To let you continue with the commands, the AutoCAD selected object is a picture of a house. Whatever rotation, distance, zoom, etc., is performed on the house, the settings will be made to your drawing when you exit the **DVIEW** command.

At the command line are the 12 choices available to you.

```
CAmera/TArget/Distance/POints/PAn/Zoom/TWist/CLip/Hide/
Off/Undo/<eXit>
```

   Type: CTRL C

This will cancel that command and return you to the command line.

The second way to choose **DVIEW** is to select it from AutoCAD's main screen menu. Pick **DISPLAY**, then pick **DVIEW**.

   Response: Select Objects:

```
<CROSSING> Select entire object and <RETURN> to confirm.
```

The 12 options are again at the command line. You can also see these options on the screen menu with pick **DVIEW OPTIONS**. Now you can choose any one from the screen menu.

   Type: CTRL C

This will cancel and return you to the command line.

The third way is to use pull-down menus. If your screen supports these, move your cursor to the pull-down menu bar and pick **DISPLAY**. Pick **DVIEW OPTIONS**.

You'll now have three options to choose from in the dialog box. They are **DVIEW CAMERA**, **DVIEW ZOOM** and **DVIEW PAN**. These are three more subcommands of **DVIEW**. Not all of the commands are available through the pull-down menus.

Pick **EXIT**.

Each time you enter **DVIEW**, you'll be given this group of prompts:

   Type: DVIEW <RETURN>

Response: Select Objects:

<CROSSING> Select entire object and <RETURN> to confirm.

You should now be in **DVIEW** with the 12 options available to you.

At this point, make sure **SNAP** is **OFF**. You can test this by typing CTRL B one or two times. If **SNAP** is **ON** while you're using **DVIEW**, you won't have total control of the object as you rotate it into view.

    Type: CAMERA <RETURN>

Move your cursor to the right until you can move it up and down inside the vertical bar that goes from **-90** to **+90**.

As you slowly move up and down, you'll see the floor plan rotate up and down in front of you. Put the small circle-like bubble on zero (or as close to zero as you can get). Now you're looking straight at the floor plan. Move the pointer to **45** degrees.

You're now at approximately a 45-degree angle, looking down at the floor plan.

Right now, it's difficult to see exactly what the object looks like. If you were to pick now, you'd be taken to the left-right rotation. So that you're using the same degrees used in the illustration in this book, don't pick the cursor at 45 degrees. Instead,

    Type: 45 <RETURN>

Notice that the top of the screen shows your angle in the number of degrees.

Now move your cursor left and right, from **-180** degrees to **0** to **+180** degrees. If you move the cursor slowly, the floor plan will start to rotate from left to right. Place your cursor at approximately **45** degrees—about halfway between **0** and **+90** degrees. Instead of picking at this point,

    Type: 45 <RETURN>

Now you're still in the **DVIEW** command and all of the options are still available to you. While in the **DVIEW** command,

Type: <HIDE>

This should produce an illustration like Figure 3-5. Notice the **UCS** icon in the lower left-hand portion of your screen. Whenever the **W** appears below the **Y**, the **User Coordinate System** and the **World Coordinate System** are one and the same. Note that from this view you can see where your original **X** and **Y** coordinates were.

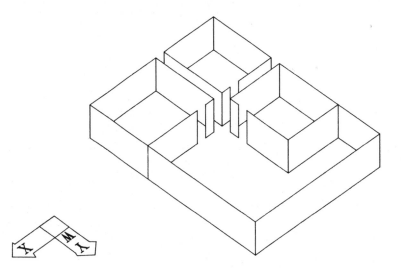

Figure 3-5: View from the top (note icon).

Now let's see if you can use **DVIEW** and some of its options.

ROTATING YOUR DRAWING WITH CAMERA (CAMERA)

In each illustration in Chapter 2, you used the **CAMERA** subcommand of **DVIEW**. We're assuming that the object referred to as the "target" by AutoCAD is stationary. The camera moves in a vertical motion above or below the object, and then left and right, rotating around the object. In Figure 3-5, your vertical inclination was **+45** degrees.
Note: In each of the following examples you'll be using a **DVIEW** subcommand. At the beginning of each example, you'll begin as though you were *not* in **DVIEW**, so that you can exit the tutorial and re-enter it

whenever you want. If you're doing all the examples in one session, then you can stay in **DVIEW** without reissuing the **DVIEW** command.

  Type: DVIEW <RETURN>

Response: Select Objects:

<CROSSING> Select entire object and <RETURN> to confirm.

  Type: CAMERA <RETURN>

Response: Enter angle from X-Y plane.

  Your vertical inclination was **+45** degrees above the object. To explore the use of vertical inclination, move your cursor to approximately **-45** degrees (notice that the exact angle is displayed at the top of the screen). Move your cursor very slowly, and as you pass **0** on the way down to **-45** degrees, notice how the picture changes.
  It's hard to imagine exactly what's happening, because the lines are not constantly being hidden; in a complex drawing, this would be nearly impossible to visualize. Place your cursor at approximately **-45** degrees and pick, or:

  Type: -45 <RETURN>

Response: Enter angle in X-Y plane from X axis.

  Let's keep the left-right rotation constant (as in the previous example) at **+45** degrees.

  Type: 45 <RETURN>

Now you can make the rotation permanent:

  Type: <RETURN>

<HIDE>

Notice that once the lines are hidden it becomes obvious that by changing the inclination of the camera from **+45** degrees to **-45** degrees you're now looking at the object from below. Therefore, by using the subcommand **CAMERA** (by changing the angle of the inclination from positive to negative) you're keeping the target still and seeing the object either from above or below.

Many times with complex objects it's hard to know whether you're looking at the object from the top down or from the bottom up. The **UCS** icon provides a solution. If the arrows crisscross at the corner, you're looking from the top down. If the arrows don't cross, you're looking from the bottom up. Notice the difference in the **UCS** icon Figures 3-5 and 3-6.

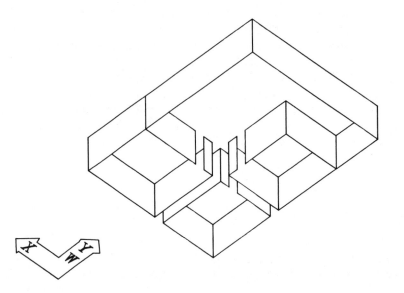

Figure 3-6: View from bottom (note icon).

Now look at the object from another angle:

Type: DVIEW <RETURN>

Response: Select Objects:

<CROSSING> Select entire object and <RETURN> to confirm.

Type: CAMERA <RETURN>

Response: Enter angle from X-Y plane.

Type: 45 <RETURN>

Response: Enter angle in X-Y plane from X axis.

Note that by sliding the bar back and forth, you can rotate the object a full **360** degrees, by going from **-180** degrees on one side to **+180** degrees on the other.

Type: -100 <RETURN>

Type: <RETURN> again to confirm the angle.

<HIDE>

As you can see from Figure 3-7, this gives you a view from a 45-degree angle. You're looking at the object almost as if it were drawn using **WCS** as indicated from the **UCS** icon.

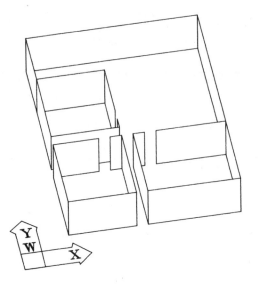

Figure 3-7: View without perspective.

ADDING PERSPECTIVE THROUGH DISTANCE (DISTANCE)

As you can see from Figure 3-7, you've been able to control both the camera angle's inclination and the camera's left-right rotation around the object. This is fine, but as you view the floor plan it's obvious that something just doesn't look right: the perspective is off.

If you could view a real room from a given height or distance, its foreground would appear larger and then the lines on each side of the floor plan would merge together the farther away the object was. Even though the distance between the lines doesn't really change, it's this optical illusion that gives the object a real-life look of depth. This is called *perspective*.

AutoCAD controls **PERSPECTIVE** under **DVIEW** and through the subcommand **DISTANCE**.

Type: DVIEW <RETURN>

Response: Select Objects:

<CROSSING> Select entire object and <RETURN> to confirm.

Type: DISTANCE <RETURN>

Response: New camera/target distance.

Now you're presented with a horizontal bar at the top of the screen. This bar goes from **0x** on the right to **16x** on the left. **1x** is your current distance from camera to target. If you move to **4x**, then the distance from camera to target is increased by a factor of four, etc., on up to **16x**. As you move to a larger number, the distance from camera to target increases, making the object look smaller or farther away. You can also type in a distance at the command line.

Type: 125' <RETURN>

Type: <RETURN>

<HIDE>

The object on your screen should look like Figure 3-8. Note how the wall lines tend to meet, making the lines at the farther end of the drawing look closer together; this gives the drawing true perspective.

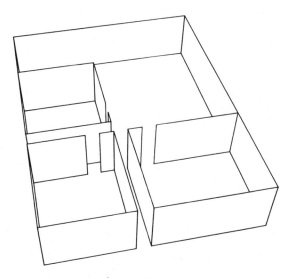

Figure 3-8: View with perspective.

In the bottom left-hand corner of your screen, the **UCS** icon has been replaced with an oblong box. This indicates that **PERSPECTIVE** is **ON**. You can't draw or edit by pointing with **PERSPECTIVE ON**. The perspective is only a view of that particular drawing. When you begin to draw or edit, you can do so as long as you enter coordinates through the keyboard, not by pointing. Pointing and zooming aren't allowed until **PERSPECTIVE** is turned **OFF**.

To save this perspective view of the drawing so that you can view it after editing, use the **VIEW, SAVE** command. After editing, use **VIEW, RESTORE**. This returns you to the saved perspective, complete with any edits.

One final word of caution. The **DISTANCE** command is intended to let you add perspective to a drawing, to give it a realistic depth. Don't use it to simply get closer to the drawing in order to perform closer, detailed work. To do this, use the **ZOOM** subcommand of **DVIEW**.

ZOOMING IN AND OUT (ZOOM)

The **ZOOM** command works differently as a subcommand of **DVIEW** than it does as an ordinary command.

Type: `DVIEW <RETURN>`

Response: `Select Objects:`

`<CROSSING> Select entire object and <RETURN> to confirm.`

Type: `ZOOM <RETURN>`

Response: `Adjust zoom lens.`
`           or`
`           Adjust zoom scale factor.`

The bar at the top is the same option bar as in **DISTANCE**. **1x** is the current distance to the object, increasing to **4x**, **9x** and **16x**. You may also type the actual distance to the object at the command line. The information entered at the command line through the keyboard performs two functions, depending on whether **PERSPECTIVE** is **ON** or **OFF**. **PERSPECTIVE** is **ON** if there is a box in the lower left-hand corner of the screen. If the **UCS** icon is present, then **PERSPECTIVE** is **OFF**.

If **PERSPECTIVE** is **ON**, enter a number that corresponds to what AutoCAD calls the camera's "lens length." If you entered 30, this would be a simulation of what you would see through a 35mm camera with a 30mm lens. Increasing the size of the lens has a similar effect to changing to a telephoto lens, thereby increasing the size of the object and bringing it closer to you. Decreasing the size of the lens makes the object seem smaller and puts it farther from the camera.

Figure 3-9 illustrates what might be seen through a 200mm lens.

Figure 3-9: Zoom with 200mm lens.

If **PERSPECTIVE** is **OFF**, **ZOOM** is the equivalent of a **ZOOM, CENTER** command. This lets you **ZOOM** at a factor of the last view. Therefore, each **ZOOM** is measured as a factor times the previous **ZOOM**'s view. Thus, if you increased the factor to **2**, then did another **ZOOM** and increased the factor again by **3**, the last view would be **6** times the original **ZOOM**. Practically speaking, it's better to use the sliding bar at the top so that you can see the exact required level of **ZOOM**.

Pick an appropriate zoom level.

Type: <RETURN> to confirm the view.

POSITIONING THE TARGET (TARGET)

AutoCAD considers the object you are drawing—such as a floor plan—as the target. There is a focal point on the target, which is an actual X Y Z coordinate. Imagine now that your camera is at a given distance from the target point; these are the beginning relative positions of the target and camera. But you can change either or both of these, since you already know how to move the camera in relation to the target.

The **TARGET** option works like **CAMERA**, except that the target moves instead of the camera. The camera remains stationary, which has the effect of reversing the positive and negative inclinations.

Under **CAMERA,** if the camera moved to a positive, 45-degree inclination, it would be on top of the object, looking down. If the camera moved to a negative, 45-degree inclination, it would be below the object, looking up.

But if you use **TARGET** and give it a positive, 45-degree inclination, then the target is moved **45** degrees above the camera and the camera is looking up at it from below. If, on the other hand, the target is given a negative, 45-degree inclination, then it is moved below the camera and the angle of view is from the top.

POSITIONING TARGET AND CAMERA (POINTS)

POINTS is a way to position two variables, the camera and the target, in relation to each other. It also has two different effects, depending on whether **PERSPECTIVE** is **ON** or **OFF**.

For this exercise, re-create the view used in Figure 3-5:

Type: DVIEW <RETURN>

Response: Select Objects:

<CROSSING> Select entire object and <RETURN> to confirm.

Response: Enter angle from X Y plane.

Type: 45 <RETURN>

Response: Enter angle in X Y plane from X axis.

Type: 45 <RETURN>

At this point, your drawing may be off the screen. If so, use **ZOOM** and **PAN** to bring the object into view at the center of the screen.

Assuming that you're still in the **DVIEW** subcommands, let's look at the effect of **POINTS**. First make sure that **PERSPECTIVE** is **OFF**. This can be confirmed by:

<OFF>

This will turn **PERSPECTIVE OFF** at any time. The oblong box should not appear at the bottom of the screen.

Type: POINTS <RETURN>

Response: Enter target point.

The **POINTS** subcommand will ask you to enter a target point, then a camera point. This lets you position yourself anywhere within the object from any angle and elevation. Look at Figure 3-10.

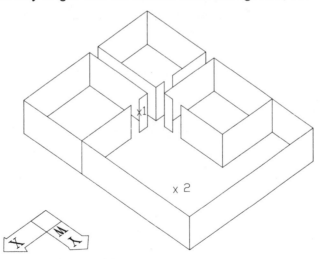

Figure 3-10: Reposition target and camera.

Pick a point at approximately point **1**.

Response: `Enter camera point.`

To get a position of about six feet elevation (about eye level), use a **FILTER** command. A **FILTER** command lets you pick any two coordinates with the cursor and then key in the third from the keyboard. Access to the **FILTER** commands is **.XY** if the two picked points are **X** and **Y. Z** will be requested from the keyboard. If you're picking two other coordinates, precede them with a decimal point.

Type: `.XY <RETURN>`

Pick a point at about point 2.

Response: `Need Z.`

Type: `6' <RETURN>`

Type: `<RETURN>`

Refer to Figure 3-11. It's not much to look at, is it? In fact, you could have done the same thing using either the **CAMERA** or **TARGET** subcommands. Save this view so that you can use it later.

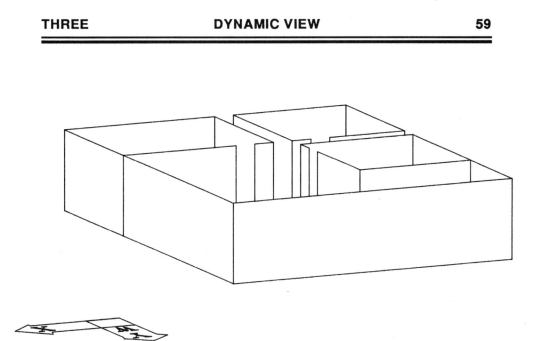

Figure 3-11: With PERSPECTIVE OFF, DISTANCE not changed.

Because **PERSPECTIVE** is **OFF**, only the angle of view is changed. The distance from camera to target remains unchanged; that's why you're still looking at the object from 125'. This is still the distance you set previously.

      Type: VIEW <RETURN>

Response: Delete, Restore, Save, Window.

      Type: S <RETURN>

Response: View name to save.

      Type: V1 <RETURN>

Return now to the view in Figure 3-10. This is the view selected with **<DVIEW, CAMERA, 45, 45>**.

Now turn **PERSPECTIVE ON**. If you're in the **DVIEW** subcommands,

   Type: `<DISTANCE>`

Response: `New camera/target distance.`

   Type: `<RETURN> to accept the current distance.`

   This will give you the same view, but in perspective. Make sure that **PERSPECTIVE** is **ON**.

`<POINTS>`

   PERSPECTIVE is temporarily turned **OFF**. Your current target is already chosen by default and permits a rubberband to the new target point.

Response: `Enter target point.`

   Type: `<RETURN>`

You want to keep the same target point as before.

Response: `Enter camera point.`

Again, use the **XY** filter.

   Type: `.XY`

Pick a point at about point **2** in Figure 3-10.

Response: `(Need Z).`

   Type: `6' <RETURN>`

`<ZOOM>`

ZOOM back and forth until you get your desired perspective. The effect now is quite dramatic, as shown in Figure 3-12. Note that you've placed yourself inside the room at point **2**. The difference between choosing points with **PERSPECTIVE ON** or **OFF** doesn't change the previous distance to the point of the camera and therefore puts you outside the figure, looking at the target point only from the angle indicated by point **2**. With **PERSPECTIVE ON**, the distance is changed to the point of the camera. You're actually placed at point **2** so that you can enter the floor plan. Then you can create dramatic effects, such as walkthroughs.

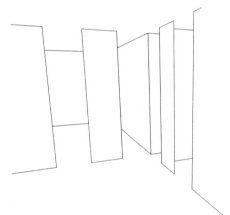

Figure 3-12: PERSPECTIVE ON, DISTANCE changed.

ROTATE THE DRAWING LEFT AND RIGHT (TWIST)

Return to the view that you previously saved.

      Type: VIEW <RETURN>

  Response: Delete, Restore, Save, Window.

      Type: R <RETURN>

Response: View name to restore.

Type: V1 <RETURN>

You should have on your screen a view that resembles Figure 3-11. The **TWIST** subcommand simply lets you rotate the view.

Type: DVIEW <RETURN>

Response: Select Objects:

<CROSSING> Select entire object and <RETURN> to confirm.

Type: TWIST <RETURN>

Response: New view twist.

Now, using your cursor, tilt the object from left to right. At a rotation of **26** degrees, you could produce Figure 3-13. Rotate the object back to **0** degrees and **CONFIRM**.

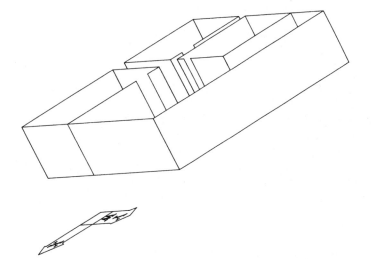

Figure 3-13: Twist the object.

REMOVING THE FRONT AND BACK CLIP

The last **DVIEW** option is **CLIP**, which lets you peel away objects from the front or back, as in Figure 3-11. Of course, if you wanted to get inside the floor plan, an easier way would be to use **POINTS**, with **PERSPECTIVE ON**.

On the other hand, the front wall of the floor plan can simply be peeled away.

      Type: DVIEW <RETURN>

    Response: Select Objects:

<CROSSING> Select entire object and <RETURN> to confirm.

      Type: CLIP <RETURN>

    Response: Back/Front/Off.

Type: F <RETURN>

Response: Eye/OFF/ON/distance from target.

   If you choose the **EYE** command, then the front clipping plane is placed at the camera (this is generally the default).
   By moving the slide bar from left to right, you see part of the front of the wall begin to disappear. The farther to the right you push the slide bar, the more the front disappears. Note the image that was created in Figure 3-14. By moving closer to the object and by increasing the clipping plane, you can move inside the floor plan, as shown in Figure 3-15.

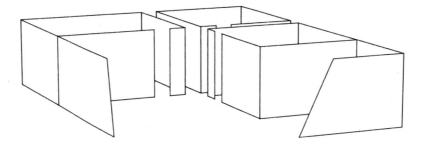

Figure 3-14: Front clipping.

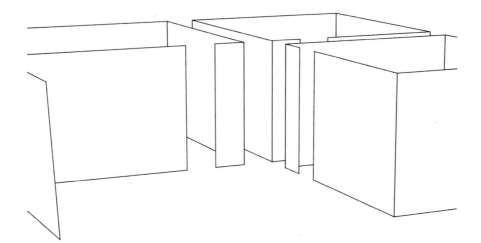

Figure 3-15: A closer look.

Now turn clipping **OFF**.

      Type: CLIP <RETURN>

Response: Back/Front/Off.

      Type: B <RETURN>

By moving the side bar to the left, you can begin stripping away part of the back of the floor plan, as shown in Figure 3-16. You can also **CLIP** both the back and the front one at a time, as in Figure 3-17.

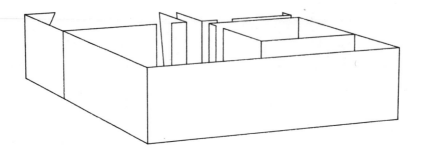

Figure 3-16: Back clipping.

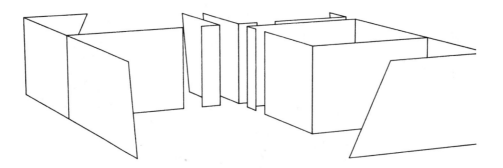

Figure 3-17: Simultaneous front and back clipping.

MISCELLANEOUS POINTS

Often, you won't need to see all of a large, complicated object. Auto-CAD lets you rotate *only* the area of the object you want to view. You do this by simply selecting the object with a **WINDOW** or by choosing only those entities you want to view. **CAMERA, TARGET, POINTS,** etc., let you select the angle from which you wish to view. When you **CONFIRM,** the entire object is rotated to the view selected. This also keeps AutoCAD from being burdened with the overhead of the entire object while it executes **DVIEW** commands.

4 AutoCAD's User Coordinate System

Before Release 10, AutoCAD had only one coordinate system, composed of two basic parts: 1) the point of origin, and 2) a series of straight lines relative to each other that formed the **X**, **Y** and **Z** axis at 90-degree angles. Now, the point of origin is in the center. If you're looking down on a piece of graph paper, positive **X** is to the right of the point of origin, positive **Y** is at the top of the paper, and positive **Z** is pointing straight at you.

AutoCAD now calls this basic system the **World Coordinate System (WCS)**. In the **WCS**, any point can be described in terms of **X**, **Y** and **Z**.

Beginning with Release 10, this coordinate system can be redefined, depending on your needs and on drafting problems. Whenever the **WCS** is redefined, it's then called the **User Coordinate System (UCS)**.

AutoCAD not only lets you redefine the **UCS** in a variety of ways, it also lets you save the current **UCS** by name and recall it at any time.

To demonstrate the **UCS**'s many benefits and features, we'll show you how to draw a 3D widget and then revise it from several viewpoints. This should give you a better understanding of the different **UCS** options.

SETTING UP YOUR DRAWING

Begin a new drawing using any name you want.

    Type: UNITS <RETURN>

    Response: Enter choice, 1 to 5.

Type: 3 <RETURN>

This is an engineering measure, in feet and inches.

Response: Number of digits to right of decimal point (0 to 8).

Type: 4 <RETURN>

Response: Systems of angle measure.

Type: 2 <RETURN>

Response: Number of fractional places for display of angles (0 to 8).

Type: 4 <RETURN>

Response: Enter direction for angle 0d0'0".

Type: 0 <RETURN>

Response: Do you want angles measured clockwise?

Type: N <RETURN>

Now set your limits.

Type: LIMITS <RETURN>

Response: ON/OFF/<Lower left corner>

Type: 0,0 <RETURN>

Response: Upper right corner.

Type: 36,24 <RETURN>

Type: ZOOM a <RETURN>

Type: GRID 1 <RETURN>

Type: SNAP 1 <RETURN>

You should now be using engineering units with degrees, minutes and seconds. Your limits should be set to 36,24. **SNAP** and **GRID** are both set to **1**.

Type: ELEV <RETURN>

Response: New current elevation.

Type: 0 <RETURN>

Response: New current thickness.

Type: .25 <RETURN>

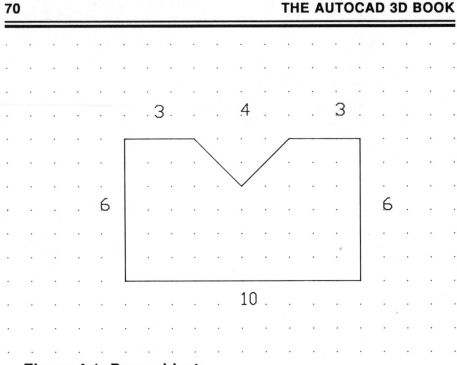

Figure 4-1: Draw object.

Draw the figure shown in Figure 4-1. Don't include the annotated numbers; they're just to help you construct the illustration properly. When the illustration is drawn,

Type: FILLET <RETURN>

Response: Polyline/Radius/<Select two objects>

Type: R <RETURN>

Response: Enter fillet radius.

Type: 2 <RETURN>

Type: <RETURN>

Response: FILLET Polyline/Radius/<Select two objects>

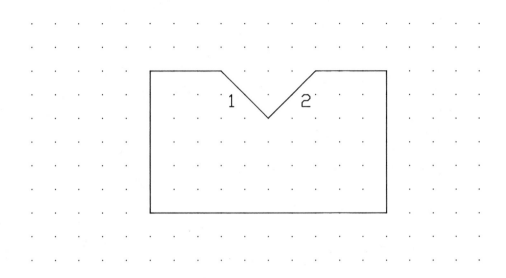

Figure 4-2: Fillet lines 1 and 2.

Pick lines **1** and **2** as shown in Figure 4-2. Your drawing should now look like Figure 4-3. Now look at your drawing using **DVIEW**.

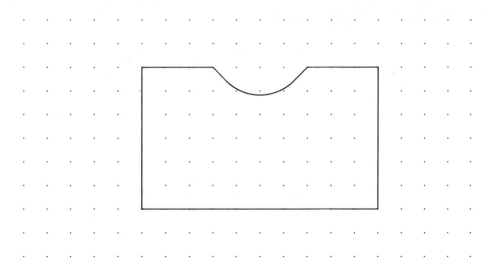

Figure 4-3: After fillet.

<DVIEW>

   Response: Select Objects:

<CROSSING> Select entire object and <RETURN> to confirm.

       Type: CAMERA <RETURN>

   Response: Enter angle from X-Y plane.

       Type: 25 <RETURN>

   Response: Enter angle in X-Y plane from X axis.

       Type: -25 <RETURN>

       Type: <RETURN>

POSITIONING THE UCS ICON

Note the position of the **UCS** icon in relation to your object, as shown in Figure 4-4. Also note that whenever the letter **W** appears below the letter **Y** in the **UCS** icon, it indicates that the **UCS** is equal to the **World Coordinate System**.

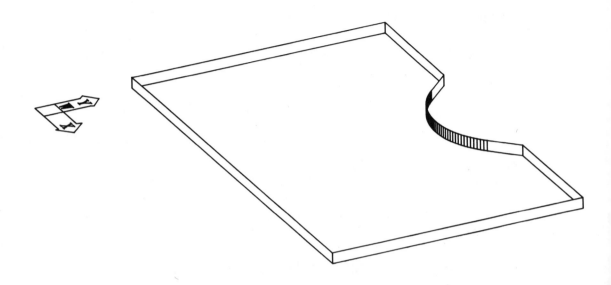

Figure 4-4: DVIEW of object.

It's often useful to attach the **UCS** icon to the object at the point of origin. Use the following command:

    Type: UCSICON <RETURN>

  Response: All/Noorigin/ORigin/OFF/ON

UCSICON is also a menu item on the screen menu, under **SET-TINGS**.

The **ON** and **OFF** options let you turn the **UCS** icon on and off at your discretion. The **ALL** option determines whether the **UCS** icon is re-adjusted in all the viewports when more than one screen is available.

Noorigin puts the **UCS** icon in the lower left portion of your screen, where it is now. The **ORigin** option places the **UCS** icon at the point of origin.

    Type: A <RETURN>

Response: Noorigin/ORigin/OFF/ON

Nothing will appear to happen. The **A** option simply says that the following command is active for all viewports.

Type: OR <RETURN>

The **ALL** option is *not* a toggle switch. It's simply activated right before you make any other selection. Therefore, if you didn't choose **ALL** before changing **ORigin** or **Noorigin,** then the viewports wouldn't be readjusted automatically. Remember to use the **ALL** command before selecting the other options if you want the **UCS** icon to move automatically in all windows.

CHANGING YOUR USER COORDINATE SYSTEM

You can choose the **UCS** command several ways: through keyboard entry, the screen menu or pull-down menus. First, let's look at the screen menu. Pick **UCS** from the AutoCAD main menu.

Response: Origin/ZAxis/3point/Entity/View/X/Y/Z/Prev/
                Restore/Save/Del/?

These are the options available to you whenever you choose **UCS**.

Type: CTRL C

This will cancel the command. Next, if pull-down menus are available on your machine, pick **SETTINGS**. Now you have several options:

UCS DIALOGUE
UCS OPTIONS
UCS PREVIOUS

Pick **UCS DIALOG.**

You should now have a dialog box called **MODIFY UCS.**
Pick **DEFINE NEW CURRENT UCS.**

This takes you to a secondary dialogue box, which gives you the various UCS options:

```
NEW ORIGIN
NEW ORIGIN Z AXIS
ORIGIN, X AXIS, PLANE
ROTATE ABOUT X AXIS
ROTATE ABOUT Y AXIS
ROTATE ABOUT Z AXIS
ALIGN WITH VIEW
ALIGN WITH ENTITY
```

You also have the option to enter a name at the top of the dialog box under which the current UCS will be saved. If you're not using pull-down menus, then you can save a **UCS** by first creating it, then issuing the **SAVE** option. The dialog box, on the other hand, wants you to name the **UCS** *before* you choose the options. If you forget to choose a name at this time, you can save the name manually by using the screen menu or keyboard. Pick **CANCEL**.

Response: You're returned to the previous dialog box.

Pick **CANCEL** again to get out of the dialog boxes.

Type: UCS <RETURN>

Response: Origin/ZAxis/3point/Entity/View/X/Y/Z/Prev/
Restore/Save/Del/?

Type: O <RETURN>

Response: Origin point.

AutoCAD now asks you to pick a new origin. The **ORIGIN** command lets you change the point of origin at any time. Changing the point of origin doesn't change the relative position of the **X, Y** or **Z**.

<OS-Intersection>

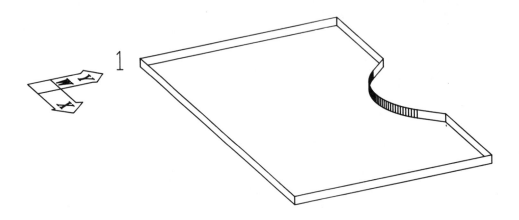

Figure 4-5: Change origin.

Pick point **1**, as shown in Figure 4-5. Note how the **UCS** icon attaches itself to the point of origin of your object. In many situations, you might want to have the **UCS** icon attached at the point of origin in order to get a better orientation of **X-Y**.

POINTING TO THE POSITIVE Z AXIS (ZAxis)

In Figure 4-6, the **X** axis goes to the right and the **Y** axis goes toward the top of the object. Use the right-hand method as discussed in Chapter 1, with your fingers pointing out. The **Z** axis is pointing toward the extrusion or the thickness of the object, as though it were pointing toward you while you were looking down at the object.

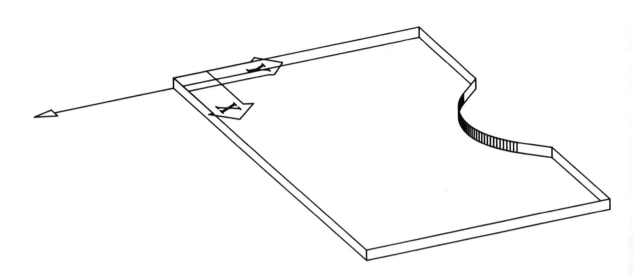

Figure 4-6: UCS ZAxis (positive Z axis).

However, you can redefine the positive direction of the **Z** axis.

Type: UCS <RETURN>

Response: Origin/ZAxis/3point/Entity/View/X/Y/Z/Prev/
Restore/Save/Del/?

Type: ZA <RETURN>

Response: Origin point <0,0,0>

Type: <RETURN>

You want your point of origin to be the same; therefore, **<RETURN>**
here.

Response: Point on positive portion of Z axis.

You'll now see a rubberband from the point of origin. You should now point to the direction of the positive **Z** axis. Turn **ORTHO** on.

Move the rubberband toward what would currently be considered negative **Y** (i.e., move it below the object) and pick. This will become the new positive **Z** axis.

Note what's happened to your **UCS** icon, as shown in Figure 4-7. **X** is now pointing to the right of the object and **Y** is pointing straight up. **Z** is therefore down from the object, toward the older negative **Y**. By pointing to a new **Z**, you've caused the **X** and **Y** to rotate.

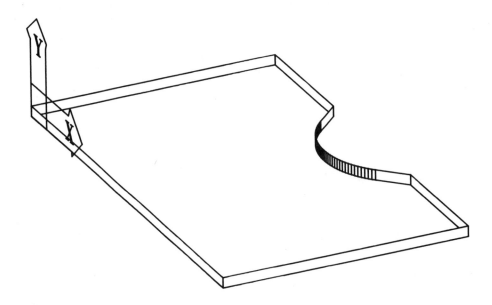

Figure 4-7: Note UCSICON rotation.

Rotating the **UCS** with **Y** pointing up can be very useful. If you wanted to copy the object on top of the original, you now know which way is "up." You simply copy @ distance and < (angle) of 90 degrees, the direction of now positive **Y**.

SAVING YOUR UCS

You can save the current **UCS** in two different ways, depending on whether you're using your screen and keyboard or the pull-down menus. If you're using the dialog box, enter the name of the **UCS** *before* defining the **UCS**. However, you can save any current **UCS** after the fact. Let's save the current **UCS**.

Type: UCS <RETURN>

Response: Origin/ZAxis/3point/Entity/View/X/Y/Z/Prev/
Restore/Save/Del/?

Type: SAVE <RETURN>

Response: ?/Name of UCS name.

If you enter ? **<RETURN>**, all currently saved **UCS**'s are displayed along with coordinate information.

Type: U1 <RETURN>

POINTING TO A NEW X AND Y (3POINT)

The most common **UCS** definition you'll use is **3POINT**. This can be a bit confusing since the *AutoCAD Reference Manual* and the *AutoCAD Release 11 Reference Manual* and the screen menus refer to this option as **3POINT**. But the dialog box refers to it as **ORIGIN, X AXIS, PLANE**. They're the same thing.

Regardless of what it's called, **3POINT** lets you designate three points: the point of origin, the direction of the positive **X** axis and the direction of the positive **Y** axis.

Now make a copy of the object and place it four inches above the current object. Since you've rotated the **Z** axis, positive **Y** is now pointing above the object.

Type: COPY <RETURN>

Response: Select Objects:

<CROSSING> Select entire object and <RETURN> to confirm.

Response: Base point or displacement:

 Type: 0,0,0 <RETURN>

Turn **ORTHO OFF** and move your cursor around. You'll see that you can move a copy of the object around and above the original. You want to be precise, so use the relative coordinate system for placing the object four inches above the existing object. Because this is the equivalent of moving straight up the **Y** axis,

 Type: @4<90 <RETURN>

As you can see, **90** degrees is the normal entry you would use to point straight up in plan view. Since the **X-Y** axis has been rotated, **Y** is now above the object. **90** degrees now points to the new **UCS Y** axis.

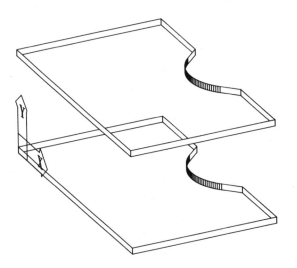

Figure 4-8: Copy in direction of positive Y.

Your drawing should now look like Figure 4-8. Split your screen so that you can view the object from two different angles.

Type: VPORTS <RETURN>

Response: Save/Restore/Delete/Join/Off/?/2/3/4

Type: 2 <RETURN>

Response: Horizontal/Vertical.

Type: V <RETURN>

Pick and make the left window active.

<DVIEW>

Response: Select Objects:

<CROSSING> Select entire object and <RETURN> to confirm.

Now use **TWIST** to rotate the object **75** degrees.

Type: TW <RETURN>

Response: New view twist.

Type: 75 <RETURN>

Type: <RETURN> (This makes the view permanent.)

Your drawing should now look like the illustration in Figure 4-9. To help you with your orientation, if you were to rotate Figure 4-9 a quarter-turn clockwise, it would be the same as in Figure 4-8. You would then see that the **UCS** icon is pointing in the same direction.

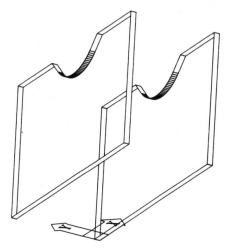

Figure 4-9: Twist object.

Compare Figure 4-9 with Figure 4-8. Look at the left and right view screens: Note that in the right view screen (Figure 4-8), the point of origin is on the bottom object with the **Y** axis pointing to the top object. In the left view screen (Figure 4-9), the object on your right is the bottom object.

Notice that the **Y** axis is pointing to the object on the top. These two screens are looking at the object from the same inclined angle, but you've twisted the rotation **75** degrees.

Just remember that in the screen on the left, the object at the right is on the bottom. It's very important for you to get this visual orientation.

Let's see what happens if you draw a circle with an elevation of **0** and a thickness of **4**, using your current **UCS**.

      Type: ELEV <RETURN>

Response: New current elevation.

      Type: 0 <RETURN>

Response: New current thickness.

Type: 4 <RETURN>

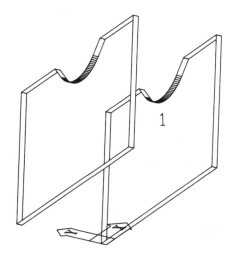

Figure 4-10: Pick center point of circle.

Draw a circle with a small radius, with the center at point **1** on the bottom object as in Figure 4-10.

<Circle, r>

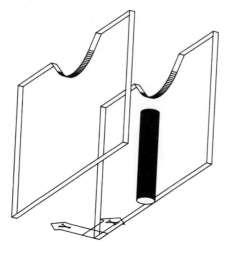

Figure 4-11: Note direction of extrusion (THICKNESS).

Pick point **1** and draw a small radius. Figure 4-11 represents the left screen and Figure 4-12 represents what you should be viewing in the right screen. Note the same relative position of the cylindrical bar. You had previously set the elevation at **0** with a thickness of **4**. The cylinder was drawn from the bottom object and extrudes toward the current **Z** axis.

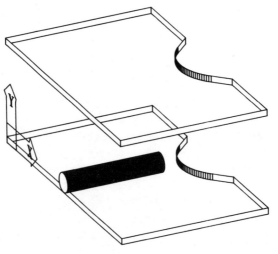

Figure 4-12: Other viewport.

But what if you wanted the cylindrical bar to connect the two objects? You could give AutoCAD enough coordinates to draw the cylinder connecting the bottom object with the top—a difficult task. It's easier to simply redefine the **UCS**.

Before continuing, erase the cylinder you've drawn.

<ERASE, L>

      Type: UCS <RETURN>

  Response: Origin/ZAxis/3point/Entity/View/X/Y/Z/Prev/
               Restore/Save/Del/?

      Type: 3 <RETURN>

You'll now change the **UCS**, using the **3POINT** option.

  Response: Origin point.

<OS-Intersection>

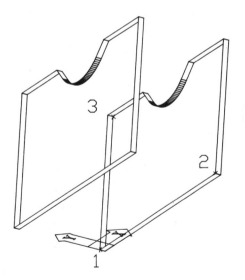

Figure 4-13: UCS 3POINT.

`<OS-Intersection>`

Pick the intersection as indicated by point **1** of Figure 4-13.

Response: `Point on positive portion of the X-Axis.`

`<OS-Intersection>`

Pick the intersection of point **2** as indicated in Figure 4-13. This is the direction of positive **X**.

Response: `Point on positive-Y portion of the UCS X-Y plane.`

Now that the **X** plane has been chosen, AutoCAD wants to know the direction of positive **Y**.

`<OS-Intersection>`

Pick point **3** as indicated in Figure 4-13. Now draw the circle.

`<CIRCLE, R>`

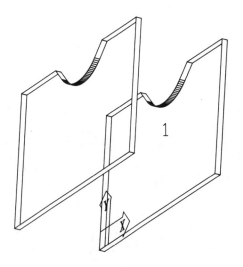

Figure 4-14: Pick center point of circle.

Pick the center point at point 1, as in Figure 4-14, and draw a small radius of not more than 1/8 inch. Note the two views in the left screen (Figure 4-15) and the right screen (Figure 4-16).

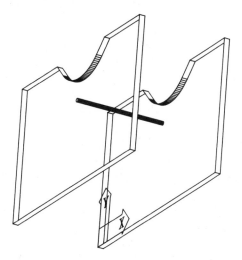

**Figure 4-15: Now note direction of extrusion
(THICKNESS).**

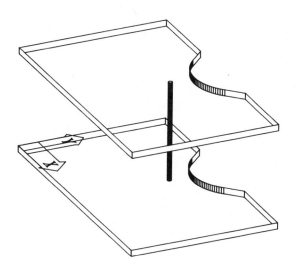

Figure 4-16: Other viewport.

Now copy the cylindrical bar one inch to the left of the current bar.

Type: COPY <RETURN>

Response: Select Objects:

Type: L <RETURN>

Type: <RETURN>

Response: Base point or displacement.

<OS-Center>

Pick any place on the cylinder.

Response: Second point of displacement.

Type: @1<180 <RETURN>

Notice in Figure 4-16 that because the **UCS** has been changed, with **X** pointing to the right and **Y** pointing to the top of the object, then **180** degrees is to the left of the current cylinder. The object in the left screen should look like Figure 4-17.

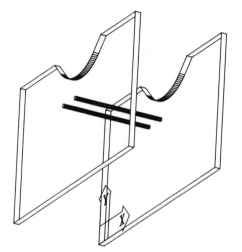

Figure 4-17: Copy cylinder <180.

ROTATING AROUND X, Y AND Z

The last options let you rotate the **UCS** icon around the **X**, **Y** or **Z** axis. Refer to Figure 4-17. If you were to rotate **180** degrees around the **Y** axis, then the current **X** (which is pointing to the right) would flip and point to the left. The **Y** would remain constant and the rotation would be around the **Y** axis. Give it a try.

      Type: UCS <RETURN>

Response: Origin/ZAxis/3point/Entity/View/X/Y/Z/Prev/
              Restore/Save/Del/?

      Type: Y <RETURN>

Response: Rotation angle about Y axis.

      Type: 180 <RETURN>

The results are confirmed in Figure 4-18. Note that the **X** arrow is now pointing to the left.

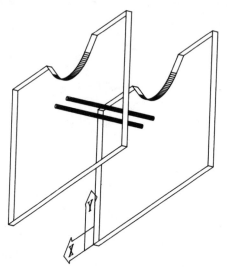

Figure 4-18: UCS Y.

You'll often make mistakes, especially in the beginning when you're just learning to use the **UCS**. And, hard as you try, you'll have a difficult time getting the **UCS** icon to point in the right direction. As you gain experience, this will become easier. But often you'll almost get there only to find that your **X** or **Y** is going in the wrong direction. By using **X**, **Y** or **Z** and rotating **90** or **180** degrees, you can often flip the **X** or the **Y** in the right direction.

Now that **X** is pointing to the left and **Y** remains constant (pointing up), what happened to **Z**? Remember the right-hand rule. Instead of pointing up toward the object on the left, **Z** is now pointing below the object on the bottom, because the orientation of **X** and **Y** have changed. Now rotate **Y** around **X**.

Type: UCS <RETURN>

Response: Origin/ZAxis/3point/Entity/View/X/Y/Z/Prev/
Restore/Save/Del/?

Type: X <RETURN>

Response: Rotation angle about X axis.

Type: 180 <RETURN>

In Figure 4-19, the **Y** axis is now rotated 180 degrees around the **X** axis and is pointing down. Again, where is **Z**? Remembering the right-hand rule, turn the book upside down so that **X** is pointing to the right and **Y** is pointing straight up. Then point your hand with the thumb going in the direction of **X** and the forefinger in the direction of **Y**. The other fingers are in the direction of **Z**.

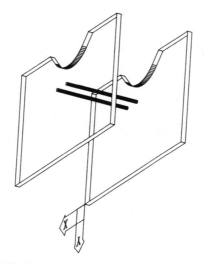

Figure 4-19: UCS X.

Before reading on, see if you can figure out what will happen when you rotate **180** degrees around the **Z** axis.

Type: UCS <RETURN>

Response: Origin/ZAxis/3point/Entity/View/X/Y/Z/Prev/
Restore/Save/Del/?

Type: Z <RETURN>

Response: Rotation angle about Z axis.

   Type: 180 <RETURN>

   Did you figure it out? Note that in Figure 4-20, you're now back where you started. The **Z** axis remained constant, still pointing toward the object on the upper left. The **X** and **Y** rotated **180** degrees counter-clockwise.

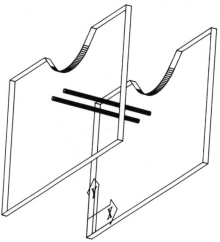

Figure 4-20: UCS Z.

   Now let's put a **3DFACE** on the object. You might be tempted at this point to change your **UCS**. Although you can create a new **UCS** at any time, it's not always required. If you'll be snapping to real objects that already have coordinates in 3D space, you don't need to change the **UCS**.
   In the following example, you'll use **3DFACE** to connect the intersections of four points.

   Type: 3DFACE <RETURN>

Response: First point.

<OS-Intersection>

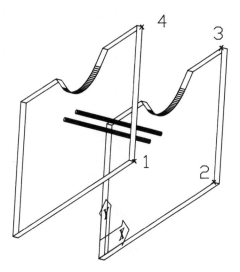

Figure 4-21: Apply 3DFACE.

Pick point 1 on Figure 4-21.

Response: Second point.

<OS-Intersection>

Pick point 2 on Figure 4-21.

Response: Third point.

<OS-Intersection>

Pick point 3 on Figure 4-21.

Response: Fourth point.

<OS-Intersection>

Pick point 4 on Figure 4-21.

Type: <RETURN>

<HIDE>

Note the effect of **3DFACE** as illustrated in Figure 4-22. Before you proceed, **SAVE** this view.

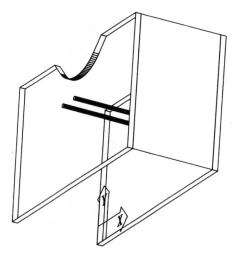

Figure 4-22: Hide lines.

Type: VIEW <RETURN>

Response: ?/Delete/Restore/Save/Window

Type: SAVE <RETURN>

Response: View name to save.

Type: V1 <RETURN>

To get a good view of this object, look at it from the other side:

<DVIEW>

Response: Select Objects:

<CROSSING> Select entire object and <RETURN> to confirm.

    Type: PO <RETURN>

Response: Enter target point.

<OS-Intersection>

  Pick point 3 in Figure 4-21.

Response: Enter camera point.

<OS-Intersection>

  Pick the intersection of one of the back legs of the object. You should be looking at the object from behind. Your view of the object may differ from Figure 4-23, depending on the position of **TARGET** and **CAMERA**.

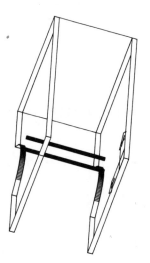

Figure 4-23: Back view.

Now, save your drawing; you'll use it again in Chapter 6.

Type: SAVE <RETURN>

Response: File name.

Type: WIDGET <RETURN>

PLACING TEXT IN THE DRAWING

Text normally goes in the direction of positive **X**. This can be really troublesome, depending on the **UCS** you've defined. Therefore, the best way to use text is to define the **UCS** as **VIEW**.

The **VIEW** option sets **X** and **Y** parallel to your screen, making the grid look normal. **X** goes to the right and positive **Y** is up, as in plan view. Your text thus comes out flat against the drawing.

Type: UCS <RETURN>

Response: Origin/ZAxis/3point/Entity/View/X/Y/Z/Prev/
Restore/Save/Del/?

Type: V <RETURN>

You may now type your text. The text should appear as in Figure 4-24.

Figure 4-24: Using text.

One word of caution when using the **VIEW** option with text: As you can see from the screen on the right, the text went crazy. The **VIEW** option will only create a **UCS** parallel to your screen. As a result, the text's location relative to the **WCS** and the rest of your object is unpredictable. Therefore, you might want to save a view of the object and put the text on a separate layer so you can turn it off.

MISCELLANEOUS HINTS

Five other options are available with **UCS: ENTITY, PREV, RESTORE, SAVE** and **DEL.**

ENTITY lets you line up the **UCS** by selecting an entity. This guarantees that the **X-Y** plane of the new **UCS** is parallel to the **X-Y** plane in effect when the entity was created.

PREV (previous) lets you bring back a **UCS** that was previously defined. As a result, you can temporarily define a **UCS** view and return with **UCS PREVIOUS <RETURN>.** AutoCAD will save ten of these previous definitions so that you can go back through them as needed.

RESTORE lets you restore a previously saved **UCS.** However, be aware that **RESTORE** won't return you to the view that was in effect when the **UCS** was saved. One trick you can use is to save a view using **<VIEW, S>** under the same name as the **<UCS, S>.** That way, you can recall the view at the same time you **RESTORE** the **UCS.**

The **SAVE** option lets you save the **UCS** definition so that you can return to it later. The name you choose may be up to 32 characters long and may contain letters, numbers, $, dash (–) and underline (_) symbols. The name can be in uppercase or lowercase. AutoCAD converts all names to uppercase.

DEL (delete) lets you delete one or more saved **UCS** definitions.

Finally, **WORLD** is always the default for any **UCS** command. Any time you enter **UCS** and **<RETURN>**, the **UCS** will be defined as the **WCS**.

VIEWING FROM PLAN

The basic definition of plan view is the view from **Z** looking straight at the **X-Y** plane. But, as you've seen, the **X-Y** plane can be redefined by the **UCS**. Therefore, if you issue the **PLAN** command, you can choose **WORLD**, current **UCS** or name the saved **UCS**. Either **UCS** will let you look straight at the newly defined **X-Y** plane.

MOVING ON

UCS will seem a little confusing at first. After working through the examples in this chapter, you should be familiar now with the workings of the **UCS** and how to change it to accommodate any 3D problem that might arise.

The trick of working with **UCS** is to be constantly aware of **Z**'s location. If you ever get confused, hold your right hand out and use the right-hand rule. If things still seem to be going backwards, chances are it's not your **UCS** that's in error, but that the object is turned around. This can often occur if the lines aren't hidden and you think you're looking at the object from a completely different angle. The key to **UCS** is to work with it and keep practicing.

Now let's add a little shape to our models with **3D MESHES**.

5   Surfaces and Meshes

The 3D mesh commands available in AutoCAD Releases 10 and 11 give you the chance to produce some of the most dramatic visual effects available in 3D. They also let you give shape and body to your drawings and transfer the shape of an object to AutoSHADE for rendering.

First, let's define what we mean by *surface* and *mesh*. If you draw a simple rectangle in 3D space, assuming no thickness, the rectangle is considered to be transparent. That is, the lines simply form the outline of a rectangular object. No lines can be hidden, because there's no surface to the rectangle. On the other hand, you can take the same rectangle and add a **3DFACE**, thus producing a solid surface behind which lines can be hidden. The **3DFACE** command is very useful for flat, rectangular objects. However, once curved surfaces are added to an object, the **3DFACE** command isn't as suitable.

Assume that **3DFACE** was the only surface modeling command available. The problem facing you involves placing a surface on a circular object. You could draw enough **3DFACES** to approximate the fill of the circle. As you reached the outer areas of the circle, you could reduce the size of each **3DFACE** so that when plotted it would come close to the fill of the circle. But as you can see, this would take a long time, and each entity would be a separate **3DFACE**.

A *mesh* lets you easily provide a 3D surface for curved entities, or any entity whose face is a single entity.

WHAT IS A 3D MESH?

A *3D mesh* is a single entity that tries to put multiple **3DFACES** on the surface of an object. It's also a series of lines or cross-grids, consisting of columns and rows. The *AutoCAD User Reference Manual* and the

AutoCAD Release 11 Reference Manual define a cross-grid as a matrix of **M** by **N**: **M** and **N** designate columns and rows.

AutoCAD lets you determine the relative spacing (resolution) between grids and lines. Two system variables let you control the resolution of the 3D mesh: **SURFTAB1** and **SURFTAB2**. (*Resolution* is the distance between the columns and rows.) AutoCAD has four 3D meshes: **RULESURF**, **TABSURF**, **REVSURF** and **EDGESURF**.

The differences between these types of meshes depend on the types of objects connecting the surfaces. **RULESURF** creates a surface connecting two known objects. **TABSURF** extends a surface in the exact shape of a single object. **REVSURF** creates a surface in the shape of a single object revolving around a center point. **EDGESURF** creates a series of vertices that connect along four sides in the shape and contour of the lines that created the four edges (sides); this may be used with curve-fitted polylines.

The system variable **SURFTAB1** controls the density of any 3D mesh generated by **RULESURF** and **TABSURF**. **REVSURF** and **EDGESURF** are controlled by both **SURFTAB1** and **SURFTAB2** to determine the density. The reason for this is that **RULESURF** and **TABSURF** aren't cross-grids. They're actually single lines forming the mesh from one point to another. However, **REVSURF** and **EDGESURF** create a cross-grid mesh that requires control of the density of the columns and rows.

You'll have to see what density you need; generally, you need a greater density if the objects are more curved than linear. The two system variables may be changed at any time and affect only the next 3D mesh drawn. However, system response slows as the density increases.

RULED SURFACES (RULESURF)

Let's set **LIMITS** to **12** by **9** and **UNITS** to **DECIMAL**. Draw two arcs like those in Figure 5-1.

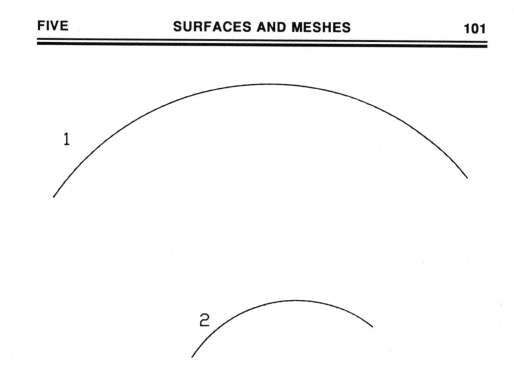

Figure 5-1: Draw two arcs.

    Type: SETVAR <RETURN>

Response: Variable name or ?

    Type: SURFTAB1 <RETURN>

Response: New value for SURFTAB1.

    Type: 2 <RETURN>

    RULESURF is one of the simplest of the 3D meshes. It forms a 3D mesh connecting two entities.

    Type: RULESURF <RETURN>

Response: Select first defining curve.

Pick the arc at the top at point 1.

Response: Select second defining curve.

Pick the arc at the bottom at point **2**.

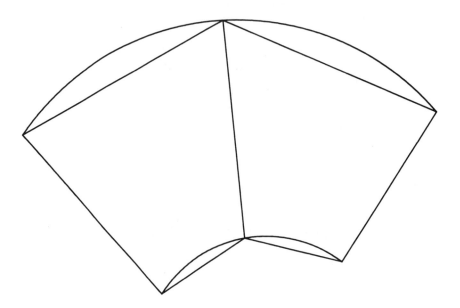

Figure 5-2: SURFTAB 1 set to 2.

It's not much to look at, is it? Figure 5-2 represents what happens when the system variable **SURFTAB1** is set too low. What you've really drawn here are two **3DFACES**. Now set **SURFTAB1** to a better density.

    Type: SETVAR <RETURN>

Response: Variable name or ?

    Type: SURFTAB1 <RETURN>

Response: New value for SURFTAB1.

    Type: 20 <RETURN>

Type: ERASE L <RETURN>

Type: <RETURN>

This erases the 3D mesh just drawn.

Type: RULESURF <RETURN>

Response: Select first defining curve. Pick the arc at the top at point 1.

Response: Select second defining curve. Pick the arc at the bottom at point 2.

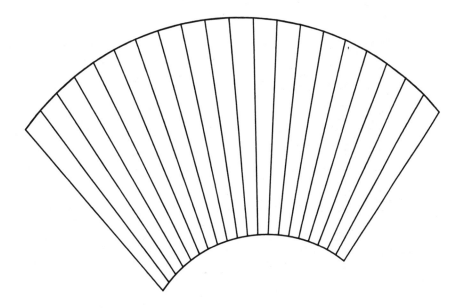

Figure 5-3: SURFTAB 1 set to 20.

Your screen should look like Figure 5-3. Now erase all entities on your screen. Remember that **RULESURF** lets you place a 3D mesh connecting any two entities; but you must have two entities. Instead of using arcs, draw two straight lines as in Figure 5-4. Don't put in the letters.

One of the peculiar aspects of **RULESURF** is that it tries to connect the vertices closest to the end points of the entities selected. Thus, the correct way to do a **RULESURF** on the two entities in Figure 5-4 is to pick a point on the larger line somewhere close to point **B** and on the smaller line close to point **A**. The two points don't actually have to be the end points of the lines. Let's see what happens if you do it the wrong way.

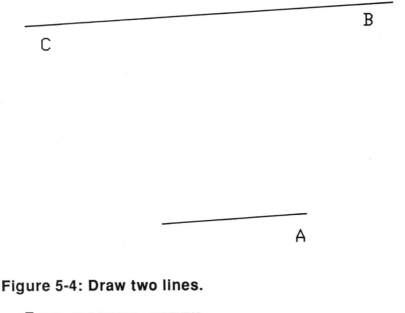

Figure 5-4: Draw two lines.

Type: RULESURF <RETURN>

Response: Select first defining curve.

Pick a point somewhere on the larger line toward point **C**. It needn't be the exact end point.

Response: Select second defining curve.

Pick the smaller line toward the end at point **A**. The result should look like Figure 5-5.

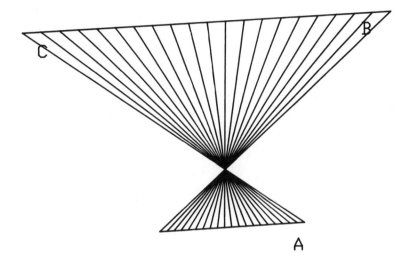

Figure 5-5: Be careful how you pick the points.

```
<ERASE L>
```

This erases the 3D mesh.

   Type: RULESURF <RETURN>

Response: Select first defining curve.

Pick the smaller line toward the end at point **A**.

Response: Select second defining curve.

Pick the larger line toward the end at point **B**. This is the proper way to do a **RULESURF**, as shown in Figure 5-6. Now, erase your entire screen.

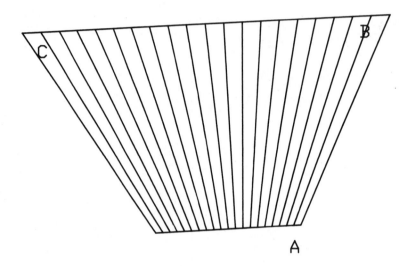

Figure 5-6: The right way.

Remember when using **RULESURF** that the larger the first entity is compared to the second, the closer the lines will merge at the smaller entity. Let's use **DVIEW** to illustrate.

Type: DVIEW <RETURN>

Response: Select Objects.

Type: <RETURN>

Response: CAmera/TArget/DIstance/POints/PAn/Zoom/TWist/
            CLip/Hide/Off/Undo/eXit

Note that because no object was selected, AutoCAD supplies you with the image of a house.

Type: CA <RETURN>

Response: Enter angle from X-Y plane.

Type: 35 <RETURN>

Response: Enter angle in X-Y plane from X axis.

Type: 35 <RETURN>

Type: <RETURN>

Draw a circle at the bottom of the screen and a point at the top of the screen as shown in Figure 5-7. Use the **POINT** command. Now connect the two entities with a **RULESURF**.

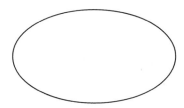

Figure 5-7: Draw a circle and a point.

Type: RULESURF <RETURN>

Response: Select first defining curve.

Pick the circle.

Response: Select second defining curve.

Pick the point.

Your drawing should look like Figure 5-8. Notice that once the **RULESURF** is added, the circle seems to be outlined more with straight line segments. This is because of the interval you selected using the system variable **SURFTAB1**. If you increase the variable to **50** from the current setting of **20**, then the 3D mesh will more closely approximate the circle.

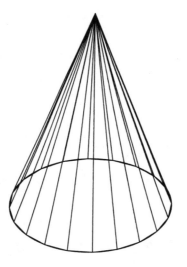

Figure 5-8: Connect the point and circle.

Erase your entire screen.

   Type: PLAN <RETURN>

Response: Current UCS/UCS/World.

Type: W <RETURN>

This takes you back to the plan view in **WCS**.

TABULATED SURFACES (TABSURF)

Unlike **RULESURF**, **TABSURF** doesn't require or connect to a second entity. **TABSURF** needs only one entity, thus creating a surface extrusion from that entity; but **TABSURF** *does* need a direction vector. This is a second entity somewhere in the drawing that points toward the direction of, and is the same length as, the 3D mesh to be drawn. Remember that the direction vector must be an entity such as a line or polyline.

Type: PLINE <RETURN>

Now draw a series of polylines as in Figure 5-9 and **CONFIRM**.

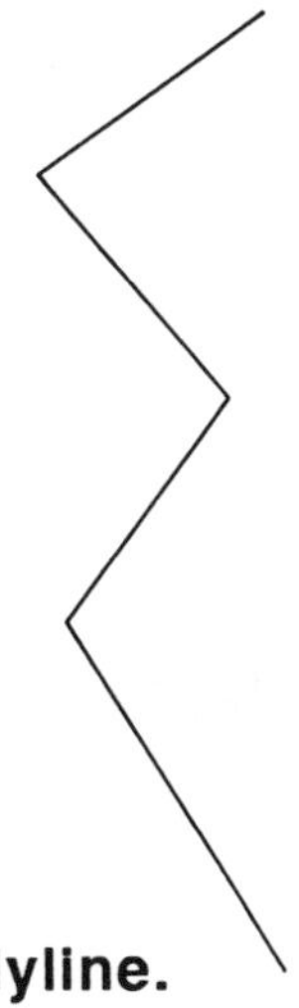

Figure 5-9: Single polyline.

Type: PEDIT <RETURN>

Response: Select polyline.

Type: L <RETURN>

Type: F <RETURN>

This will curve-fit the polyline.

Type: X <RETURN>

This exits from the **PEDIT** commands. Using the regular **LINE** command, draw a line for the direction vector as shown in Figure 5-10.

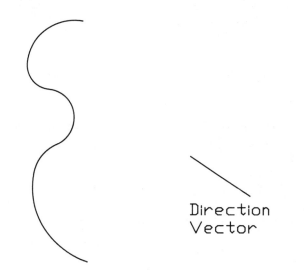

Direction
Vector

Figure 5-10: Curve-fit polylines.

Type: TABSURF <RETURN>

Response: Select path curve.

Pick the curve-fitted polyline.

Response: Select direction vector.

Pick the line drawn as the direction vector, and be sure which side you pick. If you picked the side closer to the left-end point, then the 3D mesh would be drawn to the right of the polyline. However, if you picked the side closer to the right-end point, then the 3D mesh would be drawn to the left of the polyline. The result of the **TABSURF** is shown in Figure 5-11.

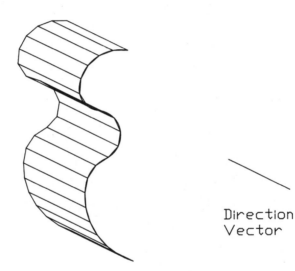

Direction
Vector

Figure 5-11: TABSURF.

SURFACES OF REVOLUTION (REVSURF)

REVSURF is a more complicated 3D mesh because it uses both columns and rows to form a complete matrix cross-grid. The key to using **REVSURF** is to remember that the surface will revolve around a fixed axis similar to a circular (polar) array.

Before proceeding, let's be sure that the second system variable, **SURFTAB2**, is properly set.

Type: SETVAR <RETURN>

Response: Variable name or ?

Type: SURFTAB2 <RETURN>

Response: New value for SURFTAB2.

Type: 20 <RETURN>

Both **SURFTAB1** and **SURFTAB2** are now set at **20**. Let's draw a simple object to demonstrate how **REVSURF** revolves a 3D mesh around a fixed axis.

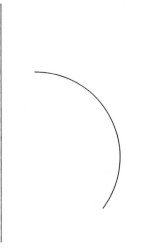

Figure 5-12: Draw a line and an arc.

Draw an arc and a straight line, as shown in Figure 5-12. During the **REVSURF** command you'll be asked for the path curve and the axis of revolution. The path curve is the entity you wish to revolve around the axis. The axis of revolution is the center point around which the entity will revolve. In our case, it's the straight line.

Type: REVSURF <RETURN>

Response: Select path curve.

Pick the arc.

Response: `Select axis of revolution.`

Pick the straight line.

Response: `Start angle <0>`

You can now supply the angle at which the 3D mesh will begin. The default is **0**. If you're going to do a full circle, it doesn't matter what you put here.

Type: `<RETURN>`

Response: `Included angle (+=ccw, -=cw) <Full circle>`

You can now specify how many degrees around the axis the 3D mesh will revolve. If you **<RETURN>**, the default is **Full circle**.

Type: `280 <RETURN>`

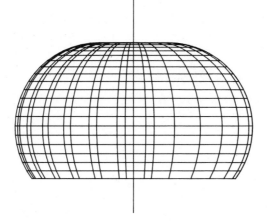

Figure 5-13: 280 degrees around the axis.

For this example, you'll draw the 3D mesh only **280** degrees around the axis so that you can see exactly what's happening. Your screen should look like Figure 5-13.

```
<DVIEW, CAMERA, 35, 20>
```

From the current view, you can't tell exactly what's happening. But by changing the view using **DVIEW**, you get a different point of view, as shown in Figure 5-14.

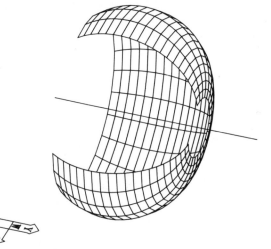

Figure 5-14: DVIEW of REVSURF.

Figure 5-14 is shown here with hidden lines. Be aware that hiding lines can take some time, depending on the speed of your computer.

As you can see, the 3D mesh revolved around the selected axis by **280** degrees. Also, it matters where you pick the axis of revolution. Look at Figures 5-15, 5-16 and 5-17. Each end of the line representing the axis of revolution is labeled **A** or **B**. In Figure 5-16, the axis of revolution was picked toward letter **A**.

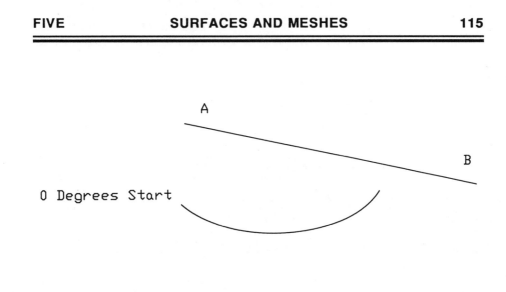

0 Degrees Start

Figure 5-15: Where you pick determines the direction.

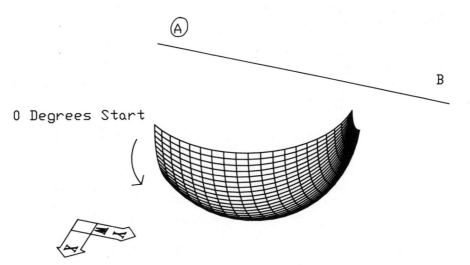

Figure 5-16: Pick a point A.

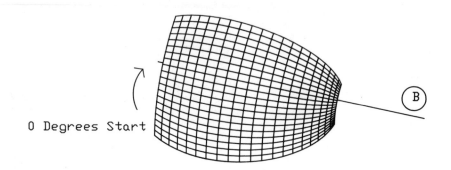

0 Degrees Start

Figure 5-17: Pick a point B.

Remember that it doesn't actually have to be the end point. In Figure 5-17, the axis of revolution was picked toward letter **B**. Note that the direction in which the 3D mesh proceeds to generate change depends on which end of the axis was chosen.

SPECIAL MODELS

You can draw nice-looking patterns with **REVSURF**, but don't forget that one of the main purposes of meshes is to fit a surface to an object for 3D modeling. These objects can then be transferred to AutoSHADE.

In many illustrations for 3D, you see bowls, glasses, goblets or teapots. But you're rarely shown what it takes to draw them.

Drawing a goblet, for example, is a simple series of steps. First, using **PLINE**, draw Figure 5-18. The curved area is a simple polyline that's been curved using **SPLINE**. If you have an AutoCAD version earlier than Release 9, you'll need to provide more points and use **FIT CURVE**.

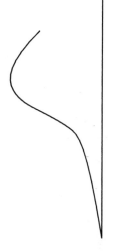

Figure 5-18: How to draw a goblet.

The straight line represents the axis of revolution around which the 3D mesh will revolve and will later be erased.
Once the figure is drawn,

    Type: REVSURF <RETURN>

Response: Select path curve.

Pick the curved object.

Response: Select axis of revolution.

Pick the straight line.

Response: Start angle <0>

Type: <RETURN>

Response: Included angle (+=ccw, -=cw) <Full circle>

Type: <RETURN>

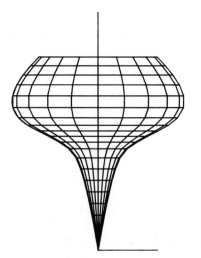

Figure 5-19: Add the base.

When your drawing looks like Figure 5-19, draw a short straight line at the bottom. You'll now use this straight line as the rotated object.

Type: REVSURF <RETURN>

Response: Select path curve.

Pick the small straight line you just drew.

Response: Select axis of revolution.

Pick the larger straight line at the top of the goblet.

Response: Start angle <0>

Type: <RETURN>

Response: Included angle (+=ccw, -=cw) <Full circle>

Type: <RETURN>

Now erase the axis line at the top of the goblet. **DVIEW** lets you rotate and tilt the goblet to get a view that looks like Figure 5-20.

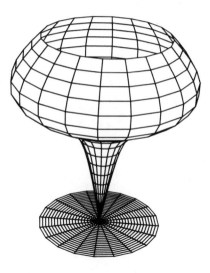

Figure 5-20: Voila!

EDGE-DEFINED SURFACE PATCHES (EDGESURF)

The last of the major 3D meshes is **EDGESURF**. This lets you draw a Coons surface patch for four adjoining edges. This means that if you have four polylines forming four adjacent edges, you can draw a 3D mesh that will find the appropriate vertices even if the polyline is complex and curved. This is particularly dramatic if you curve-fit sharp-angled polylines before using **EDGESURF**.

Draw a figure similar to Figure 5-21. Your drawing doesn't have to look exactly like the one in the book. In fact, you can make your figure look any way you want, but make sure that you use only four distinct polylines. The letters **A**, **B**, **C** and **D** show the approximate starting points of each polyline.

Once you've drawn Figure 5-21, go back and use **PEDIT** to curve-fit each polyline. This will produce an effect similar to Figure 5-22.

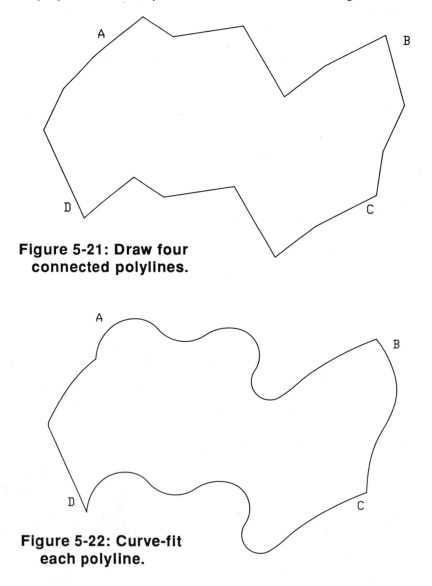

Figure 5-21: Draw four connected polylines.

Figure 5-22: Curve-fit each polyline.

You're now ready to apply **EDGESURF**.

Type: EDGESURF <RETURN>

Response: Select edge 1.

Pick a point along the line at about point **A**. One difficulty is that once the curves have been fitted, it's hard to see where one polyline begins and the other ends. Remember: It's not important that you pick a point exactly at the end point of the polyline. It *is* important that you pick a point consistently close to the beginning of that polyline. You can get some very strange results if you pick one polyline at its beginning vertex and another toward its ending vertex.

Response: Select edge 2.

Pick a point at about point **B**.

Response: Select edge 3.

Pick a point at about point **C**.

Response: Select edge 4.

Pick a point at about point **D**. This should now produce the 3D mesh as in Figure 5-23.

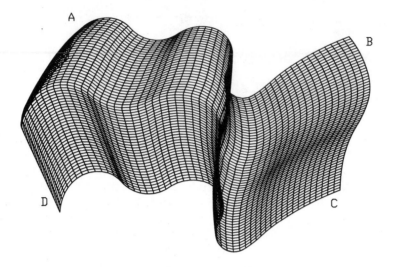

Figure 5-23: Apply EDGESURF.

You may encounter two problems using **EDGESURF**. If you have **SURFTAB1** and **SURFTAB2** set too low, your 3D mesh will not be dense enough to give you the image you need. As a result, the 3D mesh may not be accurate. The second problem occurs if you're inconsistent about where you pick each edge. Although the order in which the edges are picked doesn't matter, you must pick them all toward one end of the polyline or the other.

GENERAL POLYGON MESHES (3DMESH)

One other command produces a 3D mesh: **3DMESH**. Although the other four commands give you a wide latitude and ease of operation, **3DMESH** gives you total control of the size and density of the mesh and the placement of each vertex.

In normal AutoCAD operations **3DMESH** isn't used. Even drawing simple 3D meshes can be a time-consuming, tedious operation, so **EDGESURF**, **REVSURF**, **TABSURF** and **RULESURF** should be your usual choices. **3DMESH** is mainly used in AutoLISP programs to construct specific 3D meshes.

When you issue the **3DMESH** command, you're asked for the size of **M** and **N**. Remember that these control the density (space between the mesh lines). The total number of vertices to be specified will equal **M** x **N.** AutoCAD then asks for the 2D or 3D coordinates for each vertex.

PFACES

As you have seen so far, the various meshes provided let you put the equivalent of numerous **3DFACES** on an object with little effort. Prior to Release 11, this was the only way to place **3DFACES** on hard-to-fit objects. However, Release 11 gives you an additional method by using a command called **PFACE**. Its only restriction is that you can't use it on curved areas. Let's look at how **PFACE** can be used.

Begin by drawing an object similar in shape to the one in Figure 5-24. Place a circle in the center of the object. Now let's move the circle behind the object.

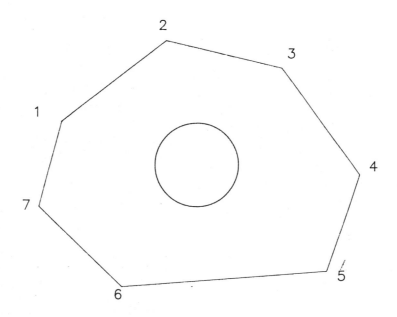

Figure 5-24: Polygon before PFACE.

      Type: Move <RETURN>

Response: Select objects:

   Select: The circle in the middle of your object.

Response: Base point of displacement:

   Type: @ <RETURN>

Response: Second point of displacement:

   Type: @0,0,-1 <RETURN>

This effectively moves the circle "behind" the object. Let's see if we've made any effect.

   Type: Hide <RETURN>

For all practical purposes, nothing happened. The circle is still visible because there's no face to the object. Now let's apply the new **PFACE** to the object. (It's of course possible to apply a series of **3DFACES** and accomplish nearly the same results.)

The biggest advantage of using the **PFACE** command is that it lets us have a single face rather than a series of faces with overlapping edges.

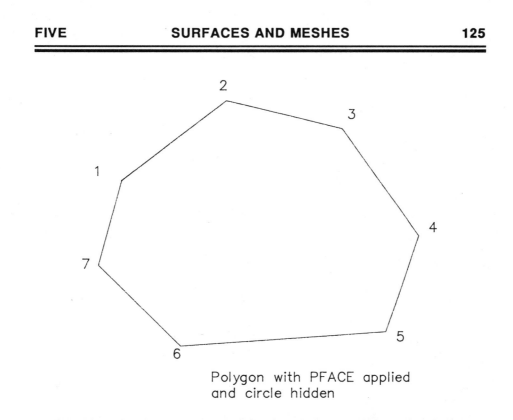

Polygon with PFACE applied
and circle hidden

Figure 5-25: Polygon with PFACE applied and circle hidden.

Type: PFACE <RETURN>

Response: Vertex 1
Vertex 2
Vertex 3
Vertex 4
Vertex 5
Vertex 6
Vertex 7

At each of the above questions, **PICK** an intersection as they are marked. You've now identified each vertex by number.

Response: Vertex 8

Type: <RETURN>

When there are no more vertices to pick, then

Type: <RETURN>

Response:	You Type:
Face 1, vertex 1	1
Face 1, vertex 2	2
Face 1, vertex 3	3
Face 1, vertex 4	4
Face 1, vertex 5	5
Face 1, vertex 6	6
Face 1, vertex 7	7
Face 1, vertex 8	<RETURN>
Face 2, vertex 1	<RETURN>

At this point, a single mesh has been placed on the entire object. Let's check this by hiding the lines to see if the circle now disappears.

Type: Hide <RETURN>

Let's look at the complete command. In the above example you placed a single face on the entire object. The **PFACE** command lets you place multiple faces on objects from any vertex to any vertex. When we finished with face 1, **PFACE** asked us about face 2, etc.

Face 1, vertex 1 really means that having previously identified each various vertex by number in the first phase of the **PFACE** command, you're specifying which vertex you want as the first vertex of face number 1. In essence, you're drawing **3DFACE** lines from point to point. For convenience, we've used the same number for the point and the vertex, but we could have drawn multiple faces from any point or group of points to any other point. They could have even overlapped if necessary.

MAKE PFACES INVISIBLE

When asked for face 1, vertex 3, answer the question with a negative number, which will make the edge of the **PFACE** invisible.

As you can see, 3D meshes aren't hard to construct, as long as you learn the rules for the four major commands and know when to use each one. It will take a little practice, but you'll soon be able to apply a surface to any entity.

6 Putting It All Together

So far, you've learned a lot about the different commands that help orient you with 3D space and how to work with 3D objects. This chapter not only gives you the tools for drawing and editing in 3D, but shows you how each of these commands works together in 3D and 2D drafting and design problems.

Let's look now at the most important command, regardless of your discipline, for increasing your productivity in Releases 10 and 11.

VIEWING YOUR DRAWING WITH WINDOWS (VPORTS)

Beginning with Release 10, you can now create up to four windows, called *viewports*, using the command **VPORTS**.

The productive application of **VPORTS** is limited only by your imagination and needs. But this invaluable tool has two distinct general uses.

First, let's look at a basic 2D application. Even if you never view a thing in 3D, this application makes Releases 10 and 11 worthwhile. Next to plotting, **ZOOM** is the biggest productivity killer in AutoCAD. Unless you have a high-speed display list processing graphics board, you know what it's like to wait for a **ZOOM ALL**. When you're in the middle of your drawing and need to **ZOOM** to another part of the drawing to continue a command, you know what it's like when AutoCAD tells you you're too deep to use transparent **ZOOM**.

Now, with multiple **VPORTS**, you can set one up with a **ZOOM EXTENTS** and the other three with areas of the drawing and various levels of zooms. You can begin a command in one **VPORT** and continue the command in any of the other **VPORTS**. You can restore various views to any **VPORT** and have an unlimited number of whole **VPORT** configurations, which can be saved and restored. With proper organization, you can almost eliminate **ZOOM ALL**s.

The second major use of **VPORTS** is with 3D modeling. The last thing you want to do is continuously rotate the object as you work on it. This can be a problem as you're drawing from one side of the object to another, where the view isn't apparent. Just set up **VPORTS** for each side and **PLAN** view. Now toggle from one **VPORT** to another, even as you're working with your commands.

To illustrate how **VPORTS** works, let's put something in the windows that you've already drawn. Starting from the AutoCAD main menu, we'll edit the drawing (2) that you saved in Chapter 4 as **WIDGET**.

You should now have your widget on the screen as it appeared when you saved it in Chapter 4.

From your screen menu, pick **SETTINGS**, then pick **NEXT,** then pick **VPORTS**. The subcommand options are:

```
Save/Restore/Delete/Join/SIngle/?/2/3/4
```

> **Type:** CTRL C

This will cancel the command. If you have pull-down menus, pick **SETTINGS**, then pick **VIEWPORTS**. You're now shown a picture of the possible viewport configurations in a dialog box. Now you can pick any of the possible configurations. From the dialog box, pick **EXIT**.

> **Type:** VPORTS <RETURN>

> **Response:** Save/Restore/Delete/Join/SIngle/?/2/3/4

To activate the viewports, choose one of the number options (**2, 3** or **4**). Note what happens with each of these options.

> **Type:** 2 <RETURN>

> **Response:** Horizontal/Vertical.

You can now split your screen into two vertical or horizontal screens of equal size.

> **Type:** V <RETURN>

Your screen should now have two windows.

Type: VPORTS <RETURN>

Response: Save/Restore/Delete/Join/SIngle/?/2/3/4

Type: SI <RETURN>

By choosing **SI** as an option, you restore the view to a single window.

Type: VPORTS <RETURN>

Response: Save/Restore/Delete/Join/SIngle/?/2/3/4

Type: 3 <RETURN>

Response: Horizontal/Vertical/Above/Below/Left/Right

Type: H <RETURN>

By choosing either **HORIZONTAL** or **VERTICAL** after the three viewports are selected, you divide the screen into three windows of equal size.

Type: VPORTS <RETURN>

Response: Save/Restore/Delete/Join/SIngle/?/2/3/4

Type: SI <RETURN>

This returns you to a single screen.

Type: VPORTS <RETURN>

Response: Save/Restore/Delete/Join/SIngle/?/2/3/4

Type: 3 <RETURN>

Response: Horizontal/Vertical/Above/Below/Left/Right

   If you choose **ABOVE**, **BELOW**, **LEFT** or **RIGHT**, the viewports will be divided into one large and two small windows. You can place the large window above, below, to the left or to the right of the two smaller windows.

Type: R <RETURN>

   You should now have one large window on the right and two smaller windows on the left.

Type: VPORTS <RETURN>

Response: Save/Restore/Delete/Join/SIngle/?/2/3/4

Type: SI <RETURN>

This returns you to a single window.

Type: VPORTS <RETURN>

Response: Save/Restore/Delete/Join/SIngle/?/2/3/4

Type: 4 <RETURN>

This creates four viewports of equal size.

Type: VPORTS <RETURN>

Response: Save/Restore/Delete/Join/SIngle/?/2/3/4

Type: S <RETURN>

Response: ?/Name for new viewport configuration.

Type: VP1 <RETURN>

SAVE lets you assign a name to the current configuration. When restored, the current view for each window is restored along with the viewport configuration. *Note*: the current view is the one that's active in a particular window when you saved the **VPORTS** configuration. As you'll see, you can have a different view for each **VPORTS** and save the whole configuration.

Type: VPORTS <RETURN>

Response: Save/Restore/Delete/Join/SIngle/?/2/3/4

Type: R <RETURN>

Type: ? <RETURN>

The I.D. numbers may differ on your screen. The following are examples.

Response: Current configuration:
id# 16
corners: 0.5000, 0.0000   1.0000, 0.5000
id# 13
corners: 0.5000, 0.5000   1.0000, 1.0000
id# 14
corners: 0.0000, 0.5000   0.5000, 1.0000
id# 15
corners: 0.0000, 0.0000   0.5000, 0.5000

```
Configuration VP1:
0.5000, 0.0000    1.0000, 0.5000
0.5000, 0.5000    1.0000, 1.0000
0.0000, 0.5000    0.5000, 1.0000
0.0000, 0.0000    0.5000, 0.5000
?/Name of viewport configuration to restore
```

Type: VP1 <RETURN>

As you can see, whenever you ask for information about a viewport configuration, you get a lot of it. You're given the identification numbers and screen positions of the active viewports. The positions of the active viewports assume limits of **0,0** for the lower left-hand corner of the screen and an upper right-hand corner limit of **1,1** (see Figure 6-1).

Therefore, screen 1 would go from **0,0** to **.5,.5**. Screen 2 would be **0,.5** to **.5,1**. Screen 3 would be **.5,0** to **1,1**. When referring to screen I.D.s, always list the current active viewport first.

You should now have restored a viewport configuration of four viewports of equal size.

Type: VPORTS <RETURN>

Response: Save/Restore/Delete/Join/SIngle/?/2/3/4

Type: J <RETURN>

Response: Select dominant viewport.

Pick the upper left-hand screen.

Response: Select viewport to join.

Pick the lower left-hand screen.

The **JOIN** subcommand lets you join two adjacent windows into one larger window. You're first asked to choose the dominant viewport and then to select the viewport to merge. The two viewports *must* be adjacent to each other. The object will take on the **VIEW**, **SNAP**, **GRID**, etc., of the dominant viewport.

The **DELETE** subcommand lets you delete a previously saved viewport.

DIVIDING VIEWPORTS

If you create a window while in a window, then the current window will be subdivided if possible. Remember that the maximum number of viewports available to you at any one time is four.

To explore the usefulness of the **VPORTS** command, create three **VPORTS** as shown in Figure 6-1. The object is the same in all three windows. Pick window **1**. The crosshairs should indicate that it is the active window.

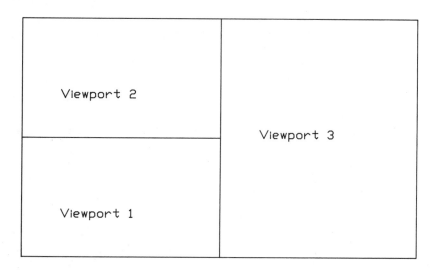

Figure 6-1: Viewports.

Now change the view in this window. Remember that in Chapter **4** you saved a view, **V1**.

Type: VIEW <RETURN>

Response: ?/Delete/Restore/Save/Window

Type: RESTORE <RETURN>

Response: View name to restore.

Type: V1 <RETURN>

A new view should now appear in window **1**. Windows **2** and **3** have the same view of the object.

REGEN AND REDRAW WITH VIEWPORTS

As you'll remember, only one viewport can be active at any time. The active viewport is always picked and the cursor is displayed with crosshairs, while in the inactive viewport(s) the cursor is displayed with an arrow. To change from one viewport to another, simply pick the one you wish to make active.

If you issue the command **REDRAW** or **REGEN,** *only the current active viewport will be affected.* If you want to **REGEN** or **REDRAW** all viewports at once, you need to use the commands **REGENALL** or **REDRAWALL**. Try these on the current windows and see how they differ.

PAPER SPACE—MODEL SPACE

Beginning with Release 11, AutoCAD introduced Paper Space. It's really more of a concept than a command. Paper Space lets you compose your drawing exactly as you want to see it—with multiple views and even at different scales—then plot those views out as one drawing.

To begin an overview of Paper Space and Model Space, it's necessary to create a new term for an old concept. Model Space is your traditional way of drawing in AutoCAD. Prior to Release 11, all work in AutoCAD was done in "Model Space," although it wasn't given that name until "Paper Space" came along.

One of Paper Space's main purposes is to let you dynamically work in an unlimited number of viewports, which operate the same as the regular viewports. You can have multiple views, different zooms, various rotated DVIEWS, and you can toggle within most commands from one viewport to another. You can also freeze and thaw selectively within each viewport. You can make as many of these special viewports as you want and dynamically size and resize them at will. They may also overlap each other as necessary.

After using the viewports within Paper Space to either develop your object or compose your views of the object, you have the ability to arrange the viewports anywhere on the screen and then plot the screen as you see it.

Because you can toggle back and forth between Paper Space and Model Space with different views, there's the danger of thinking of these two modes as being two different drawings. They are not. Anything done to any view, or any part of an entity, while in Paper Space is the same as editing that entity in reality. Remember you have only one set of entities. Paper Space just gives you more flexibility in viewing and plotting those entities.

And there's also some confusion about **TILEMODE** settings. The *AutoCAD Release 11 Reference Manual* refers simply to **TILEMODE 0** and **TILEMODE 1**. Paper Space and Model Space can both be invoked in **TILEMODE 0**. On the other hand, **TILEMODE 0** can *work* only in Model Space.

It's easier if you think of Paper Space and Model Space as two different modes of viewing and working with your drawing. Within each mode you have a series of commands specific to that mode. You must always be in one mode or the other to use specific related commands. The command that toggles you from one mode to the other is **TILEMODE**. This is a system variable rather than an actual AutoCAD command, but it's used the same way. If **TILEMODE** is set to **1**, you're in Model Space mode; if **TILEMODE** is set to **0**, you're in Paper Space mode.

To illustrate these concepts, draw some lines on your screen. At this point, you're in Model Space. Once the entities are drawn, change to Paper Space mode.

    Type: TILEMODE <RETURN>

Response: New value for TILEMODE <|>

    Type: 0 <RETURN>

Your screen should go blank. Notice the right triangle in the lower left-hand side of your screen. This is the UCS icon for Paper Space. In order to work in Paper Space, you'll need to create at least one viewport. This is done with the **MVIEW** command.

Type: MVIEW <RETURN>

Response: ON/OFF/Hideplot/Fit/2/3/4/Restore/<First Point>:

Select: A point on your screen and move your cursor to draw a window. You're creating a viewport. Notice the flexibility you have. You can create the viewport in any size or rectangular shape you want. When you've picked two points that outline the shape of the viewport, the entities from Model Space appear in the viewport.

Repeat the above command and draw two more viewports on your screen.

Notice at this point that you can't enter the viewports to change anything. This is because you're in Pspace rather than Mspace. This is where you might get confused. Once you've set **TILEMODE** to **0**, you're in Paper Space. But there are two modes of operation within Paper Space. They are called Pspace and Mspace. It's important to remember that while working in Mspace within the Paper Space mode, you're NOT working in Model Space mode. Please don't confuse the two. That is, with **TILEMODE** set to **0**, you're working in Paper Space, and Pspace and Mspace are both part of Paper Space.

Let's now enter the Mspace mode of operation within Paper Space.

Type: Mspace <RETURN>

This mode of operation is similar to that of **VPORTS** in that the normal UCS icons now appear in each one of the viewports. If you move your cursor outside the viewports, it shows the standard inactive arrow. Notice also that one of your viewports has a double outline indicating that it is your active viewport. Move your cursor inside this viewport and watch your crosshairs become active. If you move the cursor now to the other two viewports, the crosshairs turn into an arrow, indicating that the other two viewports are not active. **PICK** while inside one of the other viewports. It now becomes the active viewport.

This means that while you are in the Mspace mode of Paper Space, the viewports you created will act like the traditional viewports available to you in Model Space. But there are two big differences. First, you can have as many viewports as you need. (*Note*: only 16 may be visible at any one time.) Second, when you enter Pspace mode within Paper Space, you can move the viewports around, make them larger or smaller, annotate them anywhere on the screen with text, draw from one to another, and plot exactly what you see on the screen.

At any point in time, you can return to Model Space by changing **TILEMODE** from **0** to **1**.

    Type: TILEMODE   <RETURN>

  Response: New value for TILEMODE <0>

    Type: 1   <RETURN>

Your original drawing is now on your screen. Any changes you might have made to the drawing while in Mspace within Paper Space are retained when you return to Model Space. Annotations you made while in Pspace within Paper Space are not reflected. You may toggle back and forth at any time.

PAPER SPACE COMMANDS

Only four major commands are available to you while you're in Paper Space: **MVIEW**, **VPLAYER**, **PSPACE** and **MSPACE**. **MSPACE** and **PSPACE** control where on the screen you're able to draw. When you enter **PSPACE**, you can draw across the **VPORTS** and label text parallel to the screen without changing the **UCS**. You also can resize the viewports and move them anywhere on the screen. You may also plot exactly what you see and scale the contents of the viewports as needed. **MSPACE** simply turns the viewports into regular viewports. You're permitted to draw only inside the viewports (the same as with the Model Space **VPORT** command).

MVIEW controls the creation of Paper Space viewports. It also controls whether the lines are to be hidden in any given viewport during plot time. In this way, when you plot you can hide the lines in some viewports and not in others.

You may create up to four viewports each time you use the **MVIEW** command.

Type: MVIEW <RETURN> **(TILEMODE must be set to 0.)**

Response: ON/OFF/Hideplot/Fit/2/3/4/Restore/<First Point>:

Type: 4 <RETURN>

MVIEW now creates four viewports, each with the same view of the previous Model Space. These viewports are independent, just as if they were created one at a time. They may be moved, made larger or smaller, or activated independently within the Mspace command.

MVIEW also lets you restore any viewport configuration previously saved in Model Space. Assume you have a three-viewport configuration in Model Space called **V3**, consisting of top, plan and side views of your object.

Type: MVIEW <RETURN> **(TILEMODE must be set to 0.)**

Response: ON/OFF/Hideplot/Fit/2/3/4/Restore/<First Point>:

Type: Restore <RETURN>

Response: ?/Name of window configuration to insert <*ACTIVE>

Type: V3 <RETURN>

Now choose Fit, or pick a first and second point. The viewport configuration will be restored within Paper Space.

HIDDEN LINES IN PAPER SPACE

Remember that when you plot in Paper Space, each viewport is treated as a separate entity. You might want one viewport to hide lines, but not another. Therefore, **MVIEW** gives you the ability to choose those viewports where lines will be hidden during plot and those where the lines will not be hidden during the plot.

Type: MVIEW <RETURN> **(TILEMODE** must be set to **0.)**

Response: ON/OFF/Hideplot/Fit/2/3/4/Restore/<First Point>:

Type: H <RETURN> (Hideplot)

Response: ON/OFF

Type: ON <RETURN>

Response: Select objects:

Now pick the viewport(s) where you want the lines to be hidden during the plot. Remember to pick the lines around the viewport, not inside the viewport itself, and not the entities within the viewport. Likewise, you may choose **OFF** and pick the viewports where you don't want the lines to be hidden during the plot.

TURNING VIEWPORTS ON AND OFF

There are several reasons why you may want to turn a viewport on or off. First, if you're not working in a viewport currently, it may save you some time to turn it off. This will let you move and change the size of several viewports without having to wait for each one to regenerate. Second, you're allowed to have only 16 viewports on at one time. This doesn't mean you can't have more than 16 viewports, but only 16 will be seen on the screen at one time. When you exceed the maximum number, AutoCAD will begin automatically turning off certain viewports. You can choose which will be turned off and which turned on.

Type: MVIEW <RETURN> **(TILEMODE** must be set to **0.)**

Response: ON/OFF/Hideplot/Fit/2/3/4/Restore/<First Point>:

Type: OFF <RETURN>

Response: ON/OFF

Type: ON <RETURN>

Response: Select objects:

Now pick the viewport(s) where you want the lines to be off.

REGULAR AUTOCAD COMMANDS IN PSPACE

One of the main reasons for using Paper Space is to compose different views on the screen and plot them all out at once. Therefore, you need to be able to move the views around on the screen as well as to resize them as needed. To do this, you use regular AutoCAD commands such as **MOVE** and **SCALE**.

First, **TILEMODE** must be **0** and you must be in Pspace. Assume that you have several viewports on the screen and that you want to change the position of one of the viewports.

Type: Pspace <RETURN> (You must first be in Pspace.)

Type: Move <RETURN>

Response: Select objects:

Select: Along the outline of the viewport(s) you want to move. You may also use a Window or Crossing. Remember, at this point, the entire viewport is treated as though it were a single entity.

Response: 1 selected, 1 found

Select: <RETURN> (This confirms the selection set.)

Response: Base point or displacement:

Select: A base point on the viewport to be moved and drag it to the new position, then PICK.

You may move the viewport anywhere on the screen you want to. You may even overlap other viewports.

Multiple Scales on the Same Sheet

Assume you have four viewports and **TILEMODE** is set to **0**. You are in Paper Space. What you want to do is plot each of four separate views to a different scale at the time of plotting.

The first consideration is the scale factor you're going to use at the time you plot. If it's 1=1, you must do all of your scaling first within the viewports. On the other hand, if the overall scale factor at the time of plotting is 1=50 or 1/4"=1', then you can work up a general relationship of the viewports to each other.

Start with the assumption that you're going to be plotting the Paper Space viewports at 1=1 at plot time. Viewport 1 should be plotted 1=50; Viewport 2, 1=25; Viewport 3, 1=100; Viewport 4, 1=1000.

Type: Mspace <RETURN> (This assumes **TILEMODE 0.**)

PICK and make active Viewport 1.

Type: ZOOM <RETURN>

Type: 1/50xp <RETURN>

The XP at the end of the **ZOOM** factor scales the image in the active viewport by that ratio. Note that the object isn't actually changing size. Only the **ZOOM** view of that object in relation to Paper Space units has changed. That's how different scales are created.

If you're scaling 1/4"=1', you must enter 1/48.

VPLAYER (CONTROLLING LAYERS IN MULTIPLE VIEWPORTS)

The **VPLAYER** command controls the visibility of layers on individual viewports. The **FREEZE** and **THAW** commands control the visibility of layers in all viewports at once. In order to use **VPLAYER**, you must be in Paper Space; that is, the system variable **TILEMODE** must be set to **0**. You may be in either Mspace or Pspace at the time you use **VPLAYER**, but the command acts slightly differently depending on which mode you're in.

Begin with a drawing that has several layers. Set **TILEMODE** to **0**.

Type: `TILEMODE 0 <RETURN>`

Now set up several viewports.

Type: `MVIEW <RETURN>`

PICK the first and second corner. Repeat this command several times until you have at least two or three viewports on the screen.
Now enter Mspace.

Type: `MSPACE <RETURN>`

Notice that one of your viewports is the current viewport. You can confirm this in the traditional way by moving your crosshairs from viewport to viewport. When the crosshairs change from an arrow to crosshairs, then that is the current viewport.
Assume now that the layer you want to freeze is **LAYER1**.

Type: `VPLAYER  <RETURN>`

Response: `?/Freeze/Thaw/Reset/Newfrz/Vpvisdflt:`

Type: `Freeze  <RETURN>`

Response: `Layer(s) to Freeze:`

Type: Layer1 <RETURN>

(You may enter layer names separated by commas or use any of the wild-card facilities available to you in Release 11.)

Response: All/Select/<Current>:

Select: <RETURN>

By pressing **<RETURN>** at this option, only the current viewport is affected by the Freeze option of **VPLAYER**.

Select: <RETURN>

This exits you from the **VPLAYER** command and the screen is updated, with **LAYER1** frozen only in the current viewport.

You could have selected All or Select instead of Freeze. If you had chosen All, then all viewports currently on your screen would have that layer frozen.

But what about new viewports that might be created after the **VPLAYER** command? When those viewports are created, the layers previously affected through an All option aren't affected with a simple **FREEZE**.

If you had chosen Select, you would have been asked to select objects, then select the viewports where you wanted the layers frozen.

The Thaw option of **VPLAYER** works exactly like the Freeze option, but makes the selected layers visible.

The Current option of **VPLAYER** freezes or thaws the current layer only. This option is valid only if you're in Mspace instead of Pspace.

New Frozen Layers

Newfrz, an option of **VPLAYER**, lets you create a layer that is frozen in all viewports. But why would you want to do this? Assume that you had six viewports on your screen. You're in Pspace and want information placed in only one of the viewports. Use the Newfrz option of **VPLAYER** and create a new layer. Now Thaw that layer only for the current viewport. Use the regular **LAYER** command and Set the new layer as the current layer. Since it was created as frozen in all viewports, then what you draw on the new layer will appear only in the current viewport, since it was frozen on all the others.

Type: Mspace <RETURN> (This is easier to illustrate if you are in Mspace.)

Type: Vplayer <RETURN>

Response: ?/Freeze/Thaw/Reset/Newfrz/Vpvisdflt:

Type: Newfrz <RETURN>

Response: New Viewport frozen layer name(s):

Type: Layer2 <RETURN>

Response: ?/Freeze/Thaw/Reset/Newfrz/Vpvisdflt:

Type: Thaw <RETURN>

Response: Layer(s) to Thaw:

Type: Layer2 <RETURN>

Response: All/Select/<Current>:

Select: <RETURN> <RETURN>

Now set yourself to Layer2 using the regular AutoCAD **LAYER** command and you're ready to draw on that layer only in the selected viewport.

New Layer Visibility (VPVISDFLT)

AutoCAD lets you set the visibility of any layer for any specified viewport(s). But what happens when new viewports are created? What layers should be visible and what layers should not?

The **VPVISDFLT** command of **VPLAYER** lets you determine this.

Type: VPLAYER <RETURN> (**TILEMODE** must be set to **0**.)

Response: ?/Freeze/Thaw/Reset/Newfrz/Vpvisdflt:

Type: Vpvisdflt <RETURN>

Response: Layer name(s) to change default viewport visibility:

Type: Layer1 <RETURN>

(You may enter layer names separated by commas or use any of the wild-card facilities available to you in Release 11.)

Response: Change default viewport visibility to Frozen/Thawed:

Type: Frozen <RETURN>

From now on, any new viewport created will have **LAYER1** already frozen.

DRAWING IN PSPACE

You can still draw while in Pspace of Paper Space mode. Even though the viewports are not active, you can draw across them. You're not actually touching your Model Space drawing. Instead, you're drawing over your drawing. While in Pspace, you may plot these out together. This is great for such things as annotation or drawing connecting leader lines. When you return to Model Space, Paper Space entities are not there.

GET RID OF PAPER SPACE BOXES

When you create a viewport in Pspace, the outline of the viewport is created on the current layer. A good tip is to always make sure you create a viewport on a special viewport layer. When you plot, you're going to get exactly what you see on the screen, viewport outlines and all. If you don't want these outlines, then **FREEZE** the viewport layer. The outlines will be turned off and you'll be left with only your entities that you want to plot, properly placed where you need them.

As you can see, the concept of Paper Space with Release 11 opens up a new dimension in controlling the final output of your drawing.

SHADING

Shading is added with the **SHADE** command.

Type: SHADE <RETURN>

Whatever *can* be shaded *will* be shaded. There are no prompts. You can't plot the shading. You can't place light sources. Only solid colors are used. You can make a slide. The color of the shade is determined by the color of the entity being shaded.

When **3DFACES** are being shaded, the outlines of the faces are shaded in the background color. Turning off their layers to hide what's behind them will also prevent them from being shaded. If you want the faces shaded but you don't want their edges visible, use **LISP126**, which explodes meshes to faces then makes the faces invisible. Even though the faces are invisible, they still will shade.

PLAN VIEWS

PLAN sets a plan view for any coordinate system. This command changes only the viewing direction to the viewpoint of **0,0,1** for the active coordinate system. The coordinate system itself remains unchanged. You have three options:

Type: PLAN <RETURN>

Response: Current UCS/UCS/World.

CURRENT UCS generates a plan view for the current **UCS**.
UCS asks you for the name of a previously saved **UCS**. A plan view for that **UCS** is then generated.

WORLD generates a plan view of the **WCS**. Pick and make active window **3**. Now set this window to the world plan view.

> **Type:**   PLAN <RETURN>

> **Response:**   Current UCS/UCS/World.

> **Type:**   WORLD <RETURN>

Notice how the object in window **3** is now in world plan view. The important thing to remember about **VPORTS** is that each **VPORT** operates independently of the others. Remember also that **VPORTS** aren't limited to 3D. You can use them at any time to have various 2D zooms or views.

BASIC 3D DRAWING COMMANDS

3DLINE

Even though **3DLINE** is a valid command in AutoCAD, it's really a leftover from earlier versions. For all practical purposes, there's no difference between **3DLINE** and **LINE**.

In earlier versions, the regular **LINE** command wouldn't let you draw using the **Z** coordinate; **3DLINE** was the only such command available then. Beginning with Release 10, you can draw any entities with three coordinates. Therefore, **3DLINE** as a separate command serves no special purpose. Feel free to use **3DLINE** and **LINE** interchangeably.

3D POLYLINE (3DPOLY)

The **3DPOLY** command (which generates a 3D polyline) and **PLINE** are *not* one and the same, so don't confuse them with each other. **PLINE** won't accept a **Z** coordinate across planes. **PLINE**s may be drawn in 3D, but only in one plane.

3DPOLY is a general-purpose 3D polyline. This command will accept coordinates across planes. You may use **3DPOLY** only with straight line segments. Polyarcs aren't supported across planes. **PEDIT** works with both, and B-spline curves are permitted.

To fully understand the difference between **PLINE** and **3DPOLY**, let's use each one and then do a **LIST** on them.

Type: PLINE <RETURN>

Draw one small segment of a polyline without terminating the command.

Type: .XY <RETURN>

and continue the polyline in another direction and pick a point. Terminate the polyline by pressing **<RETURN>**. Notice that AutoCAD didn't ask you for the **Z** coordinate as it would if you'd used the **FILTER** commands.

Type: 3DPOLY <RETURN>

Draw one small segment similar to the first line segment previously drawn, without terminating the command.

Type: .XY <RETURN>

and continue the polyline in another direction and pick a point.

Response: (need Z)

Type: 4 <RETURN>

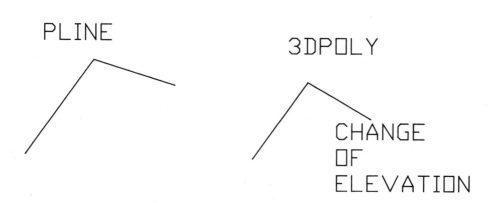

Figure 6-2: 3D polys are coplanar.

To terminate the polyline, press **<RETURN>**. You should have a drawing similar to Figure 6-2. Now list each polyline group.

    Type: LIST <RETURN>

Response: Select Objects.

Pick the entity drawn with **PLINE**. Then pick the entity drawn with **3DPOLY** and **CONFIRM**. You'll see that each **PLINE** section maintains a **Z** coordinate of zero. On the other hand, **3DPOLY** has a **Z** coordinate of zero for the two vertices of the first segment, but then changes to a **Z** of **4** in the second segment.

In brief, this means that **PLINE** polylines can be drawn in 3D, but all vertices must be on the same plane. **3DPOLY** polylines are full-purpose 3D entities whose vertices may cross planes.

A good visual example of this is Figure 6-3. Note the direction of the **UCS** icon. Remember that the polyline and the **3DPOLY** were drawn visually the same in plan view, but that the second line segment of the **3DPOLY** was drawn four units into **Z**.

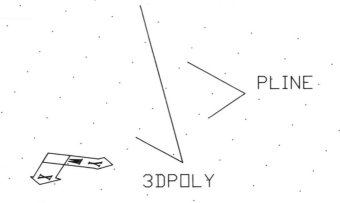

Figure 6-3: Note direction of lines.

The true **3DPOLY** will be of special interest to civil engineers. Now it's not only possible to create 3D visual topos and contours, but true coordinate, area and distance information can be extracted from the database and exact measurements taken from within the drawing.

3DFACE

You've used **3DFACE** extensively in previous chapters. **3DFACE** is used to draw objects that appear to be solid. Unlike the **SOLID** command, **3DFACE** may not be filled or shaded in AutoCAD, but both are used to pass information to AutoSHADE, which performs this function. However, you can **HATCH** a **3DFACE** as you did in Chapter 1. Take care to do all hatching on a separate layer, since hatching increases the time necessary to hide lines.

Unlike the **SOLID** command, **3DFACE** is drawn from corner to corner, clockwise or counterclockwise around the object, without the need to draw a "bow tie."

However, remember that **3DFACE** is closed after four points. If you continue, it uses the previous third point as point **1** for the next four.

Figure 6-4: Be careful when applying 3DFACE.

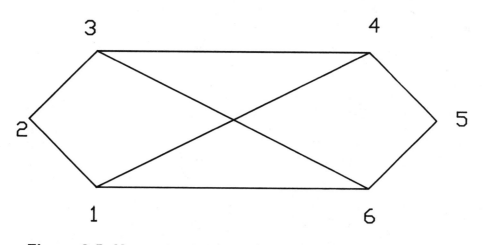

Figure 6-5: You may not get what you expect.

As long as the object is square or rectangular, there's generally no problem applying a **3DFACE**. The problem arises when the object is odd-shaped. For example, if you try to go around the six points (Figure 6-4), you would cross over, as in Figure 6-5. By going around the figure clockwise (**1, 2, 3, 4, 5** and **6**), a crisscross effect is created. That's because the command is finished when it reaches the fourth vertex. Points **1, 2, 3** and **4** return the **3DFACE** back to point **1**. When you resume at point **5**, it uses point **3** as its point **1**. Thus **3, 4, 5** and **6** return the last point back to point **3**.

You can fix this by using the invisible feature of **3DFACE**. Let's create a drawing similar to Figure 6-4.

Type: 3DFACE <RETURN>

Response: First point.

Pick point 1.

Response: Second point.

Pick point 2.

Response: Third point.

Pick point 3.

Response: Fourth point.

Type: I <RETURN>

Pick point 4.

Response: Third point.

Pick point 5.

Response: Fourth point.

Type: I <RETURN>

Pick point 6.

Type: <RETURN>

You've now put two **3DFACE**s on the object. But at the points where the lines would have crossed over, they were prefaced with **I**, which stands for "invisible." The lines weren't actually drawn, even though the **3DFACE** was added. It's possible to have all edges invisible. Then the **3DFACE** wouldn't appear at all in the wire frame view, but the items would be hidden behind them. To actually finish out the **3DFACE** on the entire object, you'll still need to go around one more level back to **1**, which will complete points **4, 5, 6** and **1**.

One final thing to note about **3DFACE** is that it can't have thickness. If you assign thickness, it's ignored when a **3DFACE** is drawn.

ELEVATION

This is a predetermined setting for the default of the **Z** coordinate. Therefore, if **ELEVATION** is set to **4** when a line is drawn from **X-Y** point **0,0** to **X-Y** point **3,5**, then the actual coordinates for each point would be **0,0,4** to **3,5,4**.

ELEVATION is set with the command **ELEV**. The responses are:

```
New current elevation     New current thickness
```

Remember that once issued, **ELEVATION** remains in effect until changed.

ELEVATION isn't just the command that precedes **THICKNESS**. Once any **UCS** that redefines the **X Y** plane is set, **ELEVATION** can act as an offset above the plane, instead of resetting your **UCS**.

THICKNESS

Think of **THICKNESS** as adding height to an entity. This "height" or "thick" entity projects toward positive **Z** if **THICKNESS** is a positive number. AutoCAD calls this projection an *extrusion*. Therefore, a line drawn with a **THICKNESS** of 4 is said to *extrude* into the **Z** axis four units.

In AutoCAD's earlier versions, this extrusion was an illusion. You couldn't **OBJECT SNAP** to the extruded portion of the object. Releases 10 and 11 allow this, and it's extremely valuable. **THICKNESS** automatically forms a *solid* (surface face) object, similar to **3DFACE** in that it creates a barrier for hidden lines for the extent of the thickness. The outline of the object isn't solid, but the thickness of the *walls* is.

When **TEXT**, **ATTRIBUTES** and **DIMENSIONS** are created, they're always initially given a thickness of **0** regardless of the original settings. Except for **ASSOCIATIVE DIMENSIONING**, the thickness may later be changed through the **CHANGE** command.

THICKNESS is set through **ELEVATION**.

Type: ELEV <RETURN>

Response: New current elevation.
New current thickness.

FILTERS

The **FILTERS** command was available in earlier versions, but is still very useful. You might call this the "Gimme a Z" concept. Before AutoCAD gave all entities the ability to have a **Z** coordinate in the database, it needed a way to produce the **Z** coordinate for the few entities that could use the coordinate. One of the methods in the earliest 3D version was **ELEVATION**. But **ELEVATION** couldn't be reset as you continued to draw a **3DLINE**. Therefore, the filtering system was used.

The way this works is simple. You start your command with a period (.) and the one or two coordinates where you'll point. For example, when pointing to an **X-Y** coordinate, you type **.XY** and pick a point on the **X-Y** plane. After selecting the **X-Y** point, AutoCAD asks you to enter the **Z** coordinate from the keyboard. If you choose a single coordinate filter (such as **.X**), then after you pick a point, it asks for **Y-Z**. Remember that the current **UCS** affects what is **X** and **Y**; that is, any change in the **UCS** redefines the **X-Y** plane.

Type: LINE <RETURN>

Response: From point.

Pick a point.

Response: To point.

Type: .XY <RETURN>

Response: Of

Pick another point.

Response: (need Z)

Type: 4 <RETURN>

<RETURN>

If you now do a listing of this line, you'll see that the **FROM** point has a **Z** coordinate of zero and the **TO** point has a **Z** coordinate of **4**.

You can also filter any one or two coordinates and supply the third coordinate from the keyboard. You might type **.YZ** and AutoCAD would respond (**NEED X**) after you pick the point.

DIMENSIONING IN 3D:
WHAT YOU SEE IS NOT WHAT YOU GET!

Be careful! There are some obvious problems with dimensioning in 3D. As you might expect with text, it can be hard to predict the exact appearance of the 3D lines and text for an object. Your first inclination might be to simply change to a **UCS VIEW** as you would with text, thus making the **X** axis parallel to the screen. You have one alternative concerning where you want the dimension lines to appear.

The problem with this approach is that the measurements won't be correct and can be off by a great deal, depending upon the angle of view to the object.

Only three available **UCS**'s will guarantee an accurate measurement: **WCS**, **UCS ENTITY** and **UCS 3POINT**, where the entity being dimensioned or measured is parallel to the **X** axis.

If you want to use the **UCS VIEW** approach, first take your measurements using the **DIST** command and write them down. Set your drawing to **UCS VIEW** and proceed to dimension the object. When the **DIMENSION** command displays the dimension text, change it to the correct dimension.

There are several things wrong with this method. It can be used only for plotting a specific view of the object. The dimensions should, of course, be saved to a special layer, so that they can be frozen if necessary. If you try to rotate the object using **DVIEW**, there's no telling where the dimensions will be or what they'll look like in the other view. Finally, **ASSOCIATIVE DIMENSIONING** will be worthless to you.

A better way to dimension an object in 3D space is to set the **UCS** parallel to the object with **UCS ENTITY** or **UCS 3POINT**. **UCS ENTITY** is easier, but has its own problems. You can't control which direction is positive **X** or positive **Y**; that was controlled for each entity when it was created. As a result, you might be surprised by the direction of the dimensioning text or dimensioning lines.

The most precise method of dimensioning is to use **UCS 3POINT**. This lets you control the direction of positive **X** and positive **Y**. Remember that your dimensioning text will follow the path of positive **X**, the same as regular text. As you go around each side of the object, you'll need to change the appropriate **UCS**.

You must be very careful using dimensioning. Unless you know the exact dimensions of each side of the drawing, it's hard to be sure of the results. If you're ever in doubt, use the **DIST** command while in **WCS** to take the measurements to check against the dimensions. When you're more comfortable with the proper **UCS**, you must be more confident of your dimension's accuracy.

CAN YOU CORRECTLY DIMENSION WITH PERSPECTIVE?

Yes, if you use some tricks. It's easiest if you set your perspective *before* dimensioning. Then save your view, **<VIEW, S, name of view>**. Now change to your **UCS 3POINT** for the first dimension. It will **REGEN** without perspective. Now dimension the object and **RESTORE** the previously saved view, **<VIEW, R, name of view>**. The restored view will be with **PERSPECTIVE ON**, complete with dimensions ready to be plotted.

EDITING IN 3D

How does editing differ in 3D? Many edit commands now need to take into account the **Z** coordinate; and there are some restrictions.

Some edit commands work better in plan view, **UCS ENTITY** or **UCS VIEW**. The **CHANGE, BREAK, TRIM, EXTEND, FILLET, CHAMFER** and **OFFSET** commands can't work on entities whose extrusion directions aren't parallel to the **Z** axis of the current **UCS**. This sometimes can be corrected by changing the **UCS** to **UCS ENTITY**. Others, like **BREAK, TRIM, EXTEND, FILLET, CHAMFER** and **OFFSET** may give unpredictable results unless you're in plan view of the current **UCS** or **WCS**. For more on how AutoCAD commands have changed with Releases 10 and 11, see Chapter 7, "New Twists to Old Commands."

3D ERROR MESSAGES WHILE EDITING

A couple of error messages can be troublesome when you use some of the above commands, such as **CHANGE** and **BREAK**.

```
Entity not parallel with UCS
```

You get this message when you try to break an entity whose extrusion direction isn't parallel to the **Z** axis of the current **UCS**. You can fix this by defining a new **UCS** using the **ENTITY** subcommand, which will force the **UCS** in the direction of the entity. The entity can be broken, and you can return to the **UCS** you were using by selecting **UCS PREVIOUS**.

```
(2 not parallel with UCS)
```

You'll get this message while trying to use the **CHANGE** command. After telling you how many objects were selected and found, this message tells you how many will *not* be affected by the **CHANGE** command. For these entities, you should probably use the **CHPROP** command, designed specifically for entities in 3D.

CHANGE PROPERTIES WITH CHPROP

The **CHPROP** command performs only four of the **CHANGE** command options: **COLOR, LAYER, LINE TYPE** and **THICKNESS**. The advantage of **CHPROP** over **CHANGE** is that it works with all entities, regardless of their extrusion direction.

HANDLES

The **HANDLES** command lets you turn handles on if they're currently off and destroy all handles in the drawing database. This command will be of primary interest to third-party software developers. The purpose of **HANDLES** is to assign a unique and permanent numeric identifier to every entity in the drawing database. You have only two choices with this command.

ON AND DESTROY

The **ON** subcommand turns **HANDLES ON** if they're not currently activated. This means that every time an entity is created, it's assigned a unique identifier in the database. You can see the **HANDLES** through **LIST** and **DBLIST** or through AutoLISP.

The **DESTROY** subcommand doesn't just turn **HANDLES OFF**; it destroys all existing **HANDLES** in the drawing database. Because this is such a powerful and permanent command, AutoCAD has gone to great lengths to keep you from doing this accidentally. In addition to presenting you with a dire warning, the confirming question isn't answered with a simple Y or N. You must enter a series of randomly selected code words.

I AGREE
UNHANDLE THAT DATABASE
MAKE MY DATA
PRETTY PLEASE
DESTROY HANDLES
GO AHEAD

You can find more information about entity handles in *The AutoCAD Database Book* (Ventana Press).

HIDDEN LINES

The **HIDE** command gives you a more realistic view of your drawing. When a drawing is created and viewed in 3D using **DVIEW**, it's displayed in wire frame. If a drawing is complex, it can often be difficult to get a realistic picture of it.

HIDE can take a long time on a complex drawing. Therefore, use **HIDE** only when necessary. Once lines are hidden, they stay hidden until the next regeneration of the drawing.

Hidden lines are treated differently, depending on the type of entity. **CIRCLES, SOLIDS, TRACES** and wide **POLYLINES** have closed tops and bottoms if they're drawn with **THICKNESS**. Other entities are transparent; you can force hidden lines by adding a **3DFACE** to them.

Text is always drawn and is never hidden. This can cause problems, so text should always be put on its own layer so that it can be **FROZEN** when necessary.

In general, don't turn layers **OFF** or **ON**. Instead, use **FREEZE** and **THAW**. This is particularly true when using **HIDE**. Entities on a layer that's turned off can hide other entities even though they, themselves, are invisible. This isn't true with frozen layers.

Sometimes you'll want an entity to be visible even though it normally would be hidden from view by another entity. You can force this by creating a **HIDDENLAYER** of the same name as the target entity's layer.

For example, assume you want an entity on layer **PRT1** to never be hidden. Create a layer called **HIDDENPRT1** (the layer's name is "HIDDEN," *plus* the name of the target layer). The entities on that layer will then be drawn according to the definition of that layer during the **HIDE** command.

LET'S PULL IT ALL TOGETHER

Let's see how many concepts you can apply in a practical application by drawing a simple object. First, be sure you're starting with a single **VPORT** and a clear screen. Erase everything on your screen or start a new drawing.

Use decimal units and limits of **36,24**. Set **SNAP** and **GRID** to **1**. (Figure 6-15 at the end of this chapter shows how your final drawing should look.)

Divide your screen into two **VPORTS**.

```
<VPORTS, 2, V>
```

Pick and make active the right window. The crosshairs should be visible in the right viewport.

Type: DVIEW <RETURN>

Response: Select objects.

Type: <RETURN>

Response: CAmera/TArget/Distance/POints/PAn/Zoom/TWist/
CLip/Hide/Off/Undo/eXit

Because you didn't select any objects, the image of a house now
appears in the right viewport.

Type: CAMERA <RETURN>

Response: Enter angle from X-Y plane.

Type: 45 <RETURN>

Response: Enter angle in X-Y plane from X axis.

Type: 45 <RETURN>

Type: <RETURN> (This exits you from DVIEW.)

The purpose of splitting the screen and changing the angle of view
in one screen is to let you see the object from a different point in 3D
space as it develops. It also lets you toggle from one screen to the other
in order to construct the object using different views.

Pick the viewport on the left. The crosshairs should now be in the
viewport on the left, indicating that it's now the active screen. Draw a
5 X 8 rectangle, as illustrated in Figure 6-6.

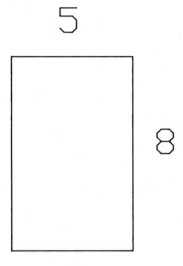

Figure 6-6: Draw rectangle.

<ZOOM, W>

You might want to **ZOOM** in on the object to enlarge it on your screen.

      Type: FILLET <RETURN>

Response: Polyline/Radius/<Select two objects>

      Type: RADIUS <RETURN>

Response: Enter fillet radius.

      Type: 1.75 <RETURN>

      Type: FILLET <RETURN>

Response: `Polyline/Radius/<Select two objects>`

Pick points **1** and **2** as indicated in Figure 6-7.

Type: `FILLET <RETURN>`

Response: `Polyline/Radius/<Select two objects>`

Pick points **3** and **4** as indicated in Figure 6-7. Then pick the right viewport. The crosshairs should now appear in the right viewport, indicating that this is the active screen.

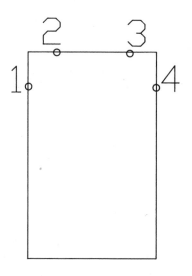

Figure 6-7: Fillet lines.

You'll now create a new **UCS** rotating **90** degrees around the **X** axis.

Type: `UCS <RETURN>`

Response: `Origin/ZAxis/3point/Entity/View/X/Y/Z/Prev/`
          `Restore/Save/Del/?/World`

Type: `X <RETURN>`

Response: Rotation angle about X-axis.

Type: 90 <RETURN>

Now make a copy of the object 18 units above the current object.

Type: COPY <RETURN>

Response: Select object.

Select the entire object and **CONFIRM**.

Response: Basepoint or displacement/Multiple.

<OS-Intersection>

Pick one of the corners of the object.

Response: 2nd point of displacement.

Type: @18<90 <RETURN>

Because the **Y** axis was rotated 90 degrees around the existing **X** axis, a copy of the object was placed directly above the existing object at a distance of 18 units. Now rotate (**TWIST**) your object using **DVIEW**.

Type: DVIEW <RETURN>

Response: Select objects.
Select both objects.

Response: CAmera/TArget/Distance/POints/PAn/Zoom/-
TWist/CLip/Hide/Off/Undo/eXit

Type: TWIST <RETURN>

Response: New view twist.

    Type: 125 <RETURN>

    Type: <RETURN>

<ZOOM, W>

Zoom in on the objects to make them larger on the screen.

Connect intersection points **1** and **2** and points **3** and **4** with a regular line. Be sure to set your **OBJECT SNAP** to **INTERSECTION** when connecting these points (Figure 6-8).

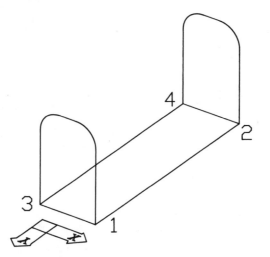

Figure 6-8: Connect objects.

The next step is to turn the five individual entities that made up the initial object (filleted top and sides) and convert them into one polyline.

    Type: PEDIT <RETURN>

Response: Select polyline.

Pick a point on the line at approximately point **1** in Figure 6-9.

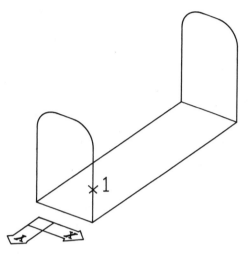

Figure 6-9: Pick object at point 1.

Response: Endpoints have different Z values.

You have now received one of the editing error messages. To correct the error, you must change the **UCS**.

Type: UCS <RETURN>

Response: Origin/ZAxis/3point/Entity/View/X/Y/Z/Prev/
Restore/Save/Del/?/World

Type: 3 <RETURN>

Response: Origin point.

<OS-Intersection>

Pick the intersection at point **1** in Figure 6-10.

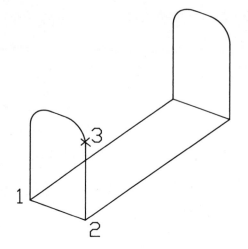

Figure 6-10: UCS 3POINT.

Response: `Point on positive portion X-axis.`

`<OS-Intersection>`

Pick the intersection at point **2** in Figure 6-10.

Response: `Point on positive-Y portion of the UCS X-Y plane.`

`<OS-Endpoint>`

Pick the end point at point **3** in Figure 6-10.

Now you can change the entities into a polyline without error.

    Type: `PEDIT <RETURN>`

Response: `Select polyline.`

Pick a point at point **1** in Figure 6-9.

Response: Entity selected is not a polyline.
Do you want to turn it into one?

Type: Y <RETURN>

Response: Close/Join/Width/Edit vertex/Fit curve/
Spline curve/Decurve/Undo/eXit

Type: JOIN <RETURN>

Response: Select objects.

Pick objects at points **2, 3, 4** and **5** in Figure 6-11. **CONFIRM** selections.

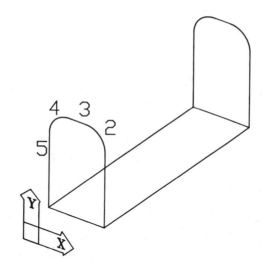

Figure 6-11: Join polyline segments.

Type: <RETURN> (to exit from PEDIT.)

Do the same thing with the entities that make up the object at the other end. Turn the first into a polyline, then join the other four entities so that each of the two ends is now a single polyline entity.

Now, let's put an **EDGESURF** over the object. But first be sure your system variables are correctly set.

168   **THE AUTOCAD 3D BOOK**

Type: SETVAR <RETURN>

Response: Variable name or ?

Type: SURFTAB1 <RETURN>

Response: New value for SURFTAB1.

Type: 20 <RETURN>

Type: SETVAR <RETURN>

Response: Variable name or ?

Type: SURFTAB2 <RETURN>

Response: New value for SURFTAB2.

Type: 20 <RETURN>

Now let's apply the **EDGESURF** mesh. As you'll remember, **EDGESURF** requires exactly four edges. The points you'll pick for each of the four edges are indicated in Figure 6-12. Don't pick the points at the intersections. Pick them on the lines approximately where the numbers are indicated.

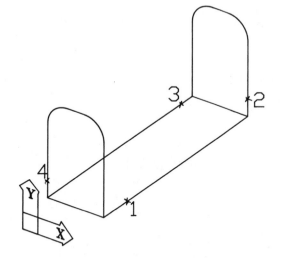

Figure 6-12: Apply EDGESURF at points 1, 2, 3 and 4.

Type: EDGESURF <RETURN>

Response: Select edge 1.

Pick point 1.

Response: Select edge 2.

Pick point 2.

Response: Select edge 3.

Pick point 3.

Response: Select edge 4.

Pick point 4.

Your drawing should now look like Figure 6-13 with hidden lines. Now turn the object so that you can add a **3DFACE** to the bottom.

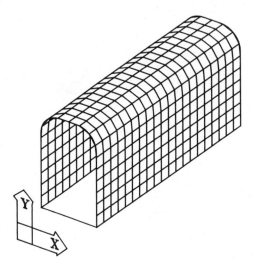

Figure 6-13: Mesh complete.

Before you change your view, save this view in order to return to it when you're finished.

```
<VIEW, S, V1>
```

      Type: DVIEW <RETURN>

Response: Select objects.
                Select the entire object.

Response: CAmera/TArget/Distance/POints/PAn/Zoom/TWist/
                CLip/Hide/Off/Undo/eXit

      Type: CAMERA <RETURN>

Response: Enter angle from X-Y plane.

Type: -30 <RETURN>

Response: Enter angle in X-Y plane from X-axis.

Type: 160 <RETURN>

You'll probably need to **PAN** two or three times to bring the object into full view.

Type: <RETURN> (in order to exit from DVIEW.)

Type: 3DFACE <RETURN>

Using **<OS-Intersection>**, pick each of the four intersections of the bottom of the object. You may need to **ZOOM** in very closely in order to pick the points; you can do this with the transparent zoom, **"ZOOM**. After you've picked your last point, **<RETURN>** one more time to exit. Return now to your previous view, which you saved as **V1**.

<VIEW, R, V1>

Now it's time to add perspective to the object.

Type: DVIEW <RETURN>

Response: Select objects.
Select entire object.

Response: CAmera/TArget/Distance/POints/PAn/Zoom/TWist/CLip/
Hide/Off/Undo/eXit

Type: DISTANCE <RETURN>

Response: New camera/target distance.

Type: 50 <RETURN>

Type: <RETURN> (to exit from DVIEW.)

Save this perspective view of the object as **V2**.

```
<VIEW, S, V2>
```

Let's dimension two sides of the object. To do this, set the **UCS** where the **X** axis is parallel to the side of the object being dimensioned and in the positive direction you want your text.

If you try to set your **UCS** by pointing, you'll be told that **OBJECT SNAP** isn't allowed in **PERSPECTIVE** view. Therefore, you must turn **PERSPECTIVE OFF** or work in the other **VPORT** when **PERSPECTIVE** is **OFF**. That's why you saved a view of the object, prior to turning **PERSPECTIVE OFF** and changing your **UCS**.

> **Type:**   DVIEW <RETURN>
>
> **Response:**   Select objects.
>
> **Type:**   <RETURN> (Do not select objects.)
>
> **Type:**   OFF <RETURN> <RETURN>

PERSPECTIVE is now **OFF** and you can change your **UCS**.

> **Type:**   UCS <RETURN>
>
> **Response:**   Origin/ZAxis/3point/Entity/View/X/Y/Z/Prev/
>   Restore/Save/del/?/World
>
> **Type:**   3POINT <RETURN>
>
> **Response:**   Origin point.

```
<OS-Intersection>
```

Pick the intersection at point **1** in Figure 6-14.

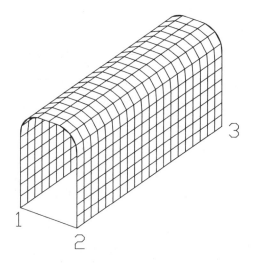

Figure 6-14: UCS 3POINT.

Response: Point on positive portion of the X axis.

<OS-Intersection>

Pick point **2** in Figure 6-14.

Response: Point on positive-Y portion of the UCS X-Y plane.

<OS-Intersection>

Pick point **3** in Figure 6-14.
At this point, **UCS** is lined up where the dimension text and lines will be, parallel to the current **X** axis. Now, dimension from points **1** to **2**, then again from points **2** to **3**.
To give your drawing a more realistic look, restore the view with the perspective that you saved.

<VIEW, R, V2>

Depending on how you've set your dimension variables, your figure should look like Figure 6-15.

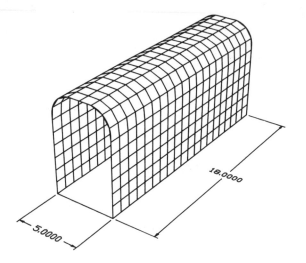

Figure 6-15: With perspective and dimensions.

MOVING ON

This simple exercise has shown you how many of the tools work together. Naturally it would be too cumbersome to design a project that would use all the concepts, but it's surprising to see just how many were necessary even with this simple design.

Each tool, each concept you've learned has a specific purpose. Go back and study this exercise at least one more time or until you're sure you know why each command was chosen to perform a specific task in constructing the model.

Remember, though, there isn't just one way to do things. See if you can find other ways to draw the object. When you're working on your own construction solutions, don't be afraid to experiment. With practice, you'll begin to see what works, and—perhaps as important—what doesn't.

7 New Twists to Old Commands

Many AutoCAD Release 10 and Release 11 features were created to support 3D. While it's true that many of these features such as **UCS**, **VPORTS** and **3D MESHES** can be used in 2D plan view, the major emphasis is on 3D.

But Releases 10 and 11 features do more than support a 3D database. Let's look at the changes that have occurred to many of the tried-and-true old commands. If you don't understand how they differ now, you not only will be missing out on many features and enhancements of Releases 10 and 11, but you'll be making assumptions that are no longer true.

In this chapter, you'll examine many changes to existing commands, and you'll be introduced to some new commands. As you've seen, many of the editing commands have changed dramatically (see Chapter 4). Those aren't discussed here unless there are additional features which we haven't presented yet.

By reading this chapter, you'll begin to understand the full benefits that Releases 10 and 11 offer.

GENERAL CHANGES TO MOST COMMANDS

Three major changes have affected most commands. Because these changes are so universal, it's easier to consider them as a group and point out exceptions where they might occur.

1.   Almost all entities now include a **Z** coordinate in the database. Because your input device is 2D, the **Z** coordinate always defaults to the current set elevation relative to the current **UCS**. You can

override it through explicit coordinate input or by using the FILTER commands (such as .XY), followed by the input of the Z coordinate.

Most of the existing commands let you input a 3D or 2D point when input is requested. A few commands, such as **PAN**, use only a 2D point and simply ignore the **Z**. **ARC**, **CIRCLE**, **TEXT**, **PLINE**, **ATTRIBUTE DEFINITIONS**, **SOLIDS** and **TRACES** accept 3D points for their initial point only. The **Z** then becomes the default. This effectively prohibits you from crossing planes. However, **3DFACE**, **3DPOLY** and **3D MESHES** accept 3D coordinates for all points input.

2. Almost everything is now relative to the current **UCS**. There are a few exceptions; we'll point them out as they occur. This doesn't mean just the direction of **X** and **Y**, but angles as well. For example, **0** degrees will always be the positive direction of **X**, and **90** degrees the positive direction of **Y**, assuming a counterclockwise rotation.

3. Many of the editing commands now have major restrictions on the extrusion direction and performing these commands in plan view. See Chapter 4 for a full explanation of these restrictions.

CONVERTING POINTS AND ANGLES TO WCS

As before, you can enter points from the keyboard as absolute coordinates such as **5,7,9**, or relative to the preceding point such as **@4<90**. If entered in this way, they're coordinates in the current **UCS**.

You can enter absolute and relative coordinates in relation to the **WCS** by preceding the input with a *. For example, *5,7,9 would place the point at those coordinates in the **WCS**, not the **UCS**. @*4<90 would cause the angular directions to be measured **90** degrees from **0** degrees (the direction of positive **X** unless changed) in the **WCS**.

INDEPENDENT SETTINGS IN EACH VIEWPORT

Each viewport is independent, which means that the settings for **GRID**, **SNAP**, **ORTHO**, **VIEWRES** for fast zooms, and **VIEWS** can be different for each one.

AXIS AND GRID

If you use **AXIS**, it may be displayed only in plan view. **AXIS** isn't available if you're using more than one viewport.

GRID will clearly show only the drawing limits if the current **UCS** is equal to the **WCS**. If the **UCS** isn't equal to the **WCS**, **GRID** encompasses the full screen or viewport.

OBJECT SNAP—THE EXCEPTION

OBJECT SNAP is one command that doesn't recognize the current **UCS**. That's because **OBJECT SNAP** finds the coordinate points of a given entity.

Remember when you drew the cube, one exercise involved drawing a line visibly over another line. By looking at the line from different angles in two viewports, you could see that unless the **UCS** was properly set, you couldn't fully depend on what you were seeing.

In order to make this mistake work, you were advised not to use **OBJECT SNAP** to the intersection. If you had, **OBJECT SNAP** would have properly picked up the coordinates of the intersection and forced you to the correct coordinates, even though your **UCS** wasn't properly set.

SPECIAL CONSIDERATIONS WITH TEXT

Text is an unusual case, and you must follow certain rules. Generally, text is created while you're using the **VIEW** suboption of **UCS** or in plan view to the current **UCS**. These will create a flat area upon which the text may be displayed; so the **UCS** is in the direction of the screen. As with dimensioning, you may also align the text with the entity using **UCS ENTITY** before the text is written.

UCS VIEW is valid only for that particular view and angle. Therefore, if you rotate the angle of view, the text may seem to disappear. *Note:* Place text on a layer of its own so that you can control its visibility. If you want text to label different views of the object, then a different layer might be set up for each group of text.

One other aspect of **TEXT** should be noted. The **HIDE** command will not hide text. If the text were ordinarily hidden, then the object would seem transparent in regard to the text only.

DISTANCE AND AREA

The performance of the **DISTANCE** command hasn't changed. It will accept 3D points and will measure the distance between those points. Instead of simply reporting **Angle,** it reports **Angle in X-Y plane** and **Angle from X-Y plane**. The **Angle in X-Y plane** is what you might normally consider to be the angle. It's relative to the **X** axis. The **Angle from X-Y plane** is the angle of the line as it extends from the **X-Y** plane. Let's say you drew a cube by drawing four lines with a thickness of **4**. If you measured the distance of any of the four original lines you drew, the **Angle in X-Y plane** would be **90** and the **Angle from X-Y plane** would be **0**. If you then measured one of the lines that creates the "height" or thickness, **Angle in X-Y plane** would be **0** and **Angle from X-Y plane** would be **90**.

In addition to giving you the delta of **X** and **Y**, the command now also displays the delta of **Z**.

The **DISTANCE** command computes the real distance in 3D without respect to the current **UCS**.

The **AREA** command works the same way as before, except that before making calculations, it projects the object onto the **X-Y** plane of the current **UCS** and then calculates area and perimeter. It doesn't make the calculations based upon which plane(s) the points may lie on.

LOAD LINETYPES ENHANCED

There have been two related enhancements to loading linetypes. You can now use a wild-card specification as you do for **LAYER** in response to the name of the linetype. Also, more than one linetype can be loaded at one time from a file. To illustrate how this works:

Type: LINETYPE <RETURN>

Response: ?/Create/Load/Set

Type: L <RETURN>

Response: Linetype(s) to load.

Type: D* <RETURN>

Response: File to search.

Type: ACAD <RETURN>

Response: Linetype Dashed loaded.
Linetype Dot loaded.
Linetype Dashdot loaded.
Linetype Divide loaded.

RENAME COMMAND ENHANCED

As before, **RENAME** lets you rename blocks, layers, linetypes, styles and views. **UCS** and **VPORTS** have been added.

SMALL CHANGE IN THE PURGE COMMAND

The **PURGE** command lets you delete unreferenced blocks, layers, linetypes, shapes and styles. Previously, the **PURGE** command would work only if it were the first command you issued after entering the drawing editor. This restriction still applies, but you may now **PURGE** until you've made a change in the drawing database (such as adding or deleting entities). So, for example, you can now **PAN** or **ZOOM** and still be able to use **PURGE**.

DIVIDE AND MEASURE

DIVIDE and **MEASURE** work essentially the same way, but with one exception: The division points were placed on the current elevation; now they're placed on the entity itself.

MISCELLANEOUS CHANGES

FILL ON will do only a solid fill in plan view of the current **UCS**.

HATCH is now available for **3DFACES** and **3DPOLY**. If you do a **HATCH** on an entity that contains a **3D MESH** then the **3D MESH** is ignored. **HATCH** is always drawn at the current elevation.

PEDIT contains new suboptions to edit **3DPOLY** and **3D MESHES**.

STATUS now has information on **UCS**.

3DLINE command is now a useless command. Use the regular **LINE** command instead. The **3DLINE** command is still supported, however.

NEW SYSTEM VARIABLES

Several system variables were introduced with Release 10. See Appendix A.

SPECIAL CONSIDERATIONS WHEN PLOTTING

Don't change your **UCS** before plotting; you could go insane trying to position your plot precisely where you want it. When you're working in **DVIEW** and want to plot a specific 3D view, it's difficult to predict exactly where on the paper it's going to plot for anything but **FIT**.

The difficulty seems to arise because the plot sequence converts your plot origin to what it sees as the plot origin in the **WCS**. Thus, even the plot origin of **0,0** might be translated to negative coordinates and throw the drawing off the page.

Let's look at a practical application of this. Assume that you've established two viewports of the same object, viewed from different angles. You want to plot both of these objects side by side, at a given scale. You might think that it's easy to run a sample plot on the active viewport to see where it will line up on the paper. Then you might readjust the plot origin up and to the right, to position the first object correctly. You'd rerun the plot on the same paper and adjust the second object accordingly. This is where you'd run into trouble. No matter what you seem to input, AutoCAD converts this plot origin to the **WCS**. Don't despair; there's an easy fix to this problem. Before plotting, change your current **UCS** to **WCS**. Then run your sample plot to see where it will line up on the paper. You can readjust the plot origin as you've done in the past, and it will work. Because the view doesn't change when you change to **WCS**, **WCS** will plot your desired view. And because the object is already using **WCS**, no conversion is necessary.

3D views of the plots cannot be rotated 90 degrees clockwise using that option. If you need to rotate your drawing, use **DVIEW** before plotting a given view.

Remember that in any AutoCAD release, it does you no good to hide lines and not remove them before you plot. The **HIDE** command for the screen and the hidden line removal option are separate. You can plot with hidden line removal only by choosing that option when you plot. So, unless you need to see on the screen what it's going to look like before you plot, there's no need to hide the lines on the screen.

8 Tips and Tricks

The following is a collection of 3D tips and tricks that have proven to be helpful when using Releases 10 and 11. It also gives some practical insights into the concepts you've just learned.

Some of these ideas have been described elsewhere in the book, but we think it's helpful to have these tips in one chapter for easy reference.

1. When using **DVIEW**, be sure **SNAP** is **OFF**. When you choose **CAMERA** or **TARGET** while in **DVIEW**, the horizontal or vertical bar is almost impossible to control if **SNAP** is **ON**. So press **CTRL B** a couple of times to make sure that **SNAP** is **OFF**.

2. When you have **PERSPECTIVE ON**, you can't edit, zoom, draw or do many other things you might want to do with the drawing by pointing. Each time you try, you'll get the message, "Pointing in **PERSPECTIVE** view not allowed here." Wouldn't it be nice if you could regen, edit or draw, then return to **PERSPECTIVE ON** exactly as it was before? Well, you can.

   Before you issue any editing or drawing commands in perspective, save the view. After the view is saved, enter **DVIEW**, defaulting with **<RETURN>** when you're asked to select objects. Choose the **OFF** subcommand and exit. **PERSPECTIVE** is now **OFF** and you can draw, edit or zoom as you like.

   After you've completed the edits, restore the view. **PERSPECTIVE** will return with the view and will include any edits that have been made.

   Another way to edit and draw while **PERSPECTIVE** is **ON** is to use the multiple viewports. Have the same view of the object in one viewport with **PERSPECTIVE ON** while another viewport has

PERSPECTIVE OFF. Do your work in the viewport with **PERSPEC-
TIVE OFF**. The changes that you make will show up in almost real
time, in perspective, in the viewport that has **PERSPECTIVE ON**.

3. You'll find that commands sometimes operate a little differently
    when **PERSPECTIVE** is **ON** than when it's **OFF**. The **POINTS**
    subcommand of **DVIEW** is a prime example.
      When changing the position of your **TARGET** and **CAMERA**
    through the **POINTS** subcommand, you can get some frustrating
    results. If you expect to be able to position the **CAMERA** at a
    specific point in relation to the **TARGET**, you might be surprised
    to find yourself somewhere in 3D outer space. At other times, it
    may seem to work perfectly well.
      To understand this, be aware that the distance of the **CAMERA**
    to the **TARGET** is set mainly by the **DISTANCE** subcommand.
    Therefore, when you issue the **POINTS** command, AutoCAD draws
    an imaginary line of sight from the **TARGET** to the **CAMERA**, but
    it doesn't change the distance. Rather, it extends that straight line
    of sight to the distance already set. This changes your viewing
    angle to the **TARGET**, but also places you somewhere unex-
    pected.
      Here's the solution. If **PERSPECTIVE** is **ON** when the **POINTS**
    command is chosen, the distance from the **CAMERA** to the **TAR-
    GET** is changed to the new point of the **CAMERA**. Therefore, you
    get the results you probably expected. So, if you want to reposition
    the **TARGET** and **CAMERA** exactly to the points chosen, be sure
    that **PERSPECTIVE** is **ON** before you issue the **POINTS** command.

4. Never use **DVIEW DISTANCE** instead of **ZOOM**, or confuse the
    two. Naturally the **DISTANCE** option of **DVIEW** lets you set the
    CAMERA to **TARGET** distance in order to add **PESPECTIVE**. This
    may seem a convenient way to **ZOOM** in on the detail, but if you're
    not careful, you can distort the **PERSPECTIVE** tremendously. If
    you need to work in detail, use **ZOOM**, not **DISTANCE**.

5. As you know, the **HIDE** command can eat up considerable time,
    depending on the complexity of your drawing. You'll often need to
    HIDE some lines in order to find out where you are in 3D space;
    but you usually don't need all the lines hidden. Unfortunately,
    there's no **HIDE WINDOW** command, but there *are* a couple of
    tricks that can speed up the process.

First, you need not include the entire object or drawing when you use the **DVIEW** command. You can put a window around only that portion you want to hide. Then use the **HIDE** command, which works as a subcommand of **DVIEW**, rather than the general-purpose **HIDE** command.

Another way is to **ZOOM** in tightly on the object, then issue **HIDE**. Only those lines visible within the **ZOOM** area will be hidden. Of course, you should **FREEZE** any hatching or meshes, since they may take too much time to **HIDE**.

6. Always use **FREEZE** and **THAW** instead of **OFF** and **ON** (which is the normal practice). You *must* observe this when hiding lines. If you use **OFF**, the lines won't be visible but they'll continue to hide anything they normally would have hidden. This can make your drawing look strange as well as eat up a lot of processing time. **FREEZE,** on the other hand, will act as though the layer doesn't exist.

7. You don't need a **UCS** when snapping to real points. The purpose of changing your **UCS** is to give AutoCAD the third coordinate as a default, because your input device, mouse or digitizer can supply only the **X** and **Y** coordinates. Therefore, changing the **UCS** redefines the **X**, **Y** and/or **Z** planes.

If you use **OBJECT SNAP** on a real object in 3D space, Auto-CAD knows all three of the coordinates and will use them no matter how you set the **UCS**. You can save time by using **OBJECT SNAP** as much as possible.

8. You can save your **UCS** definition under the name of your choice. Unfortunately, you can't tell AutoCAD to save the angle of view as well. Therefore, when you restore a **UCS** or **UCS PREVIOUS**, it restores only the **UCS**, not the view. And when you restore the view, it doesn't restore the **UCS** that was active with that view.

One way around this is to save the view and the **UCS** at the same time, which requires two operations. You might want to save **UCS** and **VIEW** under the same name, but use the prefix **V** for **VIEW** and **U** for **UCS**. When you restore the view, you're then able to restore the **UCS** that was in effect at the same time.

9. Often, you'll use a subcommand of **DVIEW** but you won't need to actually see the object to execute the command. This might be a

tighter **ZOOM**, turning **PERSPECTIVE ON**, **PAN**ning slightly to the right or keying in the two **CAMERA** or **TARGET** angles.

When this is the case, and you're prompted to select objects in your drawing, don't. Instead, simply **<RETURN>**. AutoCAD will then substitute its simple little house (or whatever drawing you've chosen) in its place. The command will be executed and your drawing will be updated on the screen with the new parameters at the end of the **DVIEW** command.

10. In many cases your drawing can get so crowded with hatching, **3DFACES** and extruded lines that it becomes difficult to **OBJECT SNAP** to an endpoint or intersection. There are two reasons for this. The **VIEW** direction might be close to looking "edge-on" at the object in relation to the current **UCS**. Pointing to locations on the screen can be difficult or impossible. When this occurs, the **UCS** icon changes to a broken pencil.

The solution to the broken pencil is to use **DVIEW CAMERA** and change your vertical inclination by as little as one degree. But another problem may arise with picking with **OBJECT SNAP** if the area is too crowded. There are three possible solutions if that happens. First, try choosing endpoint, but don't put your box directly over the intersection or endpoint itself. Simply touch the entity close to the endpoint. Then AutoCAD isn't confused as to which entity you want.

If that doesn't work, try a transparent zoom (**ZOOM** to get in a little closer to a crowded area). If the above two don't work, **FREEZE** some layers so that the area isn't as crowded.

11. Sometimes, you might want to capture a 3D-view angle of an object and combine it on the same drawing with other 3D-view angles of the same object or of different objects.

First, using **DVIEW**, create the desired view of the object. Next, change **UCS** to **UCS VIEW**, which makes the **X-Y** plane parallel to the screen. Third, **BLOCK** and **WBLOCK** the object. Do this with each of the objects you want to place on the single sheet.

Now start with the sheet on which you want to compile the objects. Insert and place each of the objects where you want it to go. They can be rescaled as you bring them in, or later, using the **SCALE** command.

Note: If you don't change to **UCS VIEW** before the object is blocked, it will be inserted parallel to the current **UCS** of the new sheet and at the correct rotated **DVIEW** viewing angle.

12. If you're not careful, you can run into some serious trouble while dimensioning an object from a 3D view. If you set the **UCS** arbitrarily, then the measurement taken for the dimension may not be correct.

    If you want the dimension to be displayed as the correct distance, align your **UCS** with the entity before dimensioning, using the **UCS ENTITY** or the **UCS 3POINT** command. **UCS ENTITY** might cause a minor problem by adding an extra step, because you can't be sure of the direction of positive **X**. Therefore, you might have to rotate an additional time around **Y**.

    If you use **3POINT**, set positive **X** and the top of the text will run in the direction of positive **Y**.

13. **DVIEW CAMERA** and **TARGET** can be quite unpredictable when using a **UCS**, since the angle of inclination is above the **X-Y** plane of the current **UCS**. That may be different from your current view of the object. Remember that the **VIEW** and the **UCS** aren't tied together, so it's entirely possible to look down on the object with a negative inclination.

    The solution to this is simple. Change your **UCS** to **WORLD** before using **DVIEW**. When you exit **DVIEW**, change the **UCS** back to **UCS PREVIOUS**.

    This is so important that Releases 10 and 11 are shipped with a system variable, called **WORLDVIEW**, set to **1**. This automatically sets you to **UCS WORLD** every time you enter **DVIEW**. When you exit **DVIEW**, you're automatically returned to your previous **UCS**. If **DVIEW** starts acting really strange, check **WORLDVIEW** to make sure it's set to **1**, not **0**. Otherwise, **DVIEW** can drive you absolutely crazy.

    You might want **WORLDVIEW** set to **0** if you want to maintain the point of origin in your current **UCS** during **DVIEW**, to enter absolute coordinates for **CAMERA** and **TARGET** positions as in the **POINTS** subcommand. Otherwise, the point of origin will be changed back to **WORLD** during the **DVIEW** session, with absolute coordinates based on the original **WORLD** point of origin.

14. Sometimes, when using the **DVIEW DISTANCE** command, you can move your cursor all the way in both directions of the horizontal bar and not much seems to happen. That means you're too close to the object. Therefore, the distance factor doesn't make much difference.

   The solution is simple. Move your cursor to the far right and pick. Now repeat the **DISTANCE** subcommand. Again, move the cursor to the right and pick. You may have to do this two or three times until you gain control over the object. Each time you move the cursor to the right and pick, you're increasing the distance from the **CAMERA** to the **TARGET** by the indicated factor. After two or three times, the factor is great enough to move in and out with better control.

15. If you've set a **UCS** when you enter the **PLOT** command, you can go mad trying to position your drawing on the page. A simple fix is to set **UCS WORLD** before beginning the **PLOT**. Then change to **UCS PREVIOUS** when you leave the plot.

   You might even want to set up a script file that changes to **UCS WORLD**, plots, and then changes you back to **UCS PREVIOUS**. (An AutoLISP program might be more elegant, but you can't invoke **PLOT** from AutoLISP.)

   To create the script file, use EDLIN or a text editor in the nondocument mode:

   Type: EDIT <RETURN>

   Response: File to edit:

   Type: PLOTW.SCR <RETURN>

   Response: New file

   Type: I <RETURN>

Then type in the following text. Don't type the numbers (they're the EDLIN line numbers).

1. UCS
2. World
3. Plot
4. (Blank line)
5. (Blank line)
6. (Blank line
7. (Blank line)
8. UCS
9. Previous
10. Control C

Response: *

    Type: E <RETURN>

Don't write on lines 4, 5, 6 and 7. They should be left blank. On line 10, press **CTRL C**. This will break you out of **INSERT** mode and return you to the * prompt.

You've now created the script file. To run it,

    Type: SCRIPT PLOTW <RETURN>

The script file will now change you to **UCS WORLD**, plot, then change you back to **UCS PREVIOUS**.

You can create many useful variations of this routine.

16. There are two basic ways to place **TEXT** in your drawing. Many times, the purpose of **TEXT** is simply to label the drawing from a specific view. If you want the **TEXT** to appear flat against the screen or paper, not at the same angle as the drawing, then change your **UCS** to **UCS VIEW**. Be sure to put the **TEXT** on a separate layer so that it can be frozen.

    If you want your **TEXT** to be aligned with some entity in the drawing, use the same technique used with dimensioning in Tip 12.

17. When working with **UCS 3POINT**, you needn't choose the direction of positive **Y** exactly at **90** degrees from the point of origin. You may pick a point for the direction of positive **Y** above the point where you picked positive **X** or anywhere in your drawing, even though your rubberband is still from the point of origin. You may even **<RETURN>** and AutoCAD will default positive **Y** as the current plane. It's looking for a coordinate to define the **Y** plane. As a result, you may **OBJECT SNAP** to any object on the desired plane.

18. At times, **EDGESURF** is the appropriate surface mesh to use; but it doesn't have four edges. Use **PEDIT** and turn the line into a **POLYLINE**, if it's not already one. Then **JOIN** or **BREAK** the **POLYLINES** as necessary so you have exactly four edges.

19. Drawing with **THICKNESS** is often fast and convenient. But you'll often want separate entities without extrusions. Drawing these separate lines from scratch in 3D can be a real chore. Instead, draw using **THICKNESS** on a separate layer. Then change layers. Rotate the object using **DVIEW** and begin to trace over the extruded object using **OBJECT SNAP** on the endpoints and intersections.

   Once the object has been replicated, **FREEZE** your current layer and **ERASE** the old extruded entities. Then **THAW** your current layer. What you'll be left with are the separate entities without extrusions, easily drawn in 3D, upon which you can now build.

20. Remember that **TEXT** is never hidden with the **HIDE** command. This can be good and bad. If you want to hide **TEXT**, then you must manipulate the layers to **FREEZE** it. AutoCAD needs a system variable that gives you text-hiding choices.

MOVING ON

You've now completed the 3D tutorial section of this book. But as you can imagine, you've only just begun. Now that you know the tools, it's up to you to use them and practice what you've learned. Your reward will be increased efficiency, productivity and creativity.

SOLID MODELING, ADVANCED MODELING EXTENSION AND PRESENTATION CAD

9 SOLID MODELING

From the chapters you've read so far, you can see that understanding 3D design and drafting is an evolutionary process. It's a process of model building that starts with the most basic and arrives at the finished, complete and unambiguous representation of the object. Your experience now includes techniques to create 2D wire frame models, such as isometric drawings; 2 1/2D models using elevation and thickness; 3D wire frames, using true 3D entities in space, that describe edges; and surface models, using a mesh to place a surface or "skin" around the wire frame.

It's important to note that it's not necessary to abandon forever techniques lower down the scale to achieve a desired result. For example, extruding a 2D object is often the fastest and easiest way to achieve a third dimension, rather than constructing boundaries and working with a mesh to achieve the same result. How far to go along the evolutionary scale really depends on the results you need.

SOLID THINKING

AutoCAD users normally decide to work in 3D for a few basic reasons: it's available, it provides better visualization, and it assures numeric accuracy. But you have to decide whether the end justifies the means—whether better visual representation is worth the time and effort needed to produce it. Luckily, as software matures, it should be a lot easier and faster to work higher up the evolutionary scale.

Is a surface model an accurate representation? As you work with surface models, getting that "skin" over your wire frame can be a very frustrating experience. Creating a hole pattern using extruded circles is a snap, but finding a mesh that's intelligent enough not to cover over these holes when describing a surface may take you a long time. If you try using patch over patch to achieve a realistic look when hidden lines are removed, this improvisation may result in an inaccurate surface model that won't shade properly and numerically cannot describe the object. That in turn can make surface area, volume and object properties in general impossible to analyze accurately.

When a CAD operator needs to accurately and precisely describe the surface, edges and interior of a model, a surface model is out of the question, regardless of how the parts of that surface model were created. For example, two cylinders created by extruding circles may intersect, but AutoCAD can't produce a proper visual representation of the intersection point of the two cylinders both inside and out. The user can usually find a way around the problem to make the model "look good"; but by no means is the model accurate or "unambiguous."

To show someone what two cylinders intersecting at midpoints look like, the ideal method would be to construct the two cylinders out of clay and add the solid clay pieces together to make a final model. Visually, this clay model would be the most accurate way possible to represent the "real thing." We could easily determine numerical analysis, volumes and surface areas, since we have a physical object. We could even do studies in dynamics and stress, given the right conditions.

Computer solid modeling uses techniques very much like our clay example, except that the software computes values related to analysis and visually represents the model on the screen with a high degree of accuracy.

Until recently, AutoCAD software has focused on the production and manipulation of visual representations and dimensional definitions of objects. We've used AutoCAD to *depict* objects, not truly *model* them. With Release 11, solid modeling, a natural extension of CAD, now addresses that discipline as well.

Solid modeling, then, defines *characteristics* of solid materials, not just edges, boundaries and surfaces. The benefits are visual and numeric accuracy. So the activity of solid modeling falls somewhere between design and simulation.

NUMERIC INFORMATION

The Advanced Modeling Extension (AME) in Release 11 provides the user with basic numerically accurate information such as area, volume and mass properties. Therefore, this model can be used as a start point for Finite Element Analysis of stress, vibration and heat, done either outside or inside by third-party software. The engineer can use area calculations to find heat transfer characteristics or estimate plating or coating material requirements. Since the model is true throughout, cross-sectional areas and profiles can be useful for electrical and magnetic calculations and simple strength analysis. Volumes are useful for calculating some material requirement calculations and can be used along with mass or weight for density and specific gravity calculations. AutoCAD's solid modeler provides properties such as mass (from knowing the material) and the ability to calculate center of gravity and moment of inertia used for dynamic analysis.

VISUAL REPRESENTATION

AutoCAD's Advanced Modeling Extension can provide wire frame displays with hidden lines removed (as we've seen in surface modeling) as well as shaded images to assist in visualization. AME lets you show your model as either a wire frame mesh or a shaded image. Wire frame is the default representation that shows solids as line, pline, arc and circle entities. The mesh representation shows solid objects using AutoCAD's Pface entities. The ability to rotate and tumble your model in real time is a feature yet to come (Release 12, perhaps?). The data from your model can be used in dedicated shading, rendering and animation software to take the visualization a step further.

DEFINING A SOLID

AutoCAD AME uses two methods for defining and representing a solid: Constructive Solid Geometry (CSG) and Boundary Representation (B-rep). The B-rep method uses 3D CAD techniques to define the boundaries of object edges. These methods are natural to use, since they're similar to the methods a CAD operator is accustomed to. CSG uses common solid shapes added to and subtracted from each other, as in our modeling clay analogy, to produce a desired solid. The simplicity of CSG makes it the method of choice, especially for the novice.

But CSG does have its weaknesses. As we shall see, to combine simple solids using CSG, Boolean algebra is used. This may present a problem in some situations; for surfaces of varying roundness, such as an automobile fender, B-rep would be much better suited. As you have discovered, successfully working in 3D requires using the right tool at the right time. The same is true here: CSG is more useful for the geometric portions of your model, while B-rep works better for adding things that are best defined using constructs like surfaces of extrusion or revolution and splines.

Combining solids into assemblies is a powerful AME feature. Since this usually means building from the simple to the complex, a hierarchical tree representing the composite solid can be listed and, if needed, torn apart. This CSG tree is similar to AutoCAD nested blocks, but more sophisticated. This feature's direct benefits to the end user are interference-checking between parts, confirmation of tolerances and assurance that the "insides" of a model are well defined.

CSG AND BOOLEAN ALGEBRA

The idea behind CSG is to allow the user to combine basic solid shapes to form a desired object. As shown in Figure 9-1, the combination may be additive (as in combining the two rectangular blocks to make a cross) or subtractive (as in removing the cylinder from the block to form a hole). These combinations are not really additive or subtractive in the arithmetic sense; they're actually derived through a Boolean logic operation related closely to Set theory and Venn Diagrams.

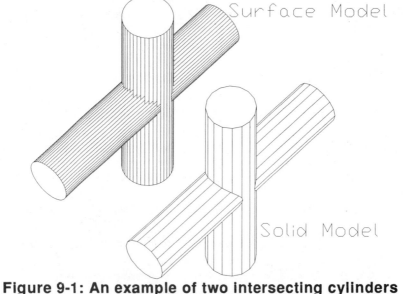

Figure 9-1: An example of two intersecting cylinders using both a surface model and a solid model. Notice the accuracy of the intersection planes in the two models.

You may have come in contact with Boolean algebra in an intermediate math or logic course, with true-false tables constructed for operations of **AND OR** and exclusive **OR**, namely **XOR**.

OPERANDS	AND	OR	XOR
00	0	0	0
01	0	1	1
10	0	1	1
11	1	1	0

This table could also be constructed with true and false instead of **1** and **0**, respectively. A direct follow-up to this is the analogy that **AND** and **OR** correspond to **INTERSECTION** and **UNION** operations in Set theory.

Boolean algebra can also be applied to graphic data—especially to solids. In Figure 9-2, notice the results of simple Boolean operations on the two solids. Combining these operations on several objects builds a CSG history tree of the final composite solid.

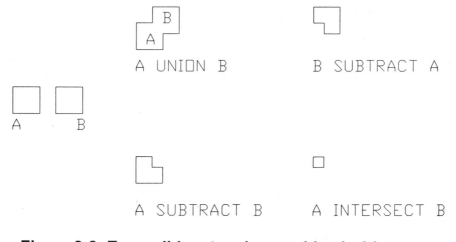

A UNION B

B SUBTRACT A

A　B

A SUBTRACT B

A INTERSECT B

Figure 9-2: Two solid rectangles combined with four Boolean algebra operations.

B-REP

Boundary representation of a solid consists of vertices' edges and surfaces that form the boundary of the model's volume. In this method, lines, plines and splines are used to extrude or resolve into solid primitives that can then be manipulated, using Boolean operations, to form new composite solids. AME also provides a way to solidify certain entities, such as extruded 2D circles, into solid entities.

Don't get the false impression that either a CSG or a B-rep method can achieve a desired solid. The correct reasoning is to think that CSG is the construction process and B-rep the display process. These two processes provide information to the drawing database to describe the solid completely and accurately.

Solid modeling provides much more than just a pretty picture. Its benefits can be realized throughout the entire process, beginning with layout and continuing with design, analysis, documentation and manufacturing. One of the limitations of early solid modelers was that, like today's analysis software, they ran outside the CAD system. In fact, AME's predecessor, Autodesk's AutoSOLID, was a separate package linked to AutoCAD only through file transfer. With AME, we get the benefits of solid modeling seamlessly inside AutoCAD so drafting and detail work can still be done.

MOVING ON

Now that you have some background on solids, let's move on to Chapter 10, where you'll create a solid model using AutoCAD's Advanced Modeling Extension. You'll find that even though solids are at the pinnacle of 3D CAD design techniques, they're the easiest to use.

10 Advanced Modeling Extension

This chapter consists of a tutorial and discussion of AutoCAD's Advanced Modeling Extension (AME). AME is a perfect example of an application executed seamlessly inside AutoCAD's drawing editor with the aid of ADS, the C language interface within AutoCAD. AME allows the user to create and manipulate true solid models with wire frame, mesh and simple rendered display techniques. In addition, the user can assign material properties to the model and perform simple analyses.

(This tutorial assumes you have AutoCAD's Advance Modeling Extension.)

MAKING A COMPOSITE SOLID

Begin a new drawing and set it up for A-size, full scale with **SNAP** set to **.1** and **GRID** set to **.5**. Our final solid model will look like Figure 10-1.

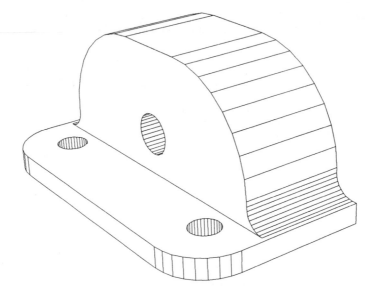

Figure 10-1: Completed solid model.

CREATE THE PRIMITIVES

Let's begin by constructing a rectangle with a **PLINE**.

    Type: PLINE <RETURN>

Response: From point:

    Type: 3,3 <RETURN>

Response: Arc/Close/Halfwidth/Length/Undo/Width/<Endpoint of Line>

    Type: @ 1.75<90 <RETURN>

    Type: @ 3.25<0

    Type: @ 1.75<270

Type: C

This closed polyline is the 2D outline of our model's base.

Type: Fillet

Response: Polyline/Radius/<Select first object>

Type: R <RETURN>

Type: .5 <RETURN>

Type: <RETURN>

Now select the segment on the left side, then the segment in front.

Type: <RETURN>

Now, select the segment on the right side and, again, the segment in front. Your drawing will look like the drawing in Figure 10-2.

Figure 10-2: Fillets used on 2D PLINE.

We can now load AME from your pull-down menu on the far right, pick Load AME, or you may type (**Xload "AME"**). AME has its own set of variables that are very much like AutoCAD's setvar variables. Several of them set the units used for mass, area and volume, as well as defaults for display. By typing **SOLVAR**, or picking it from your solids pull-down, make the following settings:"

SOLRENDER CSG

SOLWDENS   8

SOLRENDER sets rendering type, and **SOLWDENS** sets wire frame density or the number of tessellation lines displayed on a fillet or extrusion.

From your pull-down, pick Extrude or

Type: Solext <RETURN>

Response: Select objects

Pick your polyline figure.

Response: Height of the extrusion

Type: .2 <RETURN>

Response: Extrusion taper angle from Z <0>

Type: <RETURN>

The **SOLEXT** command lets you extrude a closed 2D object into a solid and taper the extrusion. This is much like adding a thickness, except that a solid is created. Those who are curious may want to use the AutoCAD **LIST** command to find out what this solid really is. They'll find out that it's a block. AME uses referenced blocks, handles (which should never be destroyed) and a layer called AME_FRZ to provide the mechanics of AME inside AutoCAD's drawing editor.

For a better view of the solid, you may want to use **VPOINT** and type in 1,1,.3 as the viewpoint. In addition, type **SOLLIST** to list information about the solid primitive.

Type: Sollist <RETURN>

Response: Edge/Face/Tree/<Solid>

Type: <RETURN>

Then pick the solid to list its properties. This listing will provide information about the initial low level of our CSG tree. Since this one primitive is only the start of the model, there are no upper-level components in the tree. The listing itself shows the solid's dimensions and any rotational or translational changes to it. Information regarding how the solid is displayed, either wire frame or mesh, as the total surface area of the solid. Another command that lists information about the solid is **SOLMASSP**.

Type: Solmassp

Response: Select objects

Pick your solid and notice the abundance of information calculated involving the static and dynamic properties of the object, assuming it was made out of mild steel. These values are all constants for this particular solid. The quantities shown are used when calculations regarding rotational or rectilinear motion or stress analysis are needed on the solid.
Use **ZOOM** Previous to get back to **PLAN** view of the model.
Let's create a UCS and place it in the back left corner of our model at the top face.

Type: UCS <RETURN>

Response: Origin/ZAxis/3Point/Entity/View/X/Y/Z/Prev/
Restore/Save/Del/?/<World>

Type: O <RETURN>

Response: .XY <RETURN>

Response: of

Using **OSNAP** Intersection, pick the back left corner of the model.

Response: of (need Z)

Type: .2 <RETURN>

Use the **UCSICON** command to get the icon to the new origin. Now we'll create another portion of our solid.

Type: SolBox <RETURN>

Response: Corner of Box

Pick a point anywhere in the upper portion of your screen, such as point 5,2.

Response: Cube/Length/<other corner>

Type: L <RETURN>

Response: Length

Type: 2.75 <RETURN>

Response: Width

Type: 1.0 <RETURN>

Response: Height

Type: 1.25 <RETURN>

Now we'll move the solid box to a new location.

Type: Move   <RETURN>

Response: Select objects

Select the created box.

Response: Base Point

Type: .XY <RETURN>

Response: of

Use **OSNAP** Int to pick the back left corner of the box.

Response: Need Z

Type: 0   <RETURN>

Response: Second point of displacement

Type: .25,0

Use **VPOINT** with a 1,1,.4 viewpoint to view the model, as shown in Figure 10-3.

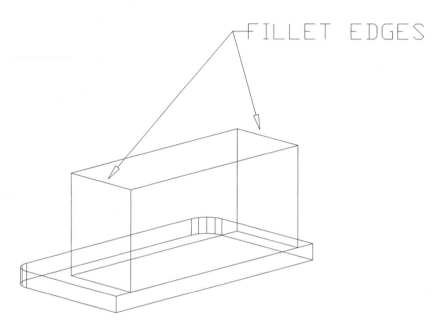

Figure 10-3: Two solid primitives viewed with VPOINT.

AME has a very powerful feature that lets you create fillets and chamfers on solids. AME's fillet and chamfer capabilities let you fillet not only edges, but entire surfaces. In fact, you can select several edges that intersect all at once for easy filleting. Using **SOLFILL**, let's do a few.

Type: Solfill   <RETURN>

Response: Select edges to be filleted
          <Press ENTER when done>

Pick the two edges as shown in Figure 10-3 and use a radius of 1.0.
Using **VPOINT** with a viewpoint of 0,-1,.4, you'll get a good working front view of the model as shown in Figure 10-4.

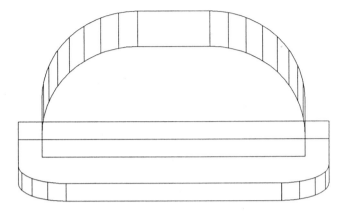

Figure 10-4: Fillets on solids.

Now, we'll put a total of three drill holes in the model.
Using the **SOLCYL** command, we'll place two solid cylinders at the filleted corners of the base.

Type:	Solcyl	
Response:	Elliptical/<centerpoint>	Use OSNAP Center to Place the center of the Cylinder at the centerpoint of the filleted corners.
Type:	Cen <RETURN>	
Response:	of	

Pick the fillet at the left front corner of the base.

Response:	Diameter/<Radius>
Type:	.15 <RETURN>

Response: Height of cylinder

    Type: -.2 <RETURN>

Do the same to the other filleted corner on the front right so the model looks like Figure 10-5.

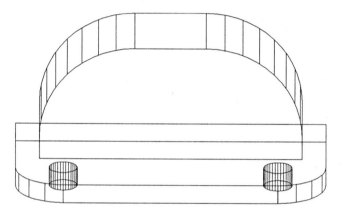

Figure 10-5: Solid modeling begins to take shape.

Use **UCS SAVE** to save the current UCS under the name **UCS1**. Now we'll create a new UCS to put a hole in the backplate.

    Type: UCS <RETURN>

Response: Origin/ZAxis/3point/Entity/View/X/Y/Z/Prev/
               Restore/Save/Del/?/<World>

    Type: O <RETURN>

OSNAP Intersection will appear at the point shown in Figure 10-6.

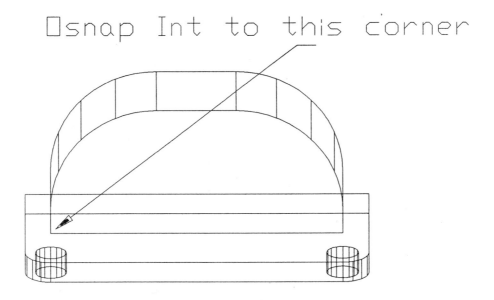

Figure 10-6: Setting the proper UCS.

Repeat the **UCS** command by pressing **<RETURN>** and

     Type: X   <RETURN>

Response: Rotational angle about the X axis <0>

     Type: 90   <RETURN>

Now let's create another **SOLCYL** to represent a hole in the back-plate.

     Type: Solcyl <RETURN>

Response: Elliptical/<Center Point>

     Type: .XZ <RETURN>

Response: of

Type: Mid

Response: of

Pick the bottom front edge of the backplate that's directly along the current X axis.

Response: of (need Y)

Type: .4 <RETURN>

Response: Diameter/<Radius>

Type: .2 <RETURN>

Response: Height of cylinder

Type: -1.0

Your model will look like Figure 10-7.

We're now ready to perform some Boolean operations to create one single solid model entity from the several primitives we now have. This in fact builds the CSG tree. In the previous chapter, we explored solid modeling's advantage of being able to perform Boolean operations—such as Union, Intersection and Subtract—on solids to achieve a single composite solid.

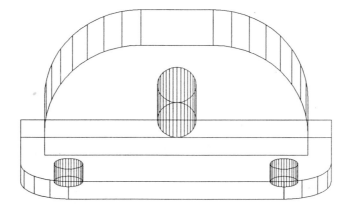

Figure 10-7: Boolean algebra.

JOINING THE SOLIDS

Our plan of attack will be first to subtract the two cylinders from the base, creating a composite solid; then subtract the cylinder from the backplate, making another composite solid. Finally, we'll use the Boolean operation Union on the backplate and base to make one composite solid.

Type: Solsub <RETURN>

Response: Source objects...
Select objects

Proceed to pick the base entity, then press the space bar or **<RETURN>**.

Response: 1 Solid selected
Objects to Subtract from them...
Select objects

Proceed to pick your two cylinders in the base, then press the space bar or **<RETURN>**. AME will update the database. Now, we'll do the same to the backplate.

Type: Solsub <RETURN>

Response: Source objects...
             Select objects:

Pick the backplate **SOLID** and press the space bar or **<RETURN>**.

Response: 1 Solid selected
             Objects to Subtract from them
             Select objects

Proceed to pick your cylinder at the center of the backplate, then press the space bar or **<RETURN>**. The database will begin to update.

Type: Solunion <RETURN>

Response: Select objects

Pick the baseplate and backplate followed by a space bar or **<RETURN>**. An update follows, and we now have a composite solid.

DISPLAY THE SOLID

To display the solid properly, let's display it as a mesh, then use HIDE to remove hidden lines.

Type: Mesh <RETURN>

Response: Select solids to be meshed...

Select our solid model. AME responds with meshing and block Dialog.

Type: Hide <RETURN>

Figure 10-8 shows our model in mesh representation with hidden lines removed and perspective turned on.

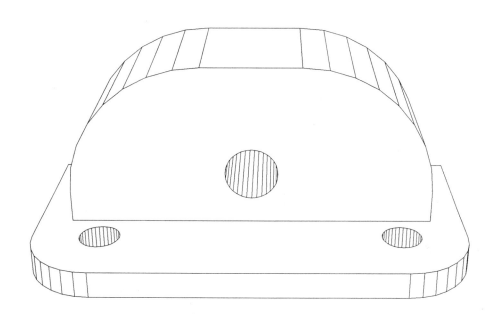

Figure 10-8: Mesh representation.

SPECIFICATIONS

Let's now use **SOLMAT** to change the material of our solid model to Brass. The **SOLMAT** command lets us specify new materials, edit old ones and generally maintain a list of materials we would like to assign to our solids. Using this feature, you can assign a material and compare mass properties between the different materials assigned.

> **Type:** Solmat   <RETURN>

> **Response:** Change/Edit/<exit>/LIst/
> LOad/New/Remove/Save/Set/?

> **Type:** C   <RETURN>   (for change.)

> **Response:** Select objects

Pick your solid model.

Response: New Material <Mild Steel>/?

Type: Brass

Response: Change/Edit/<exit>/LIst/
LOad/New/Remove/Save/Set/?

These other options should be experimented with. For example, LIST will list the definition of a solid material: density, Young's Modules, thermal conductivity, specific heat, etc. All these constants are found in handbooks if you need to create new ones with the New option. This information is kept in the **ACAD.MAT** file. You can even create a MAT file that contains your own material descriptions.

Now let's look at the CSG Tree listing of our solid. This is a non-graphical "Boolean history" of our solid model. Before we do, use **DVIEW** Off to get out of perspective mode and **SOLWIRE** to get back to wire frame display. Then,

Type: Sollist <RETURN>

Response: Edge/Face/Tree/<Solid>

Type: T <RETURN>

Response: Select objects

Pick your solid and press the space bar or **<RETURN>** when done. The text information that follows gives us the history of this solid in a "top-down" approach.

Another useful inquiry command is the **MASSP** command. Figure 10-9 shows the information the **MASSP** command provides, information needed in any analysis of dynamic or stress properties.

```
Ray projection along X axis, level of subdivision: 3.
Mass:           32.98 gm
Volume:         3.894 cu cm  (Err: 0.1083)

Bounding box:          X: -0.2504  --   3 cm
                       Y: -0.2004  --   1.25 cm
                       Z: -1       --   0.7504 cm

Centroid:              X: 1.375    cm   (Err: 0.03823)
                       Y: 0.3714   cm   (Err: 0.05662)
                       Z: -0.3977  cm   (Err: 0.06455)

Moments of inertia:    X: 20.5    gm sq cm (Err: 2.122)
                       Y: 93.75   gm sq cm (Err: 3.685)
                       Z: 93.47   gm sq cm (Err: 2.048)
Products of inertia:  XY: 16.84   gm sq cm (Err: 2.568)
                      YZ: -6.486  gm sq cm (Err: 1.143)
                      ZX: -18.04  gm sq cm (Err: 2.927)

Radii of gyration:     X: 0.7884  cm
                       Y: 1.686   cm
                       Z: 1.683   cm

Principal moments(gm sq cm) and X-Y-Z directions about centroid:
                       I: 10.73 along [0 1 0]
                       J: 24.74 along [0 0 1]
                       K: 24.74 along [1 0 0]
```

Figure 10-9: Mass properties.

Let's do two more fillets on our model.

Type: Solfill

Response: Select edges to be filleted

Pick the two edges on the left and on the right where the backplate meets the base. Use a radius of **.2**. A database update follows.

BUILD A 2D CROSS-SECTION

Now would be a good time to build a 2D cross-section of your model. This cross-section should slice the model right through the backplate. We first should orient our UCS so that it's perpendicular with the top face of the base; the orientation should be coplanar with the backplate, with the origin such that the X axis cuts the backplate. The **SOLUCS** command is used to orient the UCS with a solid edge or face. Then the **UCS** command can be used to further orient the UCS.

Type: Solucs <RETURN>

Response: Edge/<Face>

Type: <RETURN>   (This will accept the default, which is Face.)

Response: Select a Face...

Pick any edge on the top face of the baseplate on the front side. The proper face probably won't highlight. You'll be prompted for changes you want to make to a wire frame representation. You should answer yes to this prompt. In this case, the proper face is the top face of the baseplate.

Response: <OK>/Next

Now type N for next so that AME will select and highlight the top face. Once the top face highlights, press **<RETURN>** to select OK. Notice the **UCSIcon** lying flat on the top face of the baseplate at the left front corner, where the base meets the backplate. A **REGEN** may be needed before your display will give an accurate representation of the model. Now let's get that UCS oriented exactly the way we want it.

Type: UCS <RETURN>

Response: Origin/3Point/Entity/View/X/Y/Z/Prev/
Restore/Save/Del/?/<World>

Type: 0 <RETURN>

Response: Origin Point <0,0,0>

Type: -.25,-.5,0 <RETURN>

This moves the origin along the left edge.

Type: <RETURN>

Response: `Origin/3Point/Entity/View/X/Y/Z/Prev/`
`Restore/Save/Del/?/<World>`

Type: `X  <RETURN>`

Response: `Rotation angle about the X axis <0>`

Type: `90  <RETURN>`

Type: `<RETURN>`

Response: `Origin/3Point/Entity/View/X/Y/Z/Prev/`
`Restore/Save/Del/?/<World>`

Type: `Y  <RETURN>`

Response: `Rotation angle about the Y axis <0>`

Type: `90  <RETURN>`

The UCS is now oriented and placed where we can do a nice cross-section.

Using the **SOLVAR** command, we can set some **setvar** variables that are specific to solids in AME. This next one sets the hatch pattern needed for our cross-section.

Type: `Solvar <RETURN>`

Response: `Variable name or ?`

Type: `HPat  <RETURN>`

Response: `Hatch Pattern`

Type: `Ansi31  <RETURN>`

Type: `Solsect  <RETURN>`

Response: `Select objects`

Select your solid.

You'll notice that a closed entity is created in the model representing the cross-section. Use AutoCAD's **MOVE** command to move it away from the model. If prompted about hatch scale or double hatch, respond with .25 and No, respectively. You can use the Release 11 **SHADE** command to get a shaded representation of your model. But make sure you're in a mesh representation in the **MESH** command at the time.

Figure 10-10 shows the final model with hidden lines removed and perspective on.

MOVING ON

Including solids in your designs adds enormous visual appeal, makes creation easier and increases your ability to analyze. Delving this far into 3D leads us into the world of presentation CAD, a world where your models are used to produce realistic images and animations.

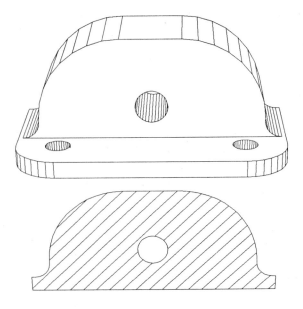

Figure 10-10: The finished solid.

11 **Presentation CAD**

From the outset, this book has stressed that for most users, one of the main benefits of drafting and designing in 3D is better visualization. Better visualization for whom? For the designer, for an audience, or both? To a CAD-proficient designer, working in 3D seems natural, comfortable and efficient. The designer can conceptualize, change and view the model as it will actually look, from any angle. Conveying the third dimension is what the techniques of multiple views and isometrics in traditional paper-and-pencil drafting have always been about. 3D drawings could adequately portray the design so that someone trained to read prints could get an accurate message.

But what if the person at the receiving end of a design concept is not well versed in reading prints, 2D views and isometrics? Most of us fall into that category. Many times, even the 3D wire frame is confusing; removing hidden lines helps, but the real thing is just not there to visualize. So, better visualization also benefits the lay person—the citizen at the town board meeting who wants to see how the proposed landfill will change the landscape. Or the marketing planner who needs more than an artist's conception of a new flashlight model. Or the homeowner who wants to know what the new kitchen will look like before remodeling begins.

SHADING AND RENDERING

Now that you've created surface and solid models in AutoCAD, you realize that surface models are what they are because entities such as 3D faces, meshes and extruded objects hide other objects behind them. These principles are the same in real life; they have to do with the effects of light sources striking surfaces.

When working with our surface models, no light sources are involved. We just see the edges of the surfaces on the screen and imagine the rest if we need to. It's a whole new ball game to ask our software to place light sources and show us with a high degree of accuracy how light reacts with our model surfaces.

Figure 11-1: The building originated as an AutoCAD model, rendered with AT&T GSL's TOPAS, and keyed with the site image, using Truevision's Vista Tips paint software.

To present our models in a way that leaves little to the imagination, we'll need software tools that can calculate and simulate the effects of reflection and refraction on surface textures where there are no color boundaries or constraints on material properties. These tools must produce a realistic rendering equal to one done by hand.

WHO NEEDS RENDERING SOFTWARE?

When and why should you use it? When can you start? Using innovative technology just to keep up with the software world can be very expensive and time-consuming, especially when you're dealing with shading/animation and imaging software. Costs can run from a few hundred to tens of thousands of dollars. And the learning curves can add cost.

Your decisions should focus on how rendering and presentation software tools fit into your business plan. Would they enhance your design process or help improve communications? Define your budget and what you expect the software to do, then if it's warranted, go ahead and fit it into your plan. Your experience with AutoCAD 3D gives you a natural segue to the world of CAD presentation graphics.

CHOOSING A PRODUCT

Before you start shopping, consider these important points. After defining your objectives, do some research to be sure you understand the differences between your AutoCAD software, a modeling/rendering package, a render-only package, an animation package and a paint package. Find out exactly what each one can and cannot do. Although you may find an overlap of features, they're all quite different.

Another consideration: you may need to add or change hardware to produce those great images. Nothing beats looking at or, better yet, working with the real thing. VGA-based rendering and animation packages are promoted with slick ad campaigns that sometimes include deceiving images. It's easy to be lured away from your original goal of meeting your own specific requirements.

Figure 11-2: This model originated as a 2D AutoCAD drawing and was rendered with AT&T GSL's TOPAS.

If you grew up in computer graphics via AutoCAD, you'll find the new world of CAD rendering with videographics/presentation software is quite different. Products are changing fast, and new products are constantly coming out to blend the features of CAD and videographics (which not too long ago were as incompatible as oil and water). You also may have trouble finding a dealer well versed in both CAD and videographics.

Much of the CAD-videographics integration work is being done by a grass-roots contingent of seasoned CAD users who've put it all together themselves and are often willing to share their knowledge and experience. Try to find these people and spend time with them; they may be able to save you from costly mistakes.

HOW DOES RENDERING SOFTWARE WORK?

Rendering software's purpose is to produce an image on an output device that shows what your surface or solid model would look like illuminated with one or more light sources. Given the complexity of simulating light behavior, you can appreciate the level of sophistication necessary to produce software that mimics the way light reacts with a model's surfaces. Reflection off surfaces, refraction through objects like glass and water, and combinations of reflection and refraction with color effects, such as dispersion, have to be taken into account to display the model accurately, as if it were a photograph of the real thing.

Figure 11-3: This model of a proposed Mobil gas station was rendered with AT&T GSL's TOPAS.

In order to do this, the software must go through a four-step process:

Step 1: Calculation of scene attributes

Your 3D model surface information must be projected onto a 2D plane. Using a camera-and-target metaphor, the software obtains a viewing angle and, through geometric calculation, creates a perspective scene with wire frame—much like AutoCAD's DVIEW. Next, the software establishes some scene attributes from the available light sources, such as ambient, cone, point and globe. You place the light sources yourself, specifying brightness, color and direction. Scene-attribute calculations might include reflected images or reflection mapping, shadows and "environment mapping." Many of these calculations must be done early, as prerequisites to the steps that follow.

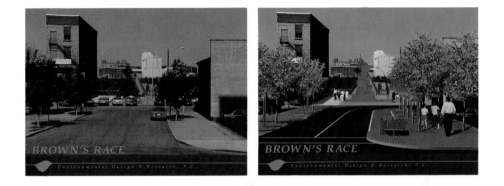

Figures 11-4 and 11-5: This before-and-after scene was created from live video and Time Art's Lumena paint software.

Step 2: Removal of hidden lines

In this computationally intensive process, the software calculates what is actually visible in the scene. Modern software uses a Z buffer technique—a 3D space array that compares entity locations. A *normal* or *perpendicular* is calculated for each surface; then it's determined which of these normals is pointing away from the camera lens. These back-plane objects are removed, and the Z buffer compares each surface with the next in the database to find out which surface is hiding which view from the camera. The Z buffer stores the data for each pixel of your video display on the screen. (A wire frame with hidden lines removed is a number-crunching process. The speed of this operation is directly proportional to the speed of your CPU.)

Step 3: Calculation of colors, textures and surface reactions to light

Good rendering software lets you assign surface characteristics to your model entities. These characteristics include color, transparency, type of shading (uniform, garaud, phong, metallic). And, if you wish, you can use a friendly user interface to map a wood or brick image on the surface. Some software offers material characteristic files, such as plastic, steel, copper, brass, etc., to choose from.

During rendering time, the software has learned the characteristics of each surface from the user's decisions. The software now begins to calculate how each surface should look. There are obvious constraints at this point on what can and cannot be displayed by your videographics adapter. It's not hard to understand why this is the most computationally taxing part of the process. That information from the previous steps must be used in conjunction with your decisions on surface characteristics to determine, for example, the precise effects of light colors and intensities shining at a particular angle from a particular camera viewpoint on a shiny or brushed aluminum surface.

Step 4: Image display

This step is primarily hardware-related. Videographics adapters designed for this type of work are often referred to as frame buffers. These video cards store each pixel, including its color, displayed on your video screen at that time. Yes, your model is vector-based, but the screen display image that's saved to a file is pixel-based. The entire frame can be saved to the disk when an image file is created. Paint software can manipulate the frame buffer, pixel by pixel if necessary, with electronic software tools such as airbrushes, color-blending and charcoal effects.

Your choice of display adapter for this application becomes very important. Yes, a VGA card can be of some help here, but the results may be disappointing. A better solution is a multifeature display adapter that can coexist with a VGA card on the same monitor. This pass-through concept, letting users share Targa-type graphics and VGA graphics on the same screen, was recently endorsed by Truevision, a leader in videographics adapters. Videographics adapters are getting so sophisticated that not only do they "hold" the rendered image, but the application software itself executes it on the board, thus freeing up the PC for other tasks. A good example of this is Truevisions' Vista Tips software, which runs on its 4mb Vista videographics adapter.

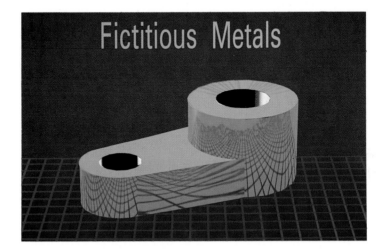

Figure 11-6: AutoCAD surface model was rendered with TOPAS, using a Truevision 4 mb ATVista.

Because presentation CAD often involves blending the real world with the rendered model, live video can be brought directly to the frame buffer by using better adapters that allow for input.

SHADING TYPES AND IMAGE QUALITY

To address Step 3, calculating colors, textures and other surface reactions to light, several types of shading algorithms can directly affect final image quality regardless of the sophistication of the hardware used. As you might guess, the higher the degree of shading quality, the longer the rendering time; the better the quality of shade, the more costly the feature.

Uniform or Gourand shading is more than 20 years old. This type of shading treats the surface, or polygon, uniformly, producing no highlights; the result is a sharply faceted appearance. Therefore, curved surfaces do not shade well using Gourand shading. Gourand shading was used in the early version of AutoSHADE.

AutoSHADE Version 2.0 uses a higher shading algorithm known as Phong shading. The Phong shading method *does* take into account levels of color and intensity around the edges of polygon facets and does produce highlights; but since the highlight color changes with different light sources at various grazing angles, a "plastic" look may result. Phong shading combined with texture mapping produces very realistic effects.

The better software lets you assign the characteristics you want to objects or individual polygons in the model. A shading algorithm called Metallic, used by AT&T GSL's TOPAS software, produces a true metallic effect and along with reflection mapping can create very realistic effects when needed.

A technique used by a more sophisticated software, Ray Tracing, brings photorealism even closer. Ray Tracing gives a faithful reproduction of reality. In this technique, a ray is projected from the camera through every pixel on the image plane until a visible surface is encountered. Then the laws of reflection and refraction take over. The subsequent reflected or refracted ray continues until it encounters another surface, and so on. A tree-structured data network checks each light source to see if a particular surface is in light or shadow or is receiving reflected light from another surface. This mathematical technique closely simulates the way things work in nature.

Ray Tracing combines hidden line removal, mapping, shadows and shading calculations into one step. But there's a drawback: only one type of light source, namely point, can be considered. This makes it difficult to simulate large light sources, such as fluorescent lights.

Ray Tracing is a popular buzz word among PC-based software vendors; but typical CAD models, whether mechanical or architectural, require calculations that are mind-boggling and out of reach for the fastest PCs today—unless you have time to burn.

STANDARDIZING SHADING AND RENDERING SOFTWARE

The PC world always demands standardization—as in page layout with PostScript. The Renderman interface, developed by Pixar, provides a published standard of object and texture descriptors of all kinds. This interface is an example of procedural rendering, where scene information is described by a procedure rather than a calculated value for color, etc. Photo-realistic Renderman is currently being bundled with software from a number of vendors. This widespread acceptance from market leaders could mean that Renderman will emerge as an industry standard for rendering software in the next few years.

ADDING MOTION: A BIG STEP

Sometimes the *essence* of a design is hard to demonstrate. Credibility and realism are usually just as important as a good-looking presentation. And how better to approach this ever-increasing demand for the real thing than by adding motion to your presentations?

But it's not as simple as it sounds. There's a hefty price to pay. Adding inexpensive animation to your design presentations may mean sacrificing the quality of the visuals. To keep the quality high and motion smooth and acceptable, this step from rendered stills to frame-accurate 32-bit animations is a quantum leap.

True animation means smooth, realistic movements on the PC's display. Smooth video is 30 frames per second; in other words, a 20-second 3D animation will require 600 rendered frames. An architectural model with texture maps, shadow, phong shading and several light sources may take 15 minutes per frame to render on a high-powered PC. Consequently, this architectural model will take more than six straight days of computer time to create this 20-second animation!

The effort to create the model is high, the effort to set up the animation is relatively low, and the human effort to create the video tape is nil. However, the post-production time factor (for edits and refinements) can be significant and costly. Therefore, there are few possible paths one can take to keep animation as an option and not waste a lot of time, effort and money doing it.

ANIMATION OPTIONS

As mentioned before, you must first look at your objectives and how much presentation CAD will benefit your business. Low-cost solutions that use your home VCR and require minimal additional hardware are certainly an option. VGA cards that allow NTSC composite video output using AutoSHADE and Autodesk's Animator can produce results that may be enough and may be a solution you can afford to outgrow. Make sure you compare time, effort, initial cost and quality of presentation to what you're doing currently.

At the other extreme, an investment in a dedicated video CAD station with 32-bit frame-accurate 3/4" video tape capabilities, along with a film recorder, scanner and appropriate software, could easily cost between $30,000 and $60,000. And this hefty investment could turn out to be far from cost-effective, since it requires a dedicated person with a lot of talent to use it properly. On the other hand, after paying your learning curve dues, this system could pay for itself with one project.

Since the videographics world continues to merge with the CAD graphics world, thanks to ADI drivers, translators and a strong demand, more and more companies are offering in-house CAD presentations. Other services include producing slides and animations for companies supplying CAD data files.

Figure 11-7: This model was created in AT&T GSL's TOPAS and rendered to a 756 x 486 resolution.

This may present an attractive option to help you get into animation. A good service bureau accepts files in various formats and provides you with prompt, quality output. You can create your animations on a low-cost VGA-based animator, like AT&T GSL's TOPAS VGA. Then, when the situation calls for it, a service bureau using the full 32-bit frame-accurate TOPAS can turn your animation files into a professional, broadcast-quality video presentation.

PRESENTATION ON A SHOESTRING

It's not necessary to invest in a lot of equipment and software to get started with animation and presentation. Your AutoCAD software itself is a good start. Techniques involving 3D wire frames, slide files and script files can be quite effective. Inexpensive utilities are available that capture VGA screens and make the files compatible with paint software. An inexpensive paint package offers 256 color images that can be translated into any format using basic shareware programs.

AutoSHADE and AutoFLIX can provide a healthy, inexpensive start, and Autodesk's Animator is a great way to catch the right person's eye. Getting management to notice and approve what you're doing will allow you to move step by step toward high-quality design presentations with presentation CAD.

In your initial approach to presentations you'll need to rely on AutoCAD customization. This will help in everything from menu picks to AutoLISP routines that use DVIEW to create a simple fly-by or walk-through. And these trials and tribulations will provide valuable experience as you progress toward more complex presentations.

PRESENTATION IN THE 1990s

Your ability to efficiently produce and effectively distribute your design work may be your biggest challenge in the years ahead. This will be especially true as competition increases. As improving technologies facilitate moving more information more quickly, your ability to get your design ideas across with speed and pizazz will be critical.

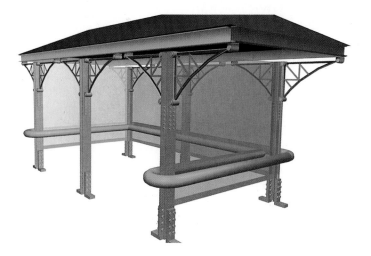

Figure 11-8: This began as an AutoCAD surface model, was translated into a TOPAS model and rendered with Truevision 4mb ATVista.

In the 1960s and early 1970s, the 35mm slide presentation was the ultimate means of presenting information. Design and illustration were all done by hand. The mid- to late 70s brought computer-generated slides produced by hardware/software systems costing hundreds of thousands of dollars. With costs ranging from $50 to $100 per slide, these systems were cost-effective only for large service bureaus.

In the 1980s, the video revolution and the CAD revolution occurred simultaneously. The VCR provided the perfect platform for information distribution and the PC, the perfect platform for design and drafting. The relatively low cost of these tools caused small-scale professional and personal video production to blossom overnight.

Even though production costs were low and the marriage of the two platforms was harmonious, high-quality computer graphics video production and reception were extremely labor- and equipment-intensive. There was also a shortage of computer software to assist in video presentations that used computer graphics as data. As a result, few companies were doing CAD presentations via the video media.

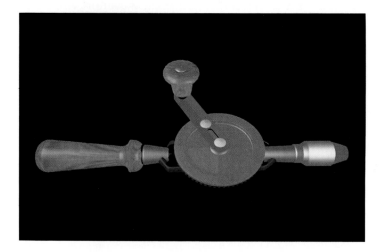

Figure 11-9: Through a DXF translator, a TOPAS model file was created of this surface model, and was rendered with TOPAS, using True-vision 4mb ATVista.

In the 1990s the buzzword is integration—integration right across the board, from software applications to hardware to operating environments to presentation formats. Since all slide images are computer-generated, it's only logical to use a PC to present the images and not go out to film at all. Video projection systems and imaging equipment such as color scanners are becoming much more affordable.

The ability to record computer images onto video tape will be a major information tool of the Nineties; already a variety of software can do just that. Computer-based audio systems that accommodate stereo, creation, editing and playback will become common when standards emerge. Using images and high-quality sound for presentations of your 3D designs will become standard practice.

Just as many companies have set aside a special class of PCs for CAD, they will probably dedicate a PC to creating presentations and another to an electronic presentation system or multimedia system. The local area network will provide an optimal distribution system for business and education. Fiber-optic networks will assist in the quick distribution of data.

In the years to come, we will see presentation CAD become an integral part of the entire design process, and your 3D surface and solid models will provide the visuals for these presentations. So keep that potential benefit in mind as you tread the learning curve of 3D design with AutoCAD.

MOVING ON

You've traveled through the entire spectrum of AutoCAD's 3D features and how they relate to presentation and analysis. However, don't forget AutoCAD's popularity can be partly attributed to its open architecture. Whether you're streamlining a drawing setup or developing a battery of 3D LISP routines to help create wire frames or a walk-through routine, customizing AutoCAD directly relates to productivity. The next section is a library of AutoLISP routines that will expedite your 3D endeavors.

Section III

THE AUTOCAD 3D LIBRARY

The AutoCAD 3D Library

As good as AutoCAD is, and with all the tools for 3D you've learned so far, more is still needed. AutoCAD by its very nature tries to be everything to everybody. As a result, it's a large, cumbersome program. These complications often get in the way of even some of the simplest tasks.

The purpose of "The AutoCAD 3D Library" is to give you some examples and programs that show how to make AutoCAD simpler and more useful for the tasks you do over and over again. The programs also let you do things in AutoCAD that can't easily be done any other way. These programs are only the beginning of your customized 3D library. Your needs and imagination are the only limits to what you can do with AutoLISP.

The programs were designed to be as simple and understandable as possible. As a result, extensive error-checking every step of the way hasn't been included. Therefore, run the programs exactly as they're described in the library. Otherwise, you might crash the program if it doesn't receive the data it's expecting. Don't worry, you can't hurt anything. Feel free to experiment, alter the programs and customize them for your needs.

It's not the purpose of this book to teach you AutoLISP. For a beginning and easy-to-understand tutorial on AutoLISP, please read George Head's *AutoLISP in Plain English* (published by Ventana Press).

However, to use the programs in this book, you'll need to know a few fundamentals on how to create, load and run AutoLISP programs.

CREATING AN AUTOLISP PROGRAM

An AutoLISP program is created as an ordinary text file. If you don't have the optional disk, you must create the file yourself.

In BASIC programming, files and programs are the same. This isn't so with an AutoLISP program; it's called a *function*. Each function begins with (**defun** and ends with a closing parenthesis. You type functions into a text file. The name of the text file is up to you, but it must end with the extension .LSP. You may have more than one function in a single file. In fact, it's possible to put all the functions into one file.

Before you can use a program (function), the file containing it must be loaded. One file, called **ACAD.LSP**, is loaded automatically. If each function is included in **ACAD.LSP**, they'll all be loaded and ready at the beginning of each drawing. When you're ready to run the program, type in the name of the program, and it will begin executing.

You'll need to make some preparations before you can use the programs. First, you must reserve some memory for AutoLISP to run. Issue the following **SET** commands from the DOS C: prompt or place these commands in the **AUTOEXEC.BAT** file:

```
SET LISPHEAP=39000
SET LISPSTACK=5000
```

If you don't issue these commands before going into AutoCAD, you'll quickly get an error message indicating you're out of node (memory) space.

Another thing that will help you with memory management is the **(vmon)** command. If you're working with AutoLISP programs you should always have an **ACAD.LSP** file, even if all of the programs aren't located in that file. Be sure that **(vmon)** is the first line in the **ACAD.LSP** file. This is necessary so that **(vmon)** is the first command issued as you go into a drawing. **(vmon)** means Virtual Memory On, and lets you run very large AutoLISP programs in a small memory environment.

As we've mentioned, programs are typed into an ordinary DOS text file whose name has the extension .LSP. You can create a text file in several ways. The easiest way is with the DOS program EDLIN.COM. If this program is in the ACAD directory or you're pathed to a directory containing EDLIN, you can access it directly from inside AutoCAD. All you need to do is type **EDIT** from the AutoCAD command line. You'll then be asked for the file to edit. When you give it the file name, you can begin editing the file using EDLIN.

Now let's try the first program and see how it works.

Type: EDIT <RETURN>

Response: File to edit.

Type: MACRO1.LSP <RETURN>

Response: New file.

Now you're ready to begin typing in the first program.

Type: I <RETURN>

This begins an insert function for the first line. Now each line will increment by one line number.

Response: 1:*

Now type in the program, ending each line with **<RETURN>**.

Type:
```
(defun C:PON ()
(command "DVIEW" "" "D" "" "")
)
^C
```

When you finish typing in the program, you must break out of Insert mode with a **CTRL-C**.

Response: *

Type: E   <RETURN>

This will end the EDLIN program and return you to the AutoCAD command line.

Now that the AutoLISP file has been created, you must load the file.

TYPE: (load "macro1") <RETURN>

Notice that the **load** command is in parentheses. This indicates to AutoCAD that the command is an AutoLISP command, not the Auto-CAD **LOAD** command. The name of the file that's being loaded is enclosed in quotation marks.

Now that the file is loaded, you can run the program simply by typing its name.

Type: PON <RETURN>

The program will now turn **PERSPECTIVE ON**.

If you have the optional disk, then each of the macro .LSP files is already created and typed in for you. You should then begin with the (**load**) command to try each program.

We hope you'll enjoy these programs and that they'll prove useful to you by themselves and in the examples they provide.

Perspective On
For Release 10 or 11

PURPOSE: The **DVIEW** command includes the prompt **DVIEW OFF** but not **DVIEW ON**. This simple routine will turn **PERSPECTIVE ON** from the current viewpoint, target and camera-to-target distance.

TO CREATE:
```
(defun C:PON ()
(command "DVIEW" "" "D" "" "")
)
```

TO INVOKE: Save this macro as an AutoLISP file (**.lsp**).

LET'S TRY IT: Get into a drawing and load **MACRO1** (**Load "MACRO1"**). Select a view by using the **DVIEW** command and either setting **CAMERA** and **TARGET** angles or using **DVIEW POints** and specifying **CAMERA** and **TARGET** points. Exit the **DVIEW** command. Type **PON**. You'll see the current view, with **PERSPECTIVE ON**.

TIPS: To use this as a menu macro, add the following line to your menu:

```
^C^C(if(null C:PON)(load "PON"));PON
```

This macro is equivalent to the non-AutoLISP macro:

```
^C^CDVIEW;;D;;;
```

We're giving you the AutoLISP version because it provides a new command, **PON**, which you can invoke from the keyboard or a menu; it's more flexible. Throughout this section, we'll present several variations for macros and suggest possible applications.

NOTE: This macro uses the current **TARGET** point, **CAMERA** point and **DISTANCE**. If you use **PON** after a **VPOINT** command, you may not see anything at all on your screen! This is because **VPOINT** uses points such as **1,1,1** for orientation and is always looking at the origin, **0,0,0**. **VPOINT** actually presents a view along a line through the point **1,1,1** and zoomed out automatically. If you just turn **PERSPECTIVE ON**, you may be inside the model and only one unit distant from the origin, and this "auto zoom" won't be performed for you. If you want to use **VPOINT** to move to new views, use **MACRO2** and **MACRO3**; **MACRO2** will use the correct **VPOINT** target and viewpoint, and **MACRO3** will provide a useful zoom option to move in and out of this extreme close-up.

Macro
2　Perspective On for VPOINTS
For Release 10 Only

PURPOSE: Turns **PERSPECTIVE ON** from the current viewpoint, when selected by the **VPOINT** command. This macro automatically supplies its own **CAMERA** and **TARGET** points. This will correct the orientation of the line of sight, but you may be zoomed in too close to the model. Correct this with the **DVIEW ZOOM** command or **MACRO3**.

TO CREATE:
```
(defun C:PONV (/ VPT)
(setq VPT(list(getvar "VPOINTX")(getvar "VPOINTY")
  (getvar "VPOINTZ")))
(command "DVIEW" "" "PO" "0,0,0" VPT "D" "" "")
)
```

TO INVOKE: Save this macro as an AutoLISP file (**.lsp**).

LET'S TRY IT: Get into a drawing and load **MACRO2** (**Load "MACRO2"**). Select a view by using the **VPOINT** command. Type **PONV**. You'll see the current view, with **PERSPECTIVE ON**.

TIPS: To use this as a menu macro, add the following line to your menu:

```
^C^C(if(null C:PONV)(load "PONV"));PONV
```

Macro 2B

PONV
For Release 11 Only

PURPOSE: Release 11 eliminates the system variables **VPOINTX**, **VPOINTY** and **VPOINTZ**. Using the new variable, VIEWDIR, this version will perform the same **PERSPECTIVE ON** command as **MACRO2**.

TO CREATE:
```
(defun C:PONV (/ VPT)
(setq VPT(getvar "VIEWDIR"))
(command "DVIEW" "" "PO" "0,0,0" VPT "D" "" "")
)
```

TO INVOKE: Save this macro as an AutoLISP file (.**lsp**)

LET'S TRY IT: Get into a drawing and load **Macro2B** (Load "MACRO2B"). Select a view by using the **VPOINT** command. Type **PONV**. You'll see the current view, with **PERSPECTIVE ON**.

TIPS: To use this as a menu macro, add the following line to your menu:

```
^C^C(if(null C:PONV)(load "PONV"));PONV
```

Macro 3

Zoom Perspective
For Release 10 Only

PURPOSE: The **DVIEW** command has a **ZOOM** option that lets you use current **TARGET** and **CAMERA** points and zoom in and out. To get controlled zooms, you must read off the current zoom distance and multiply or divide to get your new zoom distance. The onscreen graphic interface lets you zoom by approximation. This macro lets you choose the ratio to your current zoom, and does the math for you. A larger ratio will move you farther away from the current target, and a smaller ratio will move you closer—like a telephoto lens. This is useful in combination with **MACRO1** or **MACRO2**, which turn **PERSPECTIVE ON** but cannot set the proper view distance.

TO CREATE:
```
(defun C:ZP (/ RAT DI)
(setq RAT (getreal"\nWhat is ratio of current view distance?"))
(setq VPT(list(getvar "VPOINTX") (getvar "VPOINTY")
  (getvar "VPOINTZ")))
(setq TARG(getvar "TARGET"))
(setq DIS(* RAT(distance TARG VPT)))
(command "DVIEW" "" "D" DIS "")
)
```

TO INVOKE: Save this macro as an AutoLISP file (**.lsp**).

LET'S TRY IT: Get into a drawing and load **MACRO3 (Load "MACRO3")**. Select a view by using the **DVIEW** command. Turn **PERSPECTIVE ON** using **PON**. You'll see the current view with **PERSPECTIVE ON**. Type **ZP**. When prompted, provide a ratio such as **2** for zooming out twice as far or **.5** for zooming in twice as far.

TIPS: To use this as a menu macro, add the following line to your menu.

```
^C^C(in(null C:ZP) (load "ZP"));ZP
```

Macro 3B   # ZP
For Release 11 Only

PURPOSE: Release 11 eliminates the system variables **VPOINTX**, **VPOINTY** and **VPOINTZ**. Using the new variable, **VIEWDIR**, this version will perform the same **PERSPECTIVE ON** command as **MACRO3**.

TO CREATE:
```
(defun C:ZP (/ RAT VPT TARG DIS)
(setq RAT(getreal"\nWhat is ratio of current view distance?"))
(setq VPT(getvar "VIEWDIR"))
(setq TARG(getvar "TARGET"))
(setq DIS(* RAT(distance TARG VPT)))
(command "DVIEW" "" "D" DIS "")
)
```

TO INVOKE: Save this macro as an AutoLISP file (**.lsp**)

LET'S TRY IT: Get into a drawing and load **MACRO3B** (**Load "MACRO3B"**). Select a view by using the **DVIEW** command. Turn **PERSPECTIVE ON** using **PON**. You'll see the current view with **PERSPECTIVE ON**. Type ZP. When prompted, provide a ratio such as 2 for zooming out twice as far or .5 for zooming in twice as far.

TIPS: To use this as a menu macro, add the following line to your menu:

```
^C^C(if(null C:ZP)(load "ZP"));ZP
```

Macro 4

Snap to Top
Z Value
For Release 10 or 11

PURPOSE: Provides a new, 3D object snap that will supply the top **Z** value from a set of objects. This is useful in such applications as architectural modeling, in which you may want to place a typewriter on a desktop, a roof assembly on a house or construct any element "exactly" on top of another without referring to the **LIST** command.

TO CREATE:
```
(defun TOP (/ ENTS BIG COUNT ENT DESCR TH NUM ELEV A AS)
(setq ENTS(ssget) BIG 0.0 COUNT 0 NUM 0.0)
(while(< COUNT(sslength ENTS))
(setq ENT(ssname ENTS COUNT))
(setq DESCR(entget ENT))
(setq TH(assoc 39 DESCR))
(if TH
(progn
  (setq NUM(cdr TH))
  (setq ELEV(nth 3(assoc 10 DESCR)))
  (if(>(+ ELEV NUM) BIG)(setq BIG(+ ELEV NUM)))
)
)
```

```
(foreach A '(10 11 12 13)
(setq AS(assoc A DESCR))
(if AS(setq NUM(nth 3 AS)))
(if(> NUM BIG)(setq BIG NUM))
)
(setq COUNT(1+ COUNT))
)
(setq TOPZ(rtos BIG(getvar "lunits")(getvar "luprec")))
)
```

TO INVOKE: Save this macro as an AutoLISP file (**.lsp**).

LET'S TRY IT: Get into a new drawing and load **MACRO4 (Load "MACRO4")**. Create a series of objects of different elevations and thicknesses. To create a new object at the topmost elevation, type **ELEV !(TOP)**, select the group for determining the highest Z value, then type the thickness to end the **ELEV** command. Succeeding objects will have their baselines at the top Z value in the selection set.

TIPS: You can insert this macro in a menu as a transparent object snap. Copy the following to your menu: **!(TOP)**. You may then use **TOP** in conjunction with the **.XY** filters. For instance, type **LINE .XY** (choose X-Y position) **!(TOP)** (select objects for finding top Z value), and the highest Z in the group will become the Z value for the first line's endpoint.

WARNING: This macro works on all the "simple" AutoCAD entities, since it grabs the insertion point or endpoint and also elevation and thickness of objects in the selection set. However, when used with polylines, 3D polylines (including meshes) or blocks, it evaluates the Z value of only the insertion point, not the true top of the complex object. Use **EXPLODE** on these compound objects if you want to use the **TOP** snap.

Macro 5

Snap to Bottom Z Value
For Release 10 or 11

PURPOSE: Provides a new 3D object snap that will supply the bottom Z value from a set of objects. This has the opposite effect of **MACRO4**, and may be useful when you want to move one object exactly on top of another. This macro would supply the bottom Z value of the object to be placed, rather than depending on the **LIST** command.

TO CREATE:
```
(defun BOT (/ ENTS LIL COUNT ENT DESCR TH NUM ELEV A AS)
(setq ENTS(ssget) LIL 0.0 COUNT 0 NUM 0.0)
(while(< COUNT(sslength ENTS))
(setq ENT(ssname ENTS COUNT))
(setq DESCR(entget ENT))
(setq TH(assoc 39 DESCR))
(if TH
(progn
  (setq NUM(cdr TH))
  (setq ELEV(nth 3 (assoc 10 DESCR)))
  (if(<(+ ELEV NUM) LIL)(setq LIL(+ ELEV NUM)))
)
)
(foreach A '(10 11 12 13)
(setq AS(assoc A DESCR))
(if AS(setq NUM(nth 3 AS)))
(if(< NUM LIL)(setq LIL NUM))
)
(setq COUNT(1+ COUNT))
)
(setq BOTZ (rtos LIL(getvar"lunits")(getvar"luprec")))
)
```

TO INVOKE: Save this macro as an AutoLISP file (**.lsp**).

LET'S TRY IT: Get into a new drawing and load **MACRO5** (**Load "MACRO5"**). Create a series of objects of different elevations and thicknesses. To create a new object at the bottom-most elevation, type **ELEV, !(TOP),** select the group for determining the lowest Z value, then type the thickness to end the **ELEV** command. Succeeding objects will have their baselines at the bottom Z value in the selection set.

TIPS: You can insert this macro in a menu as a transparent object snap. Copy the following to your menu: **!(BOT).** You can then use **BOT** with the **.XY** filters. For instance, type **LINE .XY** (choose X-Y position) **!(BOT)** (select objects for finding bottom Z value), and the lowest Z in the group will become the Z value for the first line's endpoint.

WARNING: This macro works on all the "simple" AutoCAD entities, since it grabs the insertion point or endpoint and also elevation and thickness of objects in the selection set. However, when used with polylines, 3D polylines (including meshes) or blocks, it will evaluate the Z value of only the insertion point, not the true bottom of the complex object. Use **EXPLODE** on these compound objects if you want to use the **BOT** snap.

Macro 6 — Capture Thickness of Object
For Release 10 or 11

PURPOSE: Used in creating extruded objects at different levels but with the same thickness. If you're modeling large arrays, as in city planning, building exteriors or mechanical assemblies, it's often useful to check the extrusion thickness of an already created standard object, or "grab" it for creating the next similar object. For example, let's say you're setting thickness for chimneys on rooftops: you may want a set of chimneys to be the same height, but at different elevations. With this macro, you can "grab" the thickness of one, set your thickness, and using **ELEV** and perhaps **MACRO4, MACRO5** or **MACRO7** for **TOP, BOT** or **MIDFACE** snaps, begin drawing them in place.

TO CREATE:

```
(defun THI (/ ENT DESCR AS)
(setq ENT(car(entsel)))
(setq DESCR(entget ENT))
(setq AS(assoc 39 DESCR))
(if AS
(setq THIK(rtos(cdr AS)(getvar"lunits")(getvar"luprec")))
(setq THIK(rtos(getvar "thickness")(getvar"lunits")(getvar"
  luprec")))
)
)
```

TO INVOKE: Save this macro as an AutoLISP file (**.lsp**).

LET'S TRY IT: Get into a new drawing and create an extruded object. For instance, type **ELEV 0 3 CIRCLE 0,0,0 5** to create a circular cylinder with center at **0,0,0**, radius of **5** units, and thickness of **3** units. To create an "equal thickness" circle elsewhere in the drawing, type **ELEV 4 !(THI)** (touch edge of first circle) and draw a second circle. It will have an elevation of **4** units and the same thickness as the first circle, **3** units.

TIPS: You can inset this macro in a menu as a transparent object snap. Copy the following to your menu: **!(THI)**. You can then use **THI** with the **ELEV** command to match the thickness of an existing extruded entity. You can also use it with other object snaps. For instance, **ELEV !(TOP)** (select entities) **!(THI)** (select entities) would produce succeeding objects at the topmost Z value and with a given thickness.

Macro 7 **Capture Middle of an Entity** ⊙

For Release 10 or 11

PURPOSE: A general-purpose object snap that finds the center of a **3DFACE** at any angle and with 1, 2, 3 or 4 unique vertices. It will also snap to the center of a circle or arc, the midpoint of a line, a node of a point, the middle of a solid of 1-4 vertices, etc. In extruded objects, the snap is to the middle X, Y and Z positions (i.e., midface and halfway up an object). This macro began as an attempt to snap to the middle of a **3DFACE**, but it can find the middle of any simple entity (excluding **PLINES**).

TO CREATE:

```
(defun MIDF (/ ENT DESCR THA TH ELEV MIDZ AS10 A AS VLIST VN)
(defun MID3D (PTNUM PTLIST / XDELT YDELT ZDELT
   COUNT PT1 X1 Y1 Z1 PT2 X2 Y2 Z2 XNEW YNEW ZNEW)
(setq XDELT 0.0 YDELT 0.0 ZDELT 0.0 COUNT 0
     PT1(car PTLIST)
     X1(car PT1)
     Y1(cadr PT1)
     Z1(caddr PT1))
(while(< COUNT(length PTLIST))
(setq PT2(nth COUNT PTLIST)
     X2(car PT2)
     Y2(cadr PT2)
     Z2(caddr PT2)
     XDELT(+ XDELT(- X2 X1))
     YDELT(+ YDELT(- Y2 Y1))
     ZDELT(+ ZDELT(- Z2 Z1))
COUNT(1+ COUNT))
)
(setq XNEW(+ X1(/ XDELT COUNT))
     YNEW(+ Y1(/ YDELT COUNT))
     ZNEW(+ Z1(/ ZDELT COUNT))
     MPT(list XNEW YNEW ZNEW))
)
;
; MAIN PROGRAM
;
(setq ENT(car(entsel)))
(if ENT
(progn
(setq DESCR(entget ENT)
     THA(assoc 39 DESCR))
(if THA(setq TH(cdr THA) ELEV (cadddr(assoc 10 DESCR))
  MIDZ(+ ELEV(/ TH 2.0)))))
```

```
(setq AS10(cdr(assoc 10 DESCR)))
(if MIDZ(setq AS10(list(car AS10)(cadr AS10)MIDZ)))
(setq VLIST(cons AS10 VLIST))
(foreach A '(11 12 13)
(setq AS(cdr(assoc A DESCR)))
(if MIDZ(setq AS(list(car AS)(cadr AS)MIDZ)))
(if(and AS(car AS)(null(member AS VLIST)))(SETQ VLIST
  (CONS AS VLIST)))
)
(setq VN(length VLIST))
(MID3D VN VLIST)
)
(progn
(princ"\nOBJECT NOT FOUND...PICK AGAIN...")
(setq MPT nil)
)
)
)
```

TO INVOKE: Save this macro as an AutoLISP file (**.lsp**).

LET'S TRY IT: Get into a new drawing and create a series of objects: a circle, line, point, and solids and 3DFACES with 1, 2, 3 and 4 unique endpoints. Extrude several of the 2D entities using the **CHANGE** command. Now, load **MACRO7 (Load "MACRO7")**. Type **LINE !(MIDF)** and touch an entity on its edge. The line will be snapped to the geometric center of the object. Try viewing in isometric by typing **VPOINT 1,1,1**. Type **LINE !(MIDF)** and touch an extruded entity, **3DFACE** or **3DLINE**. The line will snap to the three-dimensional center of the entity.

TIPS: You can insert this macro in a menu as a transparent object snap. Copy the following to your menu: **!(MIDF)**. You can then use **MIDF** with an entity creation command to snap to an entity's center of mass. You can also trap the X, Y or Z values of the centerpoint by combining 3D filters with the **MIDF** snap. For instance, **.XY !(MIDF)** (select entity) **!(BOT)** (select entities) would produce a point in the middle of a chosen face and at the bottom elevation of a set of entities.

Automatic Entity Extrusion

Macro 8

For Release 10 Only

PURPOSE: Automatically extrudes 2D entities into 2 1/2 D (and back). You can accomplish this by using a series of **CHANGE** or **CHPROP** commands on selected entities; but for large drawings—for instance, entire interior space plans for architects—the use of **CHANGE** or **CHPROP** is rather tedious. Once your office standards are set up, determining the typical heights of such linear elements as interior walls, exterior walls or window mullions, this macro provides a lightning-fast way to extrude and unextrude large plans.

To use this macro, you'll need both the AutoLISP routine and the data file it will scan. The "TO CREATE" section below lists the Auto-LISP code; now let's create the data file.

This file uses a space-delimited data file. Using any ASCII editor, create the file **XTRULIST.DTA** that contains the necessary information. The following is a sample of the file included on the optional AutoCAD 3D diskette:

```
0
0
54
TEST1
0
108
TEST2
28.5
1.5
TEST3
96
2
```

Create this file in exactly the same format as the example above. The first line of an entry is the layer name, such as **0**, **TEST1**, **TEST2**, etc. The second line of an entry is the elevation or bottom Z value for extruding entities on that layer. The third line is the thickness for extruding entities on that layer. The names of the layers and their heights will depend on your system of 2D drafting. In a typical architectural application, layer **0** might contain low interior walls 54" high, while **TEST2** might contain workspace surfaces 28.5" high and 1.5" thick.

TO CREATE:

```
(defun C:XTRU (/ S FIL RM CM LAYER ELEV THIK BLOX)
(defun *ERROR* (s)
(close FIL)
(setvar "REGENMODE" RM)
(setvar "CMDECHO" CM)
(setvar "EXPERT" 0)
(princ s)
(setq *ERROR* nil)
(terpri)
)
(graphscr)
(setq RM (getvar "REGENMODE") CM (getvar "CMDECHO"))
(setvar "REGENMODE" 0)
(setvar "EXPERT" 3)
(setvar "CMDECHO" 0)
(if(null XTRUDIR)(setq XTRUDIR "2D-3D"))
(princ(strcat "\nEXTRUSION DIRECTION BEGINS: " XTRUDIR "\n"))
(setq FIL(open "XTRULIST.DTA" "r"))
(while(setq LAYER(read-line FIL))
(setq ELEV(read-line FIL))
(setq THIK(read-line FIL))
(setq BLOX(ssget "X" '((0 . "INSERT"))))
(if(and(equal XTRUDIR "2D-3D")(tblsearch "layer" LAYER))
(progn
(command "change" (ssget "X"(list(cons 8 LAYER))))
(if BLOX(command  "r" BLOX))
(command "" "p" "e" ELEV "t" THIK "")
)
)
(if(and(equal XTRUDIR "3D-2D")(tblsearch "layer" LAYER))
(progn
(command "change" (ssget "X" (list(cons 8 LAYER))))
(if BLOX(command "r" BLOX))
(command "" "p" "e" "0" "t" "0" "")
```

```
)
)
)
(close FIL)
(command "REGEN")
(setvar "REGENMODE" 1)
(setvar "CMDECHO" 1)
(setvar "EXPERT" 0)
(if(equal XTRUDIR "2D-3D")(setq XTRUDIR "3D-2D")
  (setq XTRUDIR "2D-3D"))
(princ(strcat "\nEXTRUSION DIRECTION IS NOW: "XTRUDIR))
(terpri)
)
```

TO INVOKE: Create this macro as an AutoLISP file (**.lsp**).

LET'S TRY IT: Get into a new drawing and load **MACRO8 (Load "MACRO8")**. Create objects on various layers. If you wish, use layers **0, TEST1, TEST2** and **TEST3**. Type **XTRU**. If it finds the file **XTRULIST.DTA**, it will begin. It will change the elevation and thickness of all 2D entities that aren't blocked—lines, arcs, solids, traces, etc.— to the appropriate extruded or "2 1/2 D" values. If the macro is run a second time, entities will be "unextruded" back to an elevation and thickness of 0. This macro will affect an entity regardless of whether its layer is on, off, frozen or thawed!
    You can insert this macro into a menu by including the line:

```
^C^C(if(null C:XTRU)(load "MACRO8"));XTRU
```

Macro 9

Symbol Replacement
For Release 10 or 11

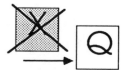

PURPOSE: Redefines blocks in your drawing. This macro will perform three useful functions: "refresh" a block definition, replacing the current block with its definition as found on hard disk; replace a block definition with the definition of a different block on hard disk; or replace a 2D symbol with its 3D counterpart from hard disk, or vice versa.

While you might use the **INSERT** command and a library of 3D symbols to create a 3D model from scratch, it's sometimes better to create a complete 2D diagram and replace each 2D symbol with its 3D counterpart. This macro shows how to use such a technique.

TO CREATE: The basic routine for symbol replacement is to use the "insert equals" command (i.e., **INSERT blockname=**, which replaces the current block definition with that of a .**DWG** file on disk, if available). At the end of the command, it will ask for a new insertion point. By pressing **<CTRL C>** you can redefine a symbol without inserting an extra instance.

An interesting feature lets you provide a .**DWG** filename on the right side of the equals sign. All instances of the first block in the drawing will be redefined using the .**DWG** file definition. For instance, if you type **INSERT CH1=CH2**, all instances of **CH1**, perhaps a symbol for a secretarial chair, will be replaced by **CH2**, perhaps a symbol for an executive chair. If the second symbol is actually a 3D or "2½ D" block, you can use this technique to perform an automatic 2D to 3D conversion. The results can help a great deal in creating complex 3D models.

TO INVOKE: Use this technique in an existing drawing by typing at the **Command:** prompt.

LET'S TRY IT: Get into an AutoCAD drawing and insert a typical symbol. Type the command **INSERT sym1=sym2**, where **sym1** is the current block name and **sym2** is the replacement symbol name. The system will respond "Block (sym1) redefined:" and request an insertion point. Press **<CTRL C>** if you don't want to insert another instance.

TIPS: You may use a symbol from another subdirectory or disk. Simply include the proper path in its name; for instance: **INSERT CH1=C:\SYM3D\CH13D.**

If you list the symbol, it will still have its original name even though it's now represented by the new symbol data. To change its name, type **RENAME BLOCKS oldname newname**, where **oldname** is the name of the original symbol and **newname** is the name of its replacement symbol. This macro will work whether the symbols' layers are on, off, frozen or thawed.

Macro 10 Automatic 2D/3D Symbol Replacement
For Release 10 or 11

PURPOSE: Replaces 2D symbols in your drawing with the appropriate 3D or "2 1/2 D" symbol. You could accomplish this by manually invoking the **INSERT=** command as in **MACRO9**, over and over. But once set up, **MACRO10** provides a repeatable and much faster exchange. It scans the current drawing for all "standard" symbols and replaces them as described in a data file you'll create. The macro eliminates the listing and fumbling of a manual technique, and if you use it with **MACRO8** and **MACRO11**, you can convert 2D plans to 3D models in moments.

This macro requires that both 2D and 3D symbols exist and reside on the current subdirectory. It also requires both the AutoLISP routine and the data file it will scan. The "TO CREATE" section below lists the AutoLISP code; now let's create the data file.

This file uses a space-delimited data file. Using any ASCII editor, create the file **SWAPLIST.DTA** that contains the necessary information. The following is a sample of the file included on the optional AutoCAD 3D diskette:

```
SYM1
SYM13D
SYM2
SYM23D
SYM3
SYM33D
```

Create this file in exactly the same format as the example above. The first line of an entry is the name of the 2D block, such as **SYM1**, **SYM2** or **SYM3**. The second line is the name of the 3D replacement block, such as **SYM13D**, **SYM23D** or **SYM33D**. The names of the 2D and 3D blocks will depend on your system of 2D drafting. In a typical architectural application, **SYM1** might be a 2D chair, while **SYM13D** would be the 3D model to replace it.

TO CREATE:
```
(defun C:SWAP (/ S FIL RM CM SYM2D SYM3D)
(defun *ERROR* (s)
```

```
(close FIL)
(setvar "REGENMODE" RM)
(setvar "CMDECHO" CM)
(setvar "EXPERT" 0)
(princ s)
(setq *ERROR* nil)
(terpri)
)
(graphscr)
(setq RM (getvar "REGENMODE") CM (getvar "CMDECHO"))
(setvar "REGENMODE" 0)
(setvar "CMDECHO" 0)
(setvar "EXPERT" 3)
(if(null SWAPDIR)(setq SWAPDIR "2D-3D"))
(princ(strcat "\nSWAP DIRECTION BEGINS: " SWAPDIR "\n"))
(setq FIL(open "SWAPLIST.DTA" "r"))
(while(setq SYM2D(read-line FIL))
(setq SYM3D(read-line FIL))
(if(and(equal SWAPDIR "2D-3D")(tblsearch "block" SYM2D))
(progn
(command "rename" "block" SYM2D SYM3D)
(command "insert" (strcat SYM3D "=") \c)
)
)
(if(and(equal SWAPDIR "3D-2D")(tblsearch "block" SYM3D))
(progn
(command "rename" "block" SYM3D SYM2D)
(command "insert" (strcat SYM2D "=") \c)
)
)
)
(close FIL)
(command "REGEN")
(setvar "REGENMODE" 1)
(setvar "CMDECHO" 1)
(setvar "EXPERT" 0)
(if(equal SWAPDIR "2D-3D")(setq SWAPDIR "3D-2D")
  (setq SWAPDIR "2D-3D"))
(princ(strcat "\nSWAP DIRECTION IS NOW: " SWAPDIR))
```

```
(terpri)
)
```

TO INVOKE: Create this macro as an AutoLISP file (**.Isp**).

LET'S TRY IT: Get into a new drawing and load **MACRO10** (**Load "MACRO10"**). If you don't have both a 2D symbol and a 3D counterpart, do the following:

Type **SOLID 0,0 1,0 0,1 1,1**. End the **SOLID** command with an extra **<RETURN>**. Now create a block. Type **BLOCK SYM1 0,0**. Select the solid and press an extra **<RETURN>** to end the **BLOCK** command. Type **OOPS** to bring it back. Type **CHANGE L** followed by a **<RETURN>** and **P E 0 T 1**. This will change the solid into a cube with its bottom Z elevation at **0** and a thickness of one unit. To prove this, type **VPOINT 1,1,1** and you'll see the cube from another angle. Type **BLOCK SYM13D 0,0**. Select the solid and press an extra **<RETURN>** to end the **BLOCK** command. There will now be no solids visible in the drawing. Insert several of the 2D blocks using **INSERT SYM1**.

Now **WBLOCK** the two blocks, 2D and 3D cubes, out to disk. Type **WBLOCK SYM1 SYM1**, then **WBLOCK SYM13D SYM13D**. Assuming you use the sample data file, you may now type **SWAP**. Each instance of **SYM1** will be replaced from disk by **SYM13D**, and the 2D cube will become 3D. Type **LIST** and select a few of the 3D cubes. Their names should be **SYM13D** now. Type **SWAP** again, and they'll become 2D again, and will list as **SYM1** insertions.

TIPS: In addition to 2D/3D swaps, this routine could show space plans with alternative sets of furniture, or replace one manufacturer's components with another's. Insert this macro into a menu by including the line:

```
^C^C(if(null C:SWAP)(load "MACRO10"));SWAP
```

Macro
11 Nonstandard Block Extrusion
For Release 10 Only

PURPOSE: If a block isn't "standard" (i.e., it isn't listed in the **SWAPLIST.DTA** file or doesn't have a ready-made 3D counterpart), you can still redefine it by inserting it, exploding, extruding its subentities and reblocking it. This macro will redefine nonstandard blocks by selection (as long as they are nested only one level deep).

This routine uses the same **XTRULIST.DTA** file as **MACRO8**. If this file doesn't already exist, create it using any ASCII editor, following the instructions in **MACRO8**.

TO CREATE:
```
(defun C:REDEF (/ S NAMLIST BLKS COUNTER NAM LAST ENT ENTS
   LAY LAY3D FIL ELEV THIK)
(defun *ERROR* (s)
(close FIL)
(setvar "HIGHLIGHT" 1)
(setvar "BLIPMODE" 1)
(setvar "REGENMODE" 1)
(setvar "CMDECHO" 1)
(setvar "EXPERT" 0)
(setq *ERROR* nil)
(terpri)
)
(setq NAMLIST nil)
(if(null RDIR)(setq RDIR "2D-3D"))
(princ"\nINDICATE BLOCKS TO REDEFINE BY EXTRUSION: ")
(setq BLKS(ssget))
(princ(strcat"\nREDEFINING DIRECTION BEGINS: " RDIR))
(initget 1 "Y N")
(setq ANS(getkword"\nREVERSE REDEFINING DIRECTION? (Y N) "))
(if(and(equal ANS "Y")(equal RDIR "2D-3D"))
(setq RDIR "3D-2D" ANS nil))
(if(and(equal ANS "Y")(equal RDIR "3D-2D"))
(setq RDIR "2D-3D"))
```

```
(princ(strcat"\nREDEFINING DIRECTION IS NOW: " RDIR))
(princ"\nABOUT TO REDEFINE ALL BLOCKS SELECTED...PLEASE WAIT!")
(setvar "HIGHLIGHT" 0)
(setvar "BLIPMODE" 0)
(setvar "REGENMODE" 0)
(setvar "CMDECHO" 0)
(setvar "EXPERT" 3)
(setq COUNTER 0)
(while(< COUNTER(sslength BLKS))
  (if(equal(cdr(assoc 0(entget(ssname BLKS COUNTER)))) "INSERT")
  (progn
  (setq NAM(cdr(assoc 2(entget(ssname BLKS COUNTER)))))
  (if(null(member NAM NAMLIST))
  (setq NAMLIST(cons NAM NAMLIST)))
)
)
(setq COUNTER(1+ COUNTER))
)
(setq LAST(entlast))
(setq COUNTER 0)
(while(< COUNTER(length NAMLIST))

  (princ(strcat"\nEXTRUDING BLOCK: " (nth COUNTER NAMLIST)
  "...WAIT!"))
  (command "insert" (strcat "*" (nth COUNTER NAMLIST))
  "0,0" "1" "0")
  (setq ENTS(ssadd))
  (setq ENT(entnext LAST))
  (while ENT
    (setq ENTS(ssadd ENT ENTS))
    (if(equal RDIR "2D-3D")
    (progn
    (setq LAY(cdr(assoc 8(entget ENT))))
    (setq FIL(open "XTRULIST.DTA" "r"))
    (setq LAY3D nil)
    (while(and(not(equal LAY LAY3D))
    (setq LAY3D(read-line FIL)))
      (setq ELEV(read-line FIL))
      (setq THIK(read-line FIL))
```

```
        (if(equal LAY LAY3D)
        (command "change" ENT "" "p" "e" ELEV "t" THIK ""))
      )
      (close FIL)
      )
      )
      (setq ENT(entnext ENT))
    )
    (if(equal RDIR "3D-2D")
    (command "change" ENTS "" "p" "e" "0" "t" "0" ""))
    (command "block" (nth COUNTER NAMLIST) "0,0" ENTS "")
    (princ(strcat"\nBLOCK: " (nth COUNTER NAMLIST)
    " REDEFINED!"))
    (setq COUNTER(1+ COUNTER))
 )
(command "REGEN")
(setvar "HIGHLIGHT" 1)
(setvar "BLIPMODE" 1)
(setvar "REGENMODE" 1)
(setvar "CMDECHO" 1)
(setvar "EXPERT" 0)
(princ "\nFINISHED!")
(terpri)
)
```

TO INVOKE: Create this macro as an AutoLISP file (**.lsp**).

LET'S TRY IT: If you're using the **XTRULIST.DTA** file listed in **MACRO8**, you've defined elevation and thickness of extrusion for layers **0**, **TEST1**, **TEST2** and **TEST3**. Type **LAYER S 0** and press an extra **<RETURN>** to exit the **LAYER** command. Draw several 2D entities, such as lines. Type **BLOCK ONE** and select an insertion point. When prompted, select each entity and press an extra **<RETURN>** to exit the **BLOCK** command. Repeat this procedure for another layer, creating **BLOCK TWO**.

Type **INSERT ONE**, and select an insertion point, X scale, Y scale and rotation angle. Create several insertions of **BLOCK ONE** at different locations and scales. Do the same for **BLOCK TWO**.

Make sure **MACRO11** is loaded, or load it now (**Load "MACRO11"**). Type **REDEF**. You'll be prompted to select blocks for redefinition.

Select at least one insertion of **BLOCK ONE** and one insertion of **BLOCK TWO**. The macro will tell you which direction you're currently extruding in, 2D-3D or 3D-2D, and you'll be asked if you want to change the current direction. Assuming this is your first run, objects will be extruded from their current elevation and thickness to their **XTRULIST.DTA** heights, so you'll be told that "Redefining direction begins: 2D-3D." When prompted for reversing direction, type **N**.

   The macro will build a list of each block in your selection set. If you accidentally select lines or nonblocked entities, they won't be affected. Also, a block will be redefined only once; a list of names is constructed and checked so no block is redefined twice.

   From the selection set, each block will be inserted, exploded, extruded and redefined for you. At the end of the macro, the drawing will **REGEN** once to display the new 3D blocks.

   If you wish, you can run the macro several different times on different nonstandard blocks in the drawing without accidentally "unextruding" your previous work. By watching the "Redefining direction" prompts and responding to the "Reverse ...direction?" prompts, you'll be in total control of the process.

TIPS: If you're converting an entire large drawing, you could thaw all layers, **ZOOM** to **EXTENTS**, and select all entities for conversion with this macro. Because the insertion points and insertion elevation of blocks aren't affected (only their subentities), this process won't interfere with symbol substitution (**MACRO10**), or with entity extrusion (**MACRO8**). After redefining all blocks, you can run **MACRO8** and **MACRO10**. The resulting drawing will have all standard, nonblocked entities extruded, standard blocks replaced and nonstandard blocks redefined. For most applications, you'd have a successful, automatic 3D conversion of your 2D drawing. By combining these routines into a "supermacro," including other levels of object revision, you could have a "one-button" 2D/3D converter.

Macro
12
3D Helix
For Release 10 or 11

PURPOSE: Creates a three-dimensional helix or "spring" using the **3DPOLY** command. It lets you control the number of revolutions, starting angle, radius and other characteristics of the spring.

TO CREATE:

```
(defun C:HELIX (/ REVS DIVS CEN RAD RINC STA HT HINC
  REVCNT R X Y A Z)
;
; function to create a 3D spiral
; in the form of a 3DPOLY (a zero-width wire spring)
;
(graphscr)
(setq REVS(getreal"\nNUMBER OF REVOLUTIONS? ")
  DIVS(getint"\nNUMBER OF DIVISIONS PER REVOLUTION? ")
  CEN(getpoint"\nCENTER OF BOTTOM LOOP? ")
  RAD(getdist"\nBEGINNING RADIUS ?" CEN)
  RINC(getdist"\nRADIUS INCREMENT ? ")
  STA(getangle"\nSTARTING ANGLE? " CEN)
  HT(getdist"\nBEGINNING HEIGHT BETWEEN LOOPS? ")
  HINC(getdist"\nHEIGHT INCREMENT ? ")
  STA (/(* STA PI)180.0) A STA Z (caddr CEN) R 0
  REVCNT 0)
(command "3dpoly")
(while(< R REVS)
(setq X(+(car CEN)(* RAD(cos A)))
  Y(+(cadr CEN)(* RAD(sin A))))
(command (list X Y Z))
(setq A(+ A(/(* 2.0 PI)DIVS))
  Z(+ Z(/ HT DIVS))
  R(+ R(/ 1.0 DIVS))
  REVCNT(1+ REVCNT)
  RAD(+ RAD(/ RINC DIVS)))
(if(equal REVCNT DIVS)
(setq HT(+ HT HINC) REVCNT 0))
)
(command "")
)
```

TO INVOKE: Create this macro as an AutoLISP file (**.lsp**).

LET'S TRY IT: Get into a new drawing and load **MACRO12** (**Load "MACRO12"**). Type **HELIX**. You'll be prompted for "Number of revolutions." Type **3**. The next prompt is for "Number of divisions per revolution." This number determines the smoothness of the X Y cross-section of the spring.

For instance, **3** would create a triangular cross-section, **4** would be square, and larger numbers would divide a circle into smoother and smoother paths. Type **15**. The resulting spring will be roughly circular when viewed from above.

Next, set the "Center of bottom loop." Type **0,0,0**. "Beginning radius" is the initial radius of the spring when viewed from above. Type **4**. "Radius increment" will let you create a spring that gets gradually wider or narrower with each revolution, depending on the value and sign of the increment. The increment represents the distance that the radius will increase (or decrease, if negative) with each revolution. Type **0**. "Beginning angle" determines the starting angle, which will correspond to the first end of the spring's "wire." Type **0**. "Beginning height between loops" is the initial distance between loops **1** and **2** of the spring. If positive, the spring will "go up" as it's created; if negative it will "go down"; if **0**, the spring will be a 2D spiral. Type **2.0**. "Height increment" is the amount of change in loop-to-loop height with each revolution. If positive, loops will get farther apart; if negative, they'll get closer together; if **0**, they'll stay a constant distance apart. Type **0**.

The macro will now build a spring centered about the X-Y point 0,0, with its base at Z=0. It will have three revolutions, beginning at 0 degrees. Each revolution will be two units apart, a constant radius of four and fifteen sections per revolution. If viewed from above, it will be roughly circular, and if you use **VPOINT** or **DVIEW**, you can see various 3D views of the spring. If you type **LIST** and select the helix, you'll see that it's a single **3DPOLY** that "goes up" from **4,0,0**.

TIPS: You can indicate point, angular and distance variables, using your cursor. By experimenting with different values at the prompts, you can create a variety of different 2D spirals and 3D springs. The **PEDIT** command will smooth the resulting helix. Type **PEDIT**, select the helix, then type **SPLINE** and a <**RETURN**> to end the command.

The helix may be used as a motion path for "walk-around" animations. (See **Macro14B**, "WTC.")

_{Macro}
13

3D to 2D—An Important Trick
For Release 10 or 11

PURPOSE: Lets you take a "photograph" of a particular 3D view. That is, you can take the 3D view of your choice, squash it flat into an identical 2D image, and insert the resulting image into drawings containing multiple 2D or 3D images.

TO CREATE: The AutoCAD configuration process lets you specify your plotter as an ADI device. If you choose this option, you'll be asked for the output format, one of which is **DXB**. If you plot to a **DXB** file, the displayed 3D image will be traced and the resulting strokes saved in a **DXB** file. If you use the **DXBIN** command, these 2D strokes will be inserted into your drawing as standard lines.

TO INVOKE: From the main menu, choose item **5** (Configure Auto-CAD). From the next menu, choose item **5** (Configure plotter). You'll be prompted with the current plotter and asked if you want to select a different one; type **Y**. If the plotter drivers aren't in the current directory, you'll be prompted for the name of their directory. If necessary, insert the driver diskette in your disk drive, then type the appropriate drive and path, as in **A:**.

You'll be presented with a list of possible plotters, one of which is ADI. Type its number. Next, you'll be asked to choose the output format for your "imaginary plotter"; type **2** for the AutoCAD **DXB** file. The remaining questions were designed to control the output resolution, size and orientation of an actual plotter. Since we're using a **DXB** plot file as an intermediary step or "imaginary plotter," your responses to these questions will affect the resulting 2D image.

"Maximum horizontal...." and "...vertical plot size in drawing units" will determine the size of the final 2D image. If you choose a maximum horizontal (**X**) plot size of **11.0** and a maximum vertical (**Y**) plot size of **8.5**, the 2D "photograph" of the 3D view will be no larger than 8.5 x 11.0 inches, regardless of actual dimensions of the 3D model. You may need to rescale the image if you're dimensioning it.

"Plotter steps per drawing unit...." controls the fineness of pen movement. In our case, this technique converts all parts of an image, whether arc, circle, text or line, into linear strokes, or lines. This number will affect the resulting resolution of arcs and circles after squashing, although simple lines are not affected by this factor. A high number such as 1,000 will result in very smooth curves after translation, but may slow down the creation of the file. We suggest an intermediate value of 256, 128 or even 64 plot units per inch.

The prompt "Do you want to change pens while plotting?" has no bearing on this technique. The resulting **DXBIN** image will be all one color, and the lines will be colored **BYLAYER** and assigned to the current layer. "Pens" don't exist in an imaginary plotter! The remaining questions determine rotation, placement in the frame, and scale of the drawing within the imaginary page. Select a plot to **Fit**. You should usually use this technique to create hidden-line images.

LET'S TRY IT: Assuming you've configured for an ADI plotter with **DXB** output as outlined, get into a new drawing. Type **SOLID 0,0 1,0 0,1 1,1**. Then type **CHANGE L** and press an extra <**RETURN**> to end object selection. Next, type **E 0 1.0**. This will extrude the solid into a one-unit cube. Type **VPOINT 1,1,1** and you'll see a typical isometric projection of the cube. Type **PLOT D** (for display) **N** and the name you want to give the **DXB** plot file; for example, **3DPLOT**. After plotting is completed, erase the cube by typing **ERASE L** and two extra <**RETURNs**>.

Now, return to a "normal" view by typing **VPOINT 0,0,1**. Next, type **DXBIN 3DPLOT** (or the name of the **DXB** file you've chosen). Type **ZOOM E** to see the entire image. You should see the hidden-line, 2D image of the cube. To prove it's a 2D "photograph," type **LIST** and choose one of the edges of the cube. It should list as a line, rather than as a solid.

TIPS: You can create multiple 3D views from within a model or from the main menu, then **DXBIN** each one into a new image sheet. By blocking each image as you **DXBIN** it and moving the blocks around, you can create a complete storyboard or visual library for the object.

Because this technique turns anything displayed into a 2D linear drawing, you may use it with **DVIEW**, perspectives, or for exploding text into vectors. If you display a piece of text, plot it and reinsert it, it'll be broken into line segments. This solves the problem of hatching outline text, or altering a font for signage.

EXTENSION: Multiple configurations are possible, so you can plot a **DXB** file or anything else whenever you want. First, make a separate directory called **DXB**. Enter AutoCAD and configure for ADI and **DXB**. Quit AutoCAD. At the DOS prompt, copy **ACAD.CFG** to the **DXB** directory. Enter AutoCAD and reconfigure to your usual plot setup.

To run AutoCAD with the standard configuration, type **SET ACADCFG=C:\ACAD** at the DOS prompt and enter AutoCAD. To run with the **DXB** configuration, type **SET ACADCFG=C:\DXB** at the DOS prompt and enter AutoCAD. You can insert these statements into batch files for faster reconfiguration.

Macro 14 # Plotting Multiple Views

For Release 10 or 11

PURPOSE: Lets you plot all the views in the current drawing, or a select group of views, automatically. It's useful when you want to plot each view in an animation. (See the AutoCAD 3D Diskette for further help on animation programs.) If you're configuring to plot to a .PLT file, the resulting images can be plotted to paper using your specifications. If you configure to plot to a .DXB file as in MACRO13, each 3D view can be squashed to 2D and reinserted in a storyboard (**MACRO16**), or saved in a new drawing (**MACRO15**).

TO CREATE:
```
(defun C:VPLOT (/ FIL TYP VPREF VW VNAM)
(initget 1 "A S")
(setq FIL(open "VPLOT.SCR" "w"))
(setq TYP(getkword"\nPlot all views or a set (A S) ? "))
(if(equal TYP "S")
(setq VPREF(strcase(getstring"\nWhat is prefix for views? "))))
(princ"\nABOUT TO PROCESS VIEWS...PLEASE WAIT!")
(setq ARROWS(ssget "X" '((2 . "ARR"))))
(if ARROWS(command "erase" ARROWS ""))
(setq VW(tblnext "view" T))
(while VW
(setq VNAM(cdr(assoc 2 VW)))
(if(or(equal TYP "A")
   (equal(substr VNAM 1(strlen VPREF))VPREF))
(progn
(princ(strcat"\nVIEW: " VNAM " WILL BE PLOTTED..."))
(write-line(strcat"PLOT V " VNAM " N") FIL)
(write-line VNAM FIL)
```

```
(write-line "" FIL)
)
)
(setq VW(tblnext "view"))
)
(close FIL)
(command "script" "VPLOT")
)
```

TO INVOKE: Create this macro as an AutoLISP file (**.lsp**).

LET'S TRY IT: Get into a new drawing. Create a series of views, naming and saving the views as **CIR1** through **CIR12**, using the same prefix for each. Now load **MACRO14 (Load "MACRO14")** and type **VPLOT**. At the prompt "Plot all views or a set (A S)?" type **S**. At the prompt "What is prefix of views?" type **CIR**. Before using this macro, you must create a one-unit cube and create a script file **VPLOT.SCR**, which will do the actual plotting. At the end of the macro, **VPLOT.SCR** is called, and **CIR1** through **CIR12** are plotted to **.PLT** or **.DXB** files according to your configuration.

　If you're configured for **.PLT** files, you may now use a plot-file spooling program to plot each drawing to paper. If you're configured for **.DXB** files as described in **MACRO13**, you may now use these output files in **MACRO15** or **MACRO16**.

Macro

14B

WTC—Walkthru, Center-of-vision

For Release 10 or 11

PURPOSE: To automatically create a "fly-by" animation. Using this macro, you can create multiple views by "batch," saving them as slides or AutoCAD VIEWS for plotting with **Macro14**.

　Before using the macro, you must create a block called **ARR** and save it to your disk. It should be directional or arrow-shaped, because its position will determine the camera point and its rotation angle will determine the viewpoint. It must be pointed to the right, since insertion with **MEASURE** or **DIVIDE** will place **ARR** blocks with their rotation along the line of movement.

Create **ARR** by entering a new drawing. Type **LINE 0,0 1,0 0.5,0.5** and press **RETURN**. Then type **LINE 1,0 0.5,-0.5**. This will create an arrow one unit long, facing to the right. Type **BLOCK ARR 0,0** and select the three lines. This will create a block called **ARR**, which inserts from the tail of the arrow. Type **WBLOCK ARR ARR**. This will save the block description to disk.

TO CREATE:
```
(defun C:WTC (/ S CM HL EX VPREF SPREF VW SLD SCRFIL HID FIL
    CONTARG TARGHGT ARROWS FRAMCNT COUNTER THISARR VIEWPT
    INSANG SLDNAM VLIST)
(defun *ERROR* (s)
(if FIL(close FIL))
(setq *ERROR* nil)
(setvar "CMDECHO" CM)
(setvar "HIGHLIGHT" HL)
(setvar "EXPERT" EX)
(terpri)
)
;
(setq CM(getvar "CMDECHO") HL(getvar "HIGHLIGHT") EX(getvar
    "EXPERT"))
(setvar "CMDECHO" 0)
(setvar "HIGHLIGHT" 0)
(setvar "EXPERT" 3)
(setq ARROWS(ssget "X" '((2 . "ARR"))))
(if ARROWS
(progn
(command "VPOINT" "0,0,1")
(initget 1 "Y N")
(setq VW(getkword"\nDO YOU WISH TO SAVE VIEWS (Y N) ? "))
(if(equal VW "Y")(setq VPREF(getstring"\nWHAT IS PREFIX
    FOR VIEWS? ")))
(initget 1 "Y N")
(setq SLD(getkword"\nDO YOU WISH TO SAVE SLIDES (Y N) ? "))
(if(equal SLD "Y")
(progn
(setq SPREF(getstring"\nWHAT IS PREFIX FOR SLIDES? ")
    SCRFIL(getstring"\nWHAT IS NAME OF SCRIPT FILE
    (omit extension) ? ")
    FIL(open(strcat SCRFIL ".SCR") "w"))
(initget 1 "Y N")
```

```
(setq HID(getkword"\n'HIDE'EACH SLIDE (Y N) ? "))
)
)
(initget 1 "C V")
(setq CONTARG(getpoint"\nPLEASE INDICATE CONSTANT
 TARGET POINT:"))
(initget 1)
(setq TARGHGT(getdist"\nPLEASE INDICATE TARGET HEIGHT: "))
(setq CONTARG(list(car CONTARG)(cadr CONTARG)TARGHGT))
(initget 1)
(setq
    FRAMCNT 1 COUNTER(sslength ARROWS))
(prompt"\nABOUT TO CREATE VIEW AND TARGET LISTS...PLEASE WAIT...")
(while(> = COUNTER 1)
(setq THISARR(ssname ARROWS(1- COUNTER))
    VIEWPT(cdr(assoc 10(entget THISARR)))
    INSANG(cdr(assoc 50(entget THISARR)))
    VLIST(cons VIEWPT VLIST))
(setq COUNTER(1- COUNTER))
)
(setq COUNTER(sslength ARROWS))
(command "erase" ARROWS "")
(while(> = COUNTER 1)
(princ(strcat"\nABOUT TO CREATE FRAME: " (itoa FRAMCNT) " OF "
  (itoa(sslength ARROWS)) "\n"))
(setq VIEWPT(nth(1- COUNTER)VLIST))
(command "DVIEW" "" "D" "" "PO" CONTARG VIEWPT "")
(if(equal VW "Y")(command "VIEW" "S" (strcat VPREF(itoa FRAMCNT))))

(if(equal SLD "Y")
(progn
(if(equal HID "Y")(command "HIDE"))
(command "MSLIDE" (strcat SPREF(itoa FRAMCNT)))
(write-line (strcat"VSLIDE " SPREF (itoa FRAMCNT)) FIL)
)
)
(setq FRAMCNT(1+ FRAMCNT) COUNTER(1- COUNTER))
)
(if FIL(close FIL))
(command "oops" "vpoint" "0,0,1")
)
(princ"\n\7NO INSERTS OF BLOCK 'ARR' IN THIS DRAWING...")
```

```
)
(setvar "CMDECHO" CM)
(setvar "HIGHLIGHT" HL)
(setvar "EXPERT" EX)
(princ"\nFINISHED!")
(if(equal SLD "Y")
(princ(strcat" TYPE 'SCRIPT " (strcase SCRFIL) "' TO ANIMATE\n"))

(terpri)
)
)
```

TO INVOKE: Create this macro as an AutoLISP file (**.lsp**).

LET'S TRY IT: Get into a new drawing. Let's create a cube. Type **SOLID 0,0 1,0 0,1 1, 1** and press **<RETURN>** to end the command. Type **CHANGE L, <RETURN>, E 0 1**. This will create a cube with length, width and height of 1. To create a circular "walk-around" path, type **CIRCLE 0.5, 0.5, 5.0**. This will create a circle centered around the cube, with a radius of five units and at a height of five units. Type **INSERT ARR 0,0 1 1 0**. This will insert **ARR** in the drawing, so it will be a defined block. Erase the **ARR** block.

Now type **DIVIDE**, choose the circle, and type **B ARR Y 12**. This will divide the circle into 12 sections, each marked by the block **ARR**. The **ARR** blocks should be aligned along the line of movement. In this macro, with a constant viewpoint, only their position is important.

Type **WTC**. When prompted "...wish to save views?" type **Y**. In response to "What is prefix for views?" type **CIR**. When prompted "...wish to save slides?" type **Y**. Choose **CIR** for the slide prefix, **CIRCLE** for the script filename and **Y** in response to "'HIDE' each slide...." When prompted for a constant target point, type **0.5,0.5** or touch the center of the cube. When prompted for target height, type **0**.

The macro will make a list of viewing positions from the insertion points of the **ARR** blocks. It will prompt you, "About to create frame: 1," "About to create frame: 2," etc. For each view, it will use **DVIEW** and move the camera point to the **X,Y** position of the arrow and Z position of your chosen camera height of three units, and pointed at the constant point **0.5,0.5,0**. At the end of the macro you'll be prompted, "Finished! Type 'Script circle' to animate."

If you type **VIEW ?**, you'll see a list of saved views, **CIR1** through **CIR12**. You can bring up a view by typing **VIEW R** and its name. In addition, the files **CIR1.SLD** through **CIR12.SLD** and **CIR.SCR** will be saved to disk.

TIPS: Although the target point is constant, you can use any path you choose. For instance, you can approach a building, circle it, etc., by drawing an initial **PLINE** and using **MEASURE** or **DIVIDE** to place the **ARR** blocks. Because the viewing point is constant, this macro is most useful for making exterior surveys of a model. The macro uses the height of the arrows to determine camera height in each view. If you wish, you may use **MACRO12** to create a 3D helix. By dividing it with **ARR** blocks, you can create an animation that circles below, around and over the "subject." Other 3D paths are possible using **3D POLYS**.

Macro
14C
WTC2—Fly-by Animation for AutoSHADE
For Release 10 or 11

PURPOSE: This macro is similar to **Macro14B**. It creates a script file for AutoSHADE, extending the functionality of **WTC** for creating fly-by animations. After "previewing" your animation, using slides or **VPLOTS** with **WTC**, you can now use AutoSHADE to create a script file for shading each image.

TO CREATE:
```
(defun C:WTC2 (/ S CM HL EX VPREF SPREF SLD SCRFIL HID FIL
   CONTARG TARGHGT ARROWS FRAMCNT COUNTER THISARR VIEWPT
   INSANG SLDNAM VLIST)
(defun *ERROR* (s)
(if FIL(close FIL))
(setq *ERROR* nil)
(setvar "CMDECHO" CM)
(setvar "HIGHLIGHT" HL)
(setvar "EXPERT" EX)
(terpri)
)
```

```
;
(setq CM(getvar "CMDECHO") HL(getvar "HIGHLIGHT") EX(getvar "EXPERT"))
(setvar "CMDECHO" 0)
(setvar "HIGHLIGHT" 0)
(setvar "EXPERT" 3)
(setq ARROWS(ssget "X" '((2 . "ARR"))))
(if ARROWS
(progn
(setq SPREF(getstring"\nWHAT IS PREFIX FOR IMAGES? ")
      SCRFIL(getstring"\nWHAT IS NAME OF SCRIPT FILE
         (omit extension) ? ")
      FIL(open(strcat SCRFIL ".SCR") "w"))
(initget 1 "FA FU")
   (setq RENDER(getkword"\n<FA>stshade or <FU>llshade ? "))
(if(equal RENDER "FA")(setq RENDER "FASTSHADE ")
   (setq RENDER "FULLSHADE "))
(write-line "RECORD ON" FIL)
(write-line "PERSPECTIVE ON" FIL)
(setq CONTARG(getpoint"\nPLEASE INDICATE CONSTANT TARGET POINT:
  "))
(initget 1)
(setq TARGHGT(getdist"\nPLEASE INDICATE TARGET HEIGHT: "))
(setq CONTARG(list(car CONTARG)(cadr CONTARG)TARGHGT))
(setq X (nth 0 CONTARG) Y (nth 1 CONTARG) Z (nth 2 CONTARG))
(setq X (rtos X 2 8) Y (rtos Y 2 8) Z (rtos Z 2 8))
(write-line(strcat "TARGET " X "," Y "," Z)FIL)
(initget 1)
(setq FRAMCNT 1 COUNTER(sslength ARROWS))
(prompt"\nABOUT TO CREATE VIEW AND TARGET LISTS...PLEASE
  WAIT...")
(while(>= COUNTER 1)
(setq THISARR(ssname ARROWS(1- COUNTER))
      VIEWPT(cdr(assoc 10(entget THISARR)))
      INSANG(cdr(assoc 50(entget THISARR)))
      VLIST(cons VIEWPT VLIST))
(setq COUNTER(1- COUNTER))
)
(setq COUNTER(sslength ARROWS))
(while(>= COUNTER 1)
(princ(strcat"\nABOUT TO WRITE FRAME: " (itoa FRAMCNT) " OF "
   (itoa(sslength ARROWS)) "\n"))
(setq VIEWPT(nth(1- COUNTER)VLIST))
```

```
(setq X (nth 0 VIEWPT) Y (nth 1 VIEWPT) Z (nth 2 VIEWPT))
(setq X (rtos X 2 8) Y (rtos Y 2 8) Z (rtos Z 2 8))
(write-line(strcat "CAMERA " X "," Y "," Z)FIL)
(write-line(strcat RENDER SPREF(itoa FRAMCNT))FIL)
(setq FRAMCNT(1+ FRAMCNT) COUNTER(1- COUNTER))
)
(close FIL)
)
(princ"\n\7NO INSERTS OF BLOCK 'ARR' IN THIS DRAWING...")
)
(setvar "CMDECHO" CM)
(setvar "HIGHLIGHT" HL)
(setvar "EXPERT" EX)
(princ"\nFINISHED!")
(princ(strcat" LOAD '" (strcase SCRFIL) ".SCR' TO SHADE\n"))
(prin1)
)
```

TO INVOKE: Create this macro as an AutoLISP file **(.lsp)**

LET'S TRY IT: Get into a new drawing. As in **WTC**, create a cube and a circular path at a height of 5 units. Divide the path with **ARR** blocks. Load AutoSHADE **(Load "ASHADE")**, and place light sources as necessary. Insert a camera and a scene clapper, and use the **FILMROLL** command to create an **.FLM** file for this model.

Now load **MACRO14C (Load "MACRO14C")**. AutoCAD will prompt, WTC2. Type WTC2 and follow the instructions. When prompted, "what is prefix for images?" type **CIR**. When prompted,"what is name of script file (omit extension)?" type **CIRCLE**. When prompted, <FA>stshade or <FU>llshade ? type **FU**. When prompted for a constant target point, type **0.5,0.5** or touch the center of the cube. When prompted for a target height, type **0**. The macro uses the height of each **ARR** block as its camera height, as well as its camera position. In this case, views circle the cube at 5 units.

The macro then writes a script file containing the commands necessary for AutoSHADE to render each view. The script, **CIRCLE.SCR**, turns **PERSPECTIVE ON** and **RECORD ON**, sets **TARGET** to the constant point (or center of the cube) and includes **CAMERA** commands for each and every view determined by **ARR** blocks.

Leave AutoCAD and enter AutoSHADE. Make sure the **CIRCLE.SCR** and **.FLM** files are copied to the correct directory for AutoSHADE. Load the **.FLM** file for this model, and choose the scene. Then choose **SCRIPT** from the **FILE** pull-down, and type the name of the script file,

CIRCLE. AutoSHADE will load the commands created by **WTC2**, performing a **FULLSHADE** of each image and recording it to a rendering file named **CIR1**, **CIR2**, etc.

If you have AutoFLIX or AutoDesk Animator, you can create a full-rendered animation of these views.

TIPS: You may use any **PLINE**, **3DPOLY** or other linear entity to create the path around the model. While the target is constant in this program, you may use Macro 12 to create a helical path that flies under, around and over the model. By modifying the code, you could also create architectural walk-through animations.

Macro
15
Automatic Conversion of DXB Files to Drawings
For Release 10 or 11

PURPOSE: After using **MACRO14**, this macro loads each **DXB** file or squashed 3D, and saves the image as a separate drawing.

TO CREATE:
```
(defun C:DXB2DWG (/ FIL TYP VPREF VW VNAM ANS)
(setvar "EXPERT" 0)
(initget 1 "A S")
(setq FIL(open "DXB2DWG.SCR" "w"))
(write-line"QUIT Y 1 DXB2DWG=" FIL)
(setq TYP(getkword"\nImport all views or a set (A S) ? "))
(if(equal TYP "S")
(setq VPREF(strcase(getstring"\nWhat is prefix for views? "))))
(princ"\nABOUT TO PROCESS VIEWS...PLEASE WAIT!")
(setq VW(tblnext "view" T))
(while VW
(setq VNAM(cdr(assoc 2 VW)))
(if(and(findfile(strcat VNAM ".DXB"))
    (or(equal TYP "A")
    (equal(substr VNAM 1(strlen VPREF))VPREF)))
```

```
(progn
(princ(strcat"\nVIEW: " VNAM " WILL BE IMPORTED AND SAVED AS
    DRAWING...\n"))
(write-line(strcat"DXBIN " VNAM)FIL)
(write-line "ZOOM E" FIL)
(if(findfile(strcat VNAM ".DWG"))
(progn
(initget 1 "Y N")
(setq ANS(getkword(strcat"\nA DRAWING NAMED " VNAM "
    ALREADY EXISTS..." "DO YOU WANT TO REPLACE IT? ")))
(if(equal ANS "Y")(write-line(strcat "WBLOCK " VNAM " Y *")FIL)))
(write-line(strcat"WBLOCK " VNAM " *")FIL)
)
(write-line(strcat"ERASE (ssget" (chr 34) "X" (chr 34) ")")FIL)
(write-line "" FIL)
)
)
(setq VW(tblnext "view"))
)
(initget 1 "Y N")
(setq ANS(getkword"\nERASE ALL SOURCE .DXB FILES ? "))
(if(equal ANS "Y")
(write-line(strcat"SHELL DEL " VPREF "*.DXB")FIL)
)
(close FIL)
(command "script" "DXB2DWG")
)
```

TO INVOKE: Create this macro as an AutoLISP file (**.lsp**).

LET'S TRY IT: Stay in the drawing with views **CIR1** through **CIR12**, as outlined in **MACRO14**. With your system configured for **DXB** plot files, load and execute **MACRO14**, plotting the files **CIR1.DXB** through **CIR12.DXB**.

Now load **MACRO15 (Load "MACRO15")**. Type **DXB2DWG**. At the prompt, "Import all views or a set (A S)?" type **S**. At the prompt, "What is prefix for views?" type **CIR**. The macro will create a script file, **DXB2DWG.SCR**, which will actually load and save the drawings **CIR1.DWG** through **CIR12.DWG**. If a drawing already exists with one of these names, you'll be asked whether it should be replaced.

At the end of this macro, the drawings **CIR1** through **CIR12** will be saved to disk. The **DXB** files are actually imported from within a temporary drawing, **DXB2DWG.DWG**, so that the original "model" file isn't changed in any way. When the process is finished, you can leave **DXB2DWG** by typing **QUIT Y**.

TIPS: If you've already created multiple **DXB** files in another session but didn't save the original "model" drawing with the views, you can still use this macro. Create a new drawing. For each **DXB** view you want to import, type **VIEW S** followed by the view name. Only the view names must appear in the current drawing to use this macro; the actual construction of the model and views aren't important now if the **DXB** files already exist.

Macro 16

Storyboard from DXBs or DWGs
For Release 10 or 11

PURPOSE: Creates a storyboard from existing **DXB** images (as made by **MACRO13** or **MACRO14**), or from existing **DWG** files. A storyboard is a drawing in which multiple images are arranged like a comic strip, showing the development of the action in animation.

This macro places the images in proper top-to-bottom, left-to-right order for you. In addition, it has two nice features: The board will always be framed as a 4 x 4, 5 x 5 or other square format; also, the frames surrounding each image and the outer frame will be automatically sized and positioned so the largest of the images can fit.

TO CREATE:
```
(defun C:SB (/ TYP FTYP VPREF VLIST VW VNAM LL UR WID HGT
  FWID FHGT ROWS COLS C XPOS YPOS V XOFFSET YOFFSET ANS ALL)
(defun *ERROR* (s)
(princ s)
(setvar "EXPERT" 0)
(setvar "HIGHLIGHT" 1)
(setvar "CMDECHO" 1)
(setq *ERROR* nil)
(terpri)
)
(setvar "EXPERT" 3)
```

```
(setvar "HIGHLIGHT" 0)
(setvar "CMDECHO" 0)
(command "elev" "0" "0")
(setq ALL(ssget "X"))
(if ALL(command "erase" ALL ""))
(initget 1 "A S")
(setq TYP(getkword"\nImport all views or a set (A S) ? "))
(if(equal TYP "S")
(setq VPREF(strcase(getstring"\nWhat is prefix for views? "))))
(initget 1 "DXB DWG")
(setq FTYP(getkword"\nImport from .DXB or .DWG files (DXB DWG) ? "))
(princ"\nABOUT TO PROCESS VIEWS...PLEASE WAIT!")
(setq VLIST nil VW(tblnext "view" T) FWID 0.0 FHGT 0.0)
(while VW
(setq VNAM(cdr(assoc 2 VW)))
(if(and(findfile(strcat VNAM "." FTYP))
    (or(equal TYP "A")
      (equal(substr VNAM 1(strlen VPREF))VPREF)))
(progn
(princ(strcat"\nVIEW: " VNAM " ABOUT TO BE INSERTED AS FRAME
      IN STORYBOARD\n"))
(princ)
(if(equal FTYP "DXB")
(command "dxbin" VNAM "zoom" "e")
(command "insert" (strcat "*" VNAM) "0,0" "1" "0" "zoom" "e")
)
(setq VLIST(cons VNAM VLIST))
(setq LL(getvar "EXTMIN")
  UR(getvar "EXTMAX")
  WID(abs(-(car UR)(car LL)))
  HGT(abs(-(cadr UR)(cadr LL)))
  )
(if(> WID FWID)(setq FWID WID))
(if(> HGT FHGT)(setq FHGT HGT))
(command "block" VNAM LL (ssget "X") "")
)
)
(setq VW(tblnext "view"))
)
(setq WID(max WID FWID) HGT(max WID FWID)
    ROWS(fix(sqrt(length VLIST)))
    COLS(fix(+ 0.5(/(length VLIST)ROWS)))
```

```
    C 0 XPOS 0.0 YPOS 0.0 V 1
    XOFFSET(* 0.1 FWID)
YOFFSET(* 0.1 FHGT)
VLIST(reverse VLIST))
(while(<= V(length VLIST))
(command "insert" (nth(1- V)VLIST)
  (list XPOS YPOS)
  "1" "1" "0" "line" (list(- XPOS XOFFSET)(- YPOS YOFFSET))
  (list(+ XPOS FWID XOFFSET)(- YPOS YOFFSET))
  (list(+ XPOS FWID XOFFSET)(+ YPOS FHGT YOFFSET))
  (list(- XPOS XOFFSET)(+ YPOS FHGT YOFFSET))
  "c")
(setq XPOS(+ XPOS FWID(* 3.0 XOFFSET))
    C(1+ C) V(1+ V))
(if(equal C COLS)
  (setq XPOS 0.0 C 0 YPOS(- YPOS FHGT(* 3 YOFFSET)))
)
)
(command "zoom" "e")
(setq LL(getvar "EXTMIN") UR(getvar "EXTMAX"))
(command "line" (list(-(car LL)XOFFSET)(-(cadr LL)YOFFSET))
  (list(+(car UR)XOFFSET)(-(cadr LL)YOFFSET))
  (list(+(car UR)XOFFSET)(+(cadr UR)YOFFSET))
  (list(-(car LL)XOFFSET)(+(cadr UR)YOFFSET))
"c" "zoom" "e")
(initget 1 "Y N")
(setq ANS(getword(strcat"\nERASE ALL SOURCE ." FTYP " FILES? ")))
(if(equal ANS "Y")
(command "shell" (strcat "DEL " VPREF "*." FTYP))
)
(setvar "EXPERT" 0)
(setvar "HIGHLIGHT" 1)
(setvar "CMDECHO" 1)
(princ"\nFINISHED!")
(terpri)
)
```

TO INVOKE: Create this macro as an AutoLISP file (**.lsp**).

LET'S TRY IT: Stay in the drawing with views **CIR1** through **CIR12** as outlined in **MACRO14**. Make your views and get the plots. Then create the **DXB** files **CIR1.DXB** through **CIR12.DXB** as described in

MACRO14. If you've already imported them to drawing files using **MACRO15**, use the drawing files **CIR1.DWG** through **CIR12.DWG**.

Now load **MACRO16 (Load "MACRO16")**. Type **SB**. When prompted "Import all views or a set (A S) ?" type **S**. When prompted "What is prefix for views ?" type **CIR**. When prompted "Import from .DXB or .DWG files (DXB DWG) ?" respond accordingly; if you've run **VPLOT** but not **DXB2DWG**, type **DXB**. If you've run **DXB2DWG**, type **DWG**. The appropriate file type will be imported.

The macro will now import each image, perform a **ZOOM E** on it, and block it. After blocking imported views **CIR1** through **CIR12**, it will insert each into a storyboard, in this case a 3 x 4 block sheet. Each image will be outlined, the final sheet will be outlined and a final **ZOOM E** will be performed.

TIPS: If you've created **DXB** files but not individual **DWG** files, you can create this storyboard, then use the following extraction macro, **MACRO17**, to **WBLOCK** the individual images out as separate **DWG** files.

The storyboard is a useful way to show animation to clients when you don't have an onscreen slide show. For this reason, you should save views while running the animation macros. You may then perform **VPLOT**, **DXB2DWG** or **SB** at a later session.

Macro 17 # Automated WBLOCKing
For Release 10 or 11

PURPOSE: Will **WBLOCK**, or create individual drawing files (**DWG**) from blocks in the current drawing. You can use it with the storyboard macro, **MACRO16**, to export individual frames to disk, or to export symbols from any drawing you wish. This can be useful in moving blocks from the current drawing into a standard symbol library.

TO CREATE:
```
(defun C:WB (/ S TYP BPREF BL BNAM ANS)
(defun *ERROR* (s)
(setvar "EXPERT" 0)
(setvar "CMDECHO" 1)
(princ s)
(terpri)
```

```
)
(setvar "EXPERT" 3)
(setvar "CMDECHO" 0)
(initget 1 "A S")
(setq TYP(getkword"\nWblock all blocks or a set (A S) ? "))
(if(equal TYP "S")
(setq BPREF(strcase(getstring"\nWhat is prefix for blocks? "))))
(princ"\nABOUT TO PROCESS BLOCKS...PLEASE WAIT!")
(setq BL(tblnext "block" T))
(while BL
(setq BNAM(cdr(assoc 2 BL)))
(if(or(equal TYP "A")
  (equal(substr BNAM 1(strlen BPREF))BPREF))
(progn
(princ(strcat"\nWBLOCKING BLOCK: " BNAM))
(if(findfile(strcat BNAM ".DWG"))
(progn
(initget 1 "Y N")
(setq ANS(getkword(strcat"\n" BNAM ".DWG ALREADY EXISTS...
  REPLACE IT? ")))
(if(equal ANS "Y")(command "WBLOCK" BNAM BNAM))
)
(command "WBLOCK" BNAM BNAM)
)
)
)
(setq BL(tblnext "block"))
)
(setvar "EXPERT" 0)
(setvar "CMDECHO" 1)
(princ"\nFINISHED!")
(terpri)
)
```

TO INVOKE: Create this macro as an AutoLISP file (**.lsp**).

LET'S TRY IT: Get into an existing storyboard drawing, with images **CIR1** through **CIR12**. Load **MACRO17 (Load "MACRO17")**.

Type **WB**. At the prompt, "Wblock all blocks or a set (A S) ?" type **S**. At the prompt "What is prefix for blocks ?" type **CIR**.

The macro will now **WBLOCK**, or export, each block to disk in the current directory. If the drawing already exists, you'll be prompted,

"Block CIR1.DWG already exists...replace it?", etc. If you wish to do so, type **Y**.

TIPS: Use this macro when creating symbol libraries, both 2D and 3D. Because it will **WBLOCK** 2D or 3D symbols, you can modify symbols in the current drawing and update a standard library on disk. The resulting 2D and 3D symbols can be useful in macros such as **SWAP**.

When used in sequence, 3D/2D "squash," **VPLOT**, storyboard and **WB** macros give you an animation toolbox for creating complete client presentations. You can present details, multi-view drawings, animations, storyboards and fully rendered images of architectural spaces or mechanical details. Of course, when used with more esoteric models, these tools have many applications.

Macro 18
Parametric 3D Windows—WIN1
For Release 10 or 11

PURPOSE: Demonstrates the power of parametric programming when applied to AutoCAD's 3D and 2 1/2 D components. It lets you create a complex 3D window frame with variable frame width, rows and columns of mullions. Because it automatically spaces vertical and horizontal mullions, correcting for the width of the frame and mullions, a nearly infinite range of 3D windows is possible. An architect will find this helpful in constructing details for 3D models, but you can extend the principle to other applications. This and the following variation may whet your appetite for more 3D construction tools.

TO CREATE:
```
(defun C:WIN1 (/ S PT1 PT2 LIN ROWS COLS FT FT2 MT MT2 BOT
  TOP LEN HT ANG COUNT MID VPTS MDIS SS STPT)
(defun *ERROR*
(s)
(if LIN(command "erase" LIN ""))
(setvar "HIGHLIGHT" 1)
(setvar "CMDECHO" 1)
(setvar "BLIPMODE" 1)
(princ s)
```

```
(setq *ERROR* nil)
(terpri)
)
(setvar "HIGHLIGHT" 0)
(setvar "CMDECHO" 0)
(setvar "BLIPMODE" 1)
(graphscr)
(setq PT1(getpoint "\nINDICATE 1st END OF GLASS LINE: ")
PT2(getpoint PT1 "\nINDICATE 2nd END OF GLASS LINE:"))
(setvar "BLIPMODE" 0)
(command "line" PT1 PT2 "")
(setq LIN(entlast))
(initget 7)
(setq ROWS(getint "\nHOW MANY PANES IN DIRECTION OF GLASS LINE
  (ROWS) ?"))
(initget 7)
(setq COLS(getint "\nHOW MANY PANES IN Z DIR. (COLS) ?")
FT(getdist "\nINDICATE FRAME THICKNESS: ")
FT2(/ FT 2.0)
MT(getdist "\nINDICATE MULLION THICKNESS: ")
MT2(/ MT 2.0)
BOT(getdist "\nWHAT IS BOTTOM (SILL) HEIGHT OF WINDOW? ")
TOP(getdist "\nWHAT IS TOP HEIGHT OF WINDOW? ")
LEN(distance PT1 PT2) HT(abs(- TOP BOT (* 2.0 FT)))
ANG(angle PT1 PT2))
(command "erase" LIN "")
(princ"\nBUILDING 3D WINDOW...PLEASE WAIT!")
;
; build bottom rail and top rail
;
(princ"\nBUILDING BOTTOM AND TOP RAILS:")
(command "solid"
(polar PT1(- ANG(/ PI 2.0))FT2)
(polar PT1(+ ANG(/ PI 2.0))FT2)
(polar PT2(- ANG(/ PI 2.0))FT2)
(polar PT2(+ ANG(/ PI 2.0))FT2) "")
(command "move" (entlast) "" (list 0 0 0) (list 0 0 BOT)
 "change" (entlast) "" "p" "t" FT "" "copy" (entlast) ""
   "0,0" "0,0" "move" (entlast) "" (list 0 0 BOT)
    (list 0 0 (- TOP FT)) "change" (entlast) "" "p" "t" FT "")
;
; build end verticals
```

```
;
(princ"\BUILDING END VERTICALS:")
(command "solid"
(polar PT1(- ANG(/ PI 2.0))FT2)
(polar PT1(+ ANG(/ PI 2.0))FT2)
(polar PT1(- ANG(atan 0.5))
(sqrt(+(expt FT 2.0)(expt FT2 2.0))))
(polar PT1(+ ANG(atan 0.5))
(sqrt(+(expt FT 2.0)(expt FT2 2.0))))
"" "move" (entlast) "" (list 0 0 0) (list 0 0 (+ BOT FT))
"change" (entlast) "" "p" "t" HT "" "solid"
(polar PT2(- ANG PI (atan 0.5))
(sqrt(+(expt FT 2.0)(expt FT2 2.0))))
(polar PT2(+ ANG PI (atan 0.5))
(sqrt(+(expt FT 2.0)(expt FT2 2.0))))
(polar PT2(+ ANG(/ PI 2.0))FT2)
(polar PT2(- ANG(/ PI 2.0))FT2) ""
"move" (entlast) "" (list 0 0 0) (list 0 0 (+ BOT FT))
"change" (entlast) "" "p" "t" HT "")
;
; build middle verticals
;
(princ"\nBUILDING MIDDLE VERTICALS:")
(setq COUNT 1 MDIS(/ LEN ROWS) STPT PT1 VPTS nil)
(while(< COUNT ROWS)
(setq MID(polar PT1 ANG (* MDIS COUNT))
VPTS(cons MID VPTS))
(command "solid" (polar MID(- ANG(* 0.75 PI))
(sqrt(* 2(expt MT2 2.0))))
(polar MID(+ ANG(* 0.75 PI))(sqrt(* 2(expt MT2 2.0))))
(polar MID(- ANG(/ PI 4.0))(sqrt(* 2(expt MT2 2.0))))
(polar MID(+ ANG(/ PI 4.0))(sqrt(* 2(expt MT2 2.0)))) ""
"move" (entlast) "" (list 0 0 0) (list 0 0 (+ BOT FT))
"change" (entlast) "" "p" "t" HT "")
(setq COUNT(1+ COUNT))
)
;
; build horizontals
;
(princ"\nBUILDING HORIZONTALS:")
(setq VPTS(cons(polar PT2(- ANG PI)(- FT MT2))VPTS)
VPTS(reverse VPTS) MDIS(/ HT COLS)
```

```
STPT(polar PT1 ANG(- FT MT2)) SS(ssadd) COUNT 0)
(while(< COUNT ROWS)
(command "solid"
(polar STPT(+ ANG(/ PI 4.0))
(sqrt(* 2(expt MT2 2.0))))
(polar STPT(- ANG(/ PI 4.0))(sqrt(* 2(expt MT2 2.0))))
(polar (nth COUNT VPTS) (+ ANG(* 0.75 PI))
(sqrt(* 2(expt MT2 2.0))))
(polar (nth COUNT VPTS) (- ANG(* 0.75 PI))
(sqrt(* 2(expt MT2 2.0)))) ""
"move" (entlast) "" (list 0 0 0) (list 0 0 (+ BOT MT2 MDIS))
"change" (entlast) "" "p" "t" MT "")
(setq STPT(nth COUNT VPTS) COUNT(1+ COUNT) SS(ssadd(entlast)SS))
)

(setq COUNT 2)
(while(< COUNT COLS)
(command "copy" SS "" "0,0" "0,0")
(command "move" SS ""
(list 0 0 (+ BOT MT2)) (list 0 0 (+ BOT MT2 MDIS)))
(command  "change" SS "" "p" "t" MT "")
(setq COUNT(1+ COUNT))
)
(setvar "HIGHLIGHT" 1)
(setvar "CMDECHO" 1)
(setvar "BLIPMODE" 1)
(princ"\nFINISHED!")
(terpri)
)
```

TO INVOKE: Create this macro as an AutoLISP file (.lsp).

LET'S TRY IT: Get into a drawing and load **MACRO18** (**Load "MACRO18"**). Type **WIN1**. When prompted, indicate the first and second glass lines (lines through glass, or "middle" of window). You might try typing **WIN1 0,0 36,0** to create a 36"-long window, or pointing to two points at any angle you choose. When prompted, supply the number of panes in the direction of the glass lines (**ROWS**), in the vertical or **Z** direction (**COLS**), the frame thickness and the bottom and top elevations (not thickness! this is calculated for you!). If you typed **4 3 1.0 30.0 45.0**, you would build a window with four panes across, three panes vertically (total 12 panes), a 1"-thick and 15"-high frame, raised to 30" off the ground (0). For each of the "distance" prompts, indicate your choice by picking two points.

After responding to these prompts, the macro will build a completed 3D window to your specifications. You can use the macro repeatedly to create sets of unique rectangular windows.

Macro
19
Parametric 3D
Windows Revisited
For Release 10 or 11

PURPOSE: After experimenting with **MACRO18**, you might want to use a macro with fewer picks and prompts. Once you've supplied the variables for frame and mullion thickness (**FT** and **MT**), **ROWS** and **COLS** of panes, bottom (**BOT**) and top (**TOP**) heights, you could "knock out" a series of variable-width and variable-angle windows by merely picking two points. This macro, when used with a set-up macro or screen menu, will accomplish this.

TO CREATE:

```
(defun C:WIN2 (/ S PT1 PT2 LIN FT2 MT2 LEN HT ANG COUNT MID
  VPTS MDIS SS STPT)
(defun *ERROR* (s)
(if LIN(command "erase" LIN ""))
(setvar "HIGHLIGHT" 1)
(setvar "CMDECHO" 1)
(setvar "BLIPMODE" 1)
(princ s)
(setq *ERROR* nil)
(terpri)
)
(setq VARLIST(list ROWS COLS BOT TOP FT MT))
(if(member nil VARLIST)
(progn (princ"\n*/Invalid/* NOT ALL VARIABLES SET!\n")
(princ "ROWS: ")(princ ROWS)(princ " COLS:")
(princ COLS)(princ " BOT:")(princ BOT)
(princ " TOP:")(princ TOP)(princ " FT:")
(princ FT)(princ " MT:")(princ MT) )
(progn (setvar "HIGHLIGHT" 0)
```

```
(setvar "CMDECHO" 0)
(setvar "BLIPMODE" 1)
(graphscr)
(setq FT2 (/ FT 2.0) MT2 (/ MT 2.0))
(setq PT1(getpoint "\nINDICATE 1st END OF GLASS LINE: ")
      PT2(getpoint PT1 "\nINDICATE 2nd END OF GLASS LINE:"))
(setvar "BLIPMODE" 0)
(command "line" PT1 PT2 "")
(setq LIN(entlast))
(setq LEN(distance PT1 PT2)
      HT(abs(- TOP BOT (* 2.0 FT)))
      ANG(angle PT1 PT2))
(command "erase" LIN "")
(princ"\nBUILDING 3D WINDOW...PLEASE WAIT!")
;
; build bottom rail and top rail
;
(princ"\nBUILDING BOTTOM AND TOP RAILS:")
(command "solid" (polar PT1(- ANG(/ PI 2.0))FT2)
(polar PT1(+ ANG(/ PI 2.0))FT2)
(polar PT2(- ANG(/ PI 2.0))FT2)
(polar PT2(+ ANG(/ PI 2.0))FT2) "")
(command "move" (entlast) "" (list 0 0 0) (list 0 0 BOT)
"change" (entlast) "" "p" "t" FT "" "copy" (entlast) ""
"0,0" "0,0" "move" (entlast) "" (list 0 0 BOT)
(list 0 0 (- TOP FT)) "change" (entlast) "" "p" "t" FT "")
;
; build end verticals
;
(princ"\BUILDING END VERTICALS:")
(command "solid" (polar PT1(- ANG(/ PI 2.0))FT2)
(polar PT1(+ ANG(/ PI 2.0))FT2)
(polar PT1(- ANG(atan 0.5))
(sqrt(+(expt FT 2.0)(expt FT2 2.0))))
(polar PT1(+ ANG(atan 0.5))
(sqrt(+(expt FT 2.0)(expt FT2 2.0)))) "" "move" (entlast) ""
(list 0 0 0) (list 0 0 (+ BOT FT)) "change" (entlast) "" "p"
  "t" HT "" "solid"
(polar PT2(- ANG PI(atan 0.5))(sqrt(+(expt FT 2.0)(expt FT2
  2.0))))
(polar PT2(+ ANG PI (atan 0.5)) (sqrt(+(expt FT 2.0)(expt
  FT2 2.0))))
```

```
(polar PT2(+ ANG(/ PI 2.0))FT2) (polar PT2(- ANG(/ PI
  2.0))FT2)
 "" "move" (entlast) "" (list 0 0 0) (list 0 0 (+ BOT FT))
  "change" (entlast) "" "p" "t" HT "")
;
; build middle verticals
;
(princ"\nBUILDING MIDDLE VERTICALS:")
(setq COUNT 1 MDIS(/ LEN ROWS) STPT PT1 VPTS nil)
(while(< COUNT ROWS)
(setq MID(polar PT1 ANG (* MDIS COUNT))
VPTS(cons MID VPTS))
(command "solid"
(polar MID(- ANG(* 0.75 PI)) (sqrt(* 2(expt MT2 2.0))))
(polar MID(+ ANG(* 0.75 PI))(sqrt(* 2(expt MT2 2.0))))
(polar MID(- ANG(/ PI 4.0))(sqrt(* 2(expt MT2 2.0))))
(polar MID(+ ANG(/ PI 4.0))(sqrt(* 2(expt MT2 2.0)))) ""
"move" (entlast) "" (list 0 0 0) (list 0 0 (+ BOT FT))
"change" (entlast) "" "p" "t" HT "")
  (setq COUNT(1+ COUNT)) )
;
; build horizontals
;
(princ"\nBUILDING HORIZONTALS:")
(setq VPTS(cons(polar PT2(- ANG PI)(- FT MT2))VPTS)
VPTS(reverse VPTS) MDIS(/ HT COLS)
STPT(polar PT1 ANG(- FT MT2))
SS(ssadd) COUNT 0)
(while(< COUNT ROWS) (command "solid"
(polar STPT(+ ANG(/ PI 4.0)) (sqrt(* 2(expt MT2 2.0))))
(polar STPT(- ANG(/ PI 4.0))(sqrt(* 2(expt MT2 2.0))))
(polar (nth COUNT VPTS) (+ ANG(* 0.75 PI)) (sqrt(* 2(expt MT2 2.0))))
(polar (nth COUNT VPTS) (- ANG(* 0.75 PI)) (sqrt(* 2(expt
  MT2 2.0)))) "" "move" (entlast) "" (list 0 0 0) (list 0 0 (
    BOT MT2 MDIS)) "change" (entlast) "" "p" "t" MT "")
  (setq STPT(nth COUNT VPTS) COUNT(1+ COUNT)
SS(ssadd(entlast)SS))
 )
 (setq COUNT 2)
 (while(< COUNT COLS) (command "copy" SS "" "0,0" "0,0"
 "move" SS "" (list 0 0 (+ BOT MT2)) (list 0 0 (+ BOT MT2 MDIS))
 "change" SS "" "p" "t" MT "")
(setq COUNT(1+ COUNT))
```

```
)
(setvar "HIGHLIGHT" 1)
(setvar "CMDECHO" 1)
(setvar "BLIPMODE" 1)
(princ"\nFINISHED!")
(terpri)
)
)
)
```

TO INVOKE: Create this macro as an AutoLISP file (**.lsp**).

LET'S TRY IT: Get into a drawing and load **MACRO19** (**Load "MACRO19"**). Before calling the macro into play, set the variables **ROWS**, **COLS**, **MT**, **BOT** and **TOP** by typing:

```
(setq ROWS 4 COLS 3 MT 1.0 FT 2.0 BOT 30.0 TOP 84.0)
```

Now, type **WIN2**. When prompted, select two points, either by typing or by indicating them with your cursor. The macro then builds a complete 3D window with no further prompts. If any of the necessary variables aren't set, the macro will detect this, stop execution and prompt you with a list of their current status. In this example, the window will have four rows and three columns of panes, a mullion thickness of 1", a frame thickness of 2", a bottom height of 30" and a top height of 84". Type **WIN2** again and choose two more points. Another window, with the same pane count, thicknesses, bottom and top will be created.

TIPS: You can set the variables in several ways. You can put the prompts into a separate macro, called only when you need to create a new window type:

Macro
19A

WINDOW SET
For Release 10 or 11

TO CREATE:
```
(defun C:WINSET ()
(initget 7)
```

```
(setq ROWS(getint "\nHOW MANY PANES IN DIRECTION OF
   GLASS LINE (ROWS) ?"))
(initget 7)
(setq COLS(getint "\nHOW MANY PANES IN Z DIR (COLS)?"))
(setq MT(getdist "\nINDICATE THICKNESS OF FRAME: "))
(setq BOT(getdist "\nWHAT IS BOTTOM (SILL) HEIGHT ?"))
(setq TOP(getdist "\nWHAT IS TOP HEIGHT OF WINDOW? "))
)
```

This routine, if you load (**Load "MACRO19A"**) and run it by typing
WINSET, will prompt you for the variables. Then you can run **WIN2**
repeatedly by typing **WIN2**, followed by picking window "glass-line"
endpoints.

You could also put the data into a screen menu format. For instance:

```
[*BOTTOM*]
[36"]^C^C(setq BOT 36.0)
[42"]^C^C(setq BOT 42.0)
[*TOP*]
[72"]^C^C(setq TOP 72.0)
[78"]^C^C(setq TOP 78.0)
[*FR WID*]
[1" FRAME]^C^C(setq FT 1.0)
[2" FRAME]^C^C(setq FT 2.0)
[*MULWID*]
[1" MULL]^C^C(setq MT 1.0)
[1.5" MUL]^C^C(setq MT 1.5)
[*PANES*]
[2x2]^C^C(setq ROWS 2 COLS 2)
[3x2]^C^C(setq ROWS 3 COLS 2)
[3x3]^C^C(setq ROWS 3 COLS 3)
[3DWINDOW]^C^C(if(null C:WIN2)(load "MACRO19"));WIN2
```

This menu is available on the optional diskette. Create this file as an
AutoCAD menu file (**3dwindow.mnu**) or copy it from the diskette. Load
the menu by typing **MENU 3DWINDOW**. You can now set and reset
variables and execute **WIN2** from the screen menu by selecting the
appropriate areas. You could expand or alter this application to provide
a wide range of 3D windows, and it would be easy to expand it to
include arched windows, brick facing, decorative 3D doors and door-
frames, and more. We hope that other developers will create other
"point-and-shoot" construction macros.

Macro
20 Save/Retrieve Complete View and Construction Setup
For Release 10 or 11

PURPOSE: In Release 10 or 11, you can request multiple viewports, change the view in each and save the configuration. You can also save the view in the current active viewport and save the current active **UCS**. These three actions are the "construction setup." This macro has two parts. When used together, they let you save **VIEW**, **VPORT** and **UCS** information as a unit, and restore them as a unit. You can have multiple construction setups in one drawing, since the macros actually store the information using standard commands.

TO CREATE:

MACRO 20A: SAVE CURRENT CONSTRUCTION PORT INFO

```
(defun C:SAVPRT (/ STR SAVNAM)
;
; function saves current UCS with VPORTS configuration and
; current active window so they can all be restored
; together
(setq STR "")
(while(null SAVNAM)
(setq SAVNAM
  (getstring"\nWHAT IS NAME FOR SAVING CURRENT VIEW
    CONFIGURATION? "))
(if(tblsearch "ucs" SAVNAM)
    (setq STR(strcat STR " UCS")))
(if(tblsearch "vport" SAVNAM)
    (setq STR(strcat STR " VPORTS")))

(if(tblsearch "view" SAVNAM)
    (setq STR(strcat STR " VIEW")))
(if(not(equal STR ""))
  (progn
    (princ(strcat"\nSORRY, THE FOLLOWING CONFIGURATIONS:"
    STR " ARE ALREADY SAVED WITH THE NAME: " SAVNAM))
```

```
        (setq SAVNAM nil STR "")
)
(command "UCS" "S" SAVNAM "VPORTS" "S" SAVNAM "VIEW" "S" SAVNAM)
)
)
)
```

MACRO 20B: RETRIEVE CONSTRUCTION PORT INFO
For Release 10 or 11

```
(defun C:GETPRT (/ STR GETNAM)
;
; function saves current UCS with VPORTS configuration and
; current active window so they can all be restored
; together
(setq STR "")
(while(null GETNAM)
(setq GETNAM
   (getstring"\nWHAT IS NAME OF VIEW CONFIGURATION TO RETRIEVE?"))
(if(null(tblsearch "ucs" GETNAM))
    (setq STR(strcat STR " UCS")))
(if(null(tblsearch "vport" GETNAM))
    (setq STR(strcat STR " VPORTS")))
(if(null(tblsearch "view" GETNAM))
    (setq STR(strcat STR " VIEW")))
(if(not(equal STR ""))
  (progn
    (princ(strcat"\nSORRY, THE FOLLOWING CONFIGURATIONS:"
      STR " ARE NOT SAVED WITH THE NAME: " GETNAM))
    (setq GETNAM nil STR "")
  )
  (command "UCS" "R" GETNAM "VPORTS" "R" GETNAM "VIEW" "R" GETNAM)
)
)
)
```

TO INVOKE: Create these two macros as AutoLISP files (.lsp).

LET'S TRY IT: Get into a new drawing and load **MACRO20A** (**Load "MACRO20A"**) and **MACRO20B** (**Load "MACRO20B"**). Create a simple object such as a cube. Set the viewports to a vertical two-view screen by typing **VPORTS 2 VERTICAL**. Now rotate the current active view by typing **VPOINT 1,1,1**. Rotate the current **UCS** by typing **UCS**

X 90. Now invoke the "saving" macro by typing **SAVPRT**. When prompted, choose a name for saving the **UCS**, **VIEW** and **VPORT** configurations; the same name will be applied to all three. You could type **SPECIAL**, for instance. If any configurations of this name already exist, you'll be prompted for a new name.

Now return to a "generic" construction setup to test the retrieval macro. Type **VPORTS SI** to return to a single viewport. Type **UCS W** to return to the "world" **UCS**. Return to a plan view by typing **VPOINT 0,0,1**. To save this generic construction, type **SAVPRT** and when prompted for a name, type **GENERIC**.

To test the retrieval process, type **GETPRT**. When prompted for a construction set name, type **SPECIAL**. The viewport, **UCS** and view will change to return you to the "special" setup. Type **GETPRT** again and the name **GENERIC** to return to the generic setup. If you type the name of a nonexistent construction setup, the macro will tell you which construction datum, **VPORTS**, **UCS** or **VIEW** doesn't exist, and prompt for a new name.

Macro 21 DVIEW with Preset Object Selection
For Release 10 or 11

PURPOSE: The **DVIEW** command asks you to choose objects for display during dynamic view selection. Unfortunately, you must choose your view set every time you use the **DVIEW** command. Since **DVIEW** is a display-only command, turning off automatically when construction commands or **VPOINT** is invoked, this macro was created to save the view set for automatic recall. In a typical drawing, it will let you select important entities such as outside lines or main structures, and display these each time you use **DVIEW**. This macro consists of two parts: the "selecting" macro, and a variation on the **DVIEW** command—a macro that calls **DVIEW** using the selection set.

TO CREATE:

MACRO 21A: DVIEW SELECTION SET CREATION

```
(defun C:DVSS ()
```

```
(prompt"\nSETTING SELECTION SET FOR DVIEWS.")
(setq DVSET(ssget))
)
```

MACRO 21B: DVIEW USING SELECTION SET

```
(defun C:DV ()
(while(null DVSET)
(princ"\nNO SELECTION SET EXISTS...")
(C:DVSS)
)
(command "DVIEW" DVSET "")
)
```

TO INVOKE: Create these two macros as AutoLISP files (**.lsp**).

LET'S TRY IT: Get into a simple drawing, or create a new one of your design. Load **MACRO21A** (**Load "MACRO21A"**) and **MACRO21B** (**Load "MACRO21B"**). Type **DVSS**. When prompted, select a group of display objects for use in **DVIEW**; if the model is small, you can select the entire model.

Type **DV**. This will invoke the **DVIEW** command, using the previous selection set for displaying. Once in the **DVIEW** command, you can select **DISTANCE, POINTS**, etc., to adjust the current view as usual. If you want to change the current display set, type **DVSS** from the **Command**: prompt and select a new group.

TIPS: These two AutoLISP macros could have been written as simple menu macros as follows:

```
^C^C(setq DVSET(ssget))
```

```
^C^CDVIEW;DVSET;;
```

However, we think that the AutoLISP solution is usually the better one. New AutoCAD commands created through AutoLISP can be inserted into any area of the menu interface without modification, as if they were "usual" commands. Also, if you call a menu macro, then type **<RETURN>** or space to repeat the macro, only the last AutoCAD command will be repeated—some of the utility may be lost.

To insert the **DV** and **DVSS** commands into a menu, use these macros:

```
^C^C(if(null C:DVSS)(load "MACRO21A"));DVSS

^C^C(if(null C:DV)(load "MACRO21B"));DV
```

In this style, a <RETURN> would repeat the entire **DV** variation or **DVSS** setup for you.

Macro 22 # Hidden Line Removal (and Other Tasks) Without Text
For Release 10 or 11

PURPOSE: Text poses peculiar problems in 3D. While it's very useful for creating 2D charts and marking areas in plan view, it often clutters the 3D viewports. In wireframe views, it generally obscures an already complicated image; and because AutoCAD doesn't perform hidden-line removal on text, during a **HIDE** command or **DVIEW HIDE** it will still be written through the displayed objects.

These two macros remove and replace text in a drawing. You can use them with commands such as **HIDE** in a menu application.

TO CREATE:

MACRO 22A: TEXT BLOCKING OUT
```
(defun C:TOUT (/ TXT)
(setvar "EXPERT" 3)
(setvar "CMDECHO" 0)
(setq TXT(ssget "X" '((0 . "TEXT"))))
(if TXT
(progn
(prompt"\nTHIS DRAWING CONTAINS TEXT...BLOCKING IT...\n")
(command "BLOCK" "TEXTXXXX" "0,0" (ssget "X" '((0 . "TEXT"))) "")
(prompt(strcat"\nUSE " (chr 34) "TRET" (chr 34)
  " TO RE-INSERT TEXT..."))
)
(progn
```

```
(prompt"\nTHIS DRAWING DOESN'T CONTAIN TEXT...")
(setq BLOCKED nil)
)
)
(setvar "EXPERT" 0)
(setvar "CMDECHO" 1)
(setq BLOCKED 1)
(terpri)
)
```

MACRO 22B: TEXT RETRIEVAL

```
(defun C:TRET ()
(setvar "CMDECHO" 0)
(if(not(null BLOCKED))
(progn
(prompt"\nREINSERTING BLOCKED-OUT TEXT...")
(command "insert" "*TEXTXXXX" "0,0" "1" "0")
)
(prompt"\nNO FURTHER TEXT HAS BEEN BLOCKED OUT...")
)
(setq BLOCKED nil)
(setvar "CMDECHO" 1)
(terpri)
)
```

TO INVOKE: Create these two macros as AutoLISP files (**.lsp**).

LET'S TRY IT: Get into an existing drawing with text, or create a new drawing with text. Load **MACRO22A (Load "MACRO22A")** and **MACRO22B (Load "MACRO22B")**. Type **TOUT**.

If there's text in the drawing, it will disappear. The macro has created a block named **TEXTXXXX** containing all the "free" text in the drawing (text that isn't part of an associated dimension or nested in another block).

You can now use **HIDE** or other commands, knowing that you can return the blocked text at will. To do this, type **TRET. MACRO22B** will re-insert an exploded version of the block **TEXTXXXX**.

TIPS: The block name **TEXTXXXX** was chosen at random, in the hope that the macro won't redefine an existing block in your drawing. Avoid using the name for another block, or, if you use the name **TEXTXXXX**

frequently for a standard block, replace the name in both **MACRO22A** and **MACRO22B** with another of your choice.

The first macro has a "bug catcher" that will not make a block if there's no text in the drawing. The second macro will avoid making multiple inserts of the text into your drawing. The macros use the variable **BLOCKED** as a flag to indicate if a text block exists, and they check and reset this variable to avoid trouble.

You can use these macros in a menu, as follows:

```
^C^C(if(null C:TOUT)(load "MACRO22A"));TOUT

^C^C(if(null C:TRET)(load "MACRO22B"));TRET
```

Macro 23 — Dual Viewports
For Release 10 or 11

PURPOSE: By using the **UCS** (User Coordinate System) and the **VPORTS** commands, you can manipulate your 3D construction more easily, but working in 3D may involve setting up standard viewport configurations. This macro presents one standard view configuration, in which the left-hand view is an orthogonal plan view, the right-hand view is rotated **45** degrees, and you work in the left viewport.

TO CREATE:
```
(defun C:2PORTS (/ UCSF VP LPRT RPRT)
; this function produces 2 standard vertical
; viewports.
;
(setvar "CMDECHO" 0)
(setvar "EXPERT" 3)
(setq UCSF(getvar "UCSFOLLOW"))
(command "vports" "si" "vports" "2" "V")
(setq VP(vports)
    RPRT(car(nth 0 VP))
    LPRT(car(nth 1 VP)))
(setvar "CVPORT" RPRT)
(command "VPOINT" "1,1,1")
(setvar "CVPORT" LPRT)
```

```
(command "VPOINT" "0,0,1")
(setvar "CMDECHO" 1)
(setvar "EXPERT" 0)
(setvar "UCSFOLLOW" UCSF)
(terpri)
)
```

TO INVOKE: Create this macro as an AutoLISP file (**.lsp**).

LET'S TRY IT: Get into an existing drawing and load **MACRO23** (**Load "MACRO23"**). Type **2PORTS**. The macro will create a dual viewport. If you want to save the configuration for automatic recall, use the **VPORTS SAVE** command and give it a name. You can also choose your active window by picking with your cursor, and manipulate your view using the **VPOINT** or **DVIEW** commands.

Macro 24   Quadruple Viewports
For Release 10 or 11

PURPOSE: Presents another standard view configuration, in which there are four viewports. The upper left window is an orthogonal plan view, the lower left window is a front view, the upper right window is a right-side view, and the lower right window is an isometric view rotated **45** degrees around the **Z** axis. You work in the upper left (plan) view. This is a standard layout adopted by many engineering firms for standard drafting.

TO CREATE:
```
(defun C:4PORTS ()
; this function produces 4 standard
; viewports.
;
(setvar "CMDECHO" 0)
(setvar "EXPERT" 3)
(setq UCSF(getvar "UCSFOLLOW"))
(command "vports" "si" "vports" "4")
(setq VP(vports)
    LRPRT(car(nth 0 VP))
    URPRT(car(nth 1 VP))
```

```
    ULPRT(car(nth 2 VP))
    LLPRT(car(nth 3 VP)))
(setvar "CVPORT" LLPRT)
(command "VPOINT" "0,-1,0")
(setvar "CVPORT" URPRT)
(command "VPOINT" "1,0,0")
(setvar "CVPORT" LRPRT)
(command "VPOINT" "1,1,1")
(setvar "CVPORT" ULPRT)
(command "VPOINT" "0,0,1")
(setvar "CMDECHO" 1)
(setvar "EXPERT" 0)
(setvar "UCSFOLLOW" UCSF)
(terpri)
)
```

TO INVOKE: Create this macro as an AutoLISP file (**.lsp**).

LET'S TRY IT: Get into an existing drawing and load **MACRO23** (**Load "MACRO23"**). Type **4PORTS**. The macro will create a quadruple viewport. If you want to save the configuration for automatic recall, use the **VPORTS SAVE** command and give it a name. You can also choose your active window by picking with your cursor, and manipulate your view using the **VPOINT** or **DVIEW** commands.

Macro 25

Solid-to-3DFACE Transformation
For Release 10 or 11

PURPOSE: An easy way to construct 3D objects is by extruding them using the techniques available in "2½ D" prior to Release 10. For instance, many models are constructed using extruded solids; **3D-FACES** would be more practical. For example, if two solids touch on an edge, those two faces will require additional computation time during the **HIDE** command. In addition, if you wanted to remove those common edges or any edge on the solids, you'd have to reconstruct the cubes as sets of **3DFACES**. This routine transforms them for you, on either a selected set of solids or on all solids in the drawing file.

TO CREATE:

```
(defun C:SF (/ LA HI BL SEL SOLIDS COUNTER SOL DESCR TYP THIK
  ELEV LAY PT1 PT2 PT3 PT4 PT5 PT6 PT7 PT8 FL)
(setvar "CMDECHO" 0)
(setq FL (getvar "FLATLAND"))
(setvar "FLATLAND" 0)
(setq EL(getvar "ELEVATION") TH(getvar "THICKNESS")
  LA (getvar "CLAYER")
  HI(getvar"HIGHLIGHT") BL(getvar "BLIPMODE"))
(initget 1 "A S")
(setq SEL(getkword"\nCONVERT ALL SOLIDS OR A SELECTION ? (A S)"))
(if(equal SEL "A")(setq SOLIDS(ssget "X" '((0 . "SOLID")))))
(progn
(princ"\nPLEASE CHOOSE SOLIDS: ")
(setq SOLIDS(ssget))
)
)
(setvar "HIGHLIGHT" 0)
(setvar "BLIPMODE" 0)
(princ"\nCONVERTING SOLIDS TO 3DFACES...PLEASE WAIT!")
(setq COUNTER 0)
(if SOLIDS
(progn
(while(< COUNTER(sslength SOLIDS))
  (setq SOL(ssname SOLIDS COUNTER)
    DESCR(entget SOL)
    TYP(cdr(assoc 0 DESCR)))
  (if(equal TYP "SOLID")
    (progn
    (setq THIK(cdr(assoc 39 DESCR))
      ELEV(cadddr(assoc 10 DESCR))
      LAY(cdr(assoc 8 DESCR))
      PT1(cdr(assoc 10 DESCR))
      PT2(cdr(assoc 11 DESCR))
      PT3(cdr(assoc 12 DESCR))
      PT4(cdr(assoc 13 DESCR)))
(if THIK(setq PT5(list(car PT1)(cadr PT1)
    (+ THIK(caddrPT1)))
    PT6(list(car PT2)(cadr PT2)
    (+ THIK(caddr PT2)))
      PT7(list(car PT3)(cadr PT3)
      (+ THIK(caddr PT3)))
```

```
        PT8(list(car PT4)(cadr PT4)
        (+ THIK(caddr PT4))))
        )
        (setq PT1(trans PT1 SOL 1)
        PT2(trans PT2 SOL 1)
        PT3(trans PT3 SOL 1)
        PT4(trans PT4 SOL 1)
        PT5(trans PT5 SOL 1)
        PT6(trans PT6 SOL 1)
        PT7(trans PT7 SOL 1)
        PT8(trans PT8 SOL 1))
        (command "layer" "s" LAY ""
        "erase" SOL "" "3dface" PT1 PT2 PT4 PT3 "")
        (if THIK
        (command "3dface" PT5 PT6 PT8 PT7 ""
        "3dface" PT1 PT3 PT7 PT5 ""
        "3dface" PT2 PT4 PT8 PT6 ""
        "3dface" PT1 PT2 PT6 PT5 ""
        "3dface" PT3 PT4 PT8 PT7 "")
        )
        )
        )
        (setq COUNTER(1+ COUNTER))
        )
    )
(princ"\nTHERE ARE NO SOLIDS IN THIS DRAWING!"
)
        (command "layer" "s" LA "")
        (setvar "CMDECHO" 1)
        (setvar "HIGHLIGHT" HI)
        (setvar "BLIPMODE" BL)
        (princ "\nFINISHED!")
        (terpri)
        )
```

TO INVOKE: Create this macro as an AutoLISP file (**.lsp**).

TO USE: This macro includes a **UCS** transformation routine that lets it operate on solids created on different **User Coordinate Systems**. It also transforms both extruded and unextruded solids to **3DFACES**.

Get into a new drawing. Type **SOLID 0,0 1,0 0,1 1,1 CHPROP L <RETURN> T 1**. This will create a one-unit extruded cube. Create another cube on another **UCS** by typing: **UCS X 45 SOLID 0,0 1,0 0,1 1,1 CHPROP L <RETURN> T 1**. To view the model, type **VPOINT 1,1,1**. You'll see two rotated cubes that intersect. Load **MACRO25 (Load "MACRO25")**. Type **SF**. At the prompt, "Convert all solids or a selection? (A S)," type **A**. The macro will erase each of the extruded solids and replace them with **3DFACES** in the appropriate coordinates and layers. You can check them by using the **LIST** command.

Macro 26 Object Tweening

PURPOSE: Will aid in 3D animation where an object "metamorphoses." A complex object, constructed entirely of **3DFACES**, will evolve into another shape, based on "keyframe animation." The resulting forms may be saved as slides for viewing as animation or loading into Autodesk Animator. Resulting "tween" models may be rendered with AutoSHADE and, optionally, viewed with Animator.

TO CREATE:

```
(defun C:TWEENIT (/ S SAVESLD SAVEDW LAYFILE LAYBEGIN FRAMEFILE AS1
   DELTFILE SCRPT LAY1 LAY2 FRAMENUM PREF SCRNAM SSET1 SSET2 COUNT AS2
   ENTNUM POINTER DELT DELTSTR FRAME VAL FRAMENAM ASNEWFRAMEN HID)
   ;
(defun *ERROR* (s)
(close LAYFILE)(close DELTFILE)(close SCRPT)
(redraw)(print s)(setvar "HIGHLIGHT" 1)
(setvar "CMDECHO" 1)(setq *ERROR* nil))
   ;
(setvar "HIGHLIGHT" 0)(setvar "CMDECHO" 0)
(setq SAVESLD(strcase(substr
(getstring"\n\nDo you wish to save slides? ")1 1))
     SAVEDWG(strcase(substr
(getstring"\n\nDo you wish to save drawings? ")1 1))
     PREF(strcase
(getstring"\n\nWhat is the prefix name for your slides/drawings? ")))
(if(equal SAVESLD "Y")(progn(initget 1 "Y N")
(setq HID(getkword"\nDo you wish to Hide slides? <Y N> "))
(setq SCRNAM(strcase
(getstring "\n\nWhat is the name for the script-file? ")))))
(princ(strcat"\nPLEASE SUPPLY NAMES OF FRAME LAYERS...ANSWER "
        " WITH  <return>  TO END LISTING"))
```

```
(setq LAYFILE(open "LAYERS.XXX" "w") LAY1(strcase
(getstring "\n\nWhat is name of first layer? ")) LAY2(strcase
(getstring "\n\nWhat is name of second layer? ")))
(write-line LAY1 LAYFILE)(write-line LAY2 LAYFILE)
(while(not(equal LAY1 ""))
(setq LAY1(strcase(getstring(strcat "\n\nWhat is name of next layer after "
(strcase LAY2) "? "))))
(if(not(equal LAY1 ""))(write-line LAY1 LAYFILE))
(setq LAY2 LAY1))(close LAYFILE)
(setq LAYFILE(open "LAYERS.XXX" "r") FRAMEFILE(open "FRAMES.XXX"
   "w")
     LAY2(read-line LAYFILE))
(while(setq LAYTEMP(read-line LAYFILE))
(setq LAY1 LAY2 LAY2 LAYTEMP FRAMENUM (+(getint
(strcat"\n\nHow many frames BETWEEN image on layer "
             LAY1 " and image on layer " LAY2 "? ")) 2))
(write-line(itoa FRAMENUM) FRAMEFILE))
(close FRAMEFILE)(close LAYFILE)
(setq LAYFILE(open "LAYERS.XXX" "r") FRAMEFILE(open "FRAMES.XXX"
   "r") LAYBEGIN
(read-line LAYFILE) SSET1(ssget "X"(list(cons 8 LAYBEGIN)))
   FRAMEN 1)
(if(equal SAVESLD "Y")
(setq SCRPT(open(strcat SCRNAM ".SCR") "w")))
(while(setq LAY2(read-line LAYFILE))
(setq FRAMENUM(atoi(read-line FRAMEFILE)))
(princ "\nSORTING ENTITIES...PLEASE WAIT!...")
(setq SSET2(ssget "X"(list(cons 8 LAY2))) COUNT
(min(sslength SSET1)(sslength SSET2)))
(command "LAYER" "T" "*" "S" LAYBEGIN "F" "*" "")
(princ "\nCALCULATING MOTION VECTORS...PLEASE WAIT!...");
(setq ENTNUM 0)(setq DELTFILE(open "DELTAXXX.XXX" "w"))
(while( <ENTNUM COUNT)
(princ (strcat"\nEVALUATING ENTITY #"  (itoa (1+ ENTNUM)) " OF "
   (itoa COUNT)))
(foreach A '(10 11 12 13)
(if(and(setq AS1(assoc A(entget(ssname SSET1 ENTNUM))))
(setq AS2(assoc A(entget (ssname SSET2 ENTNUM)))))
(progn(setq POINTER(1-(length AS1)))
(while( >POINTER 0)(setq DELT(/(-(nth POINTER AS2)(nth POINTER
   AS1))
```

```
(1- FRAMENUM)))(setq DELTSTR(rtos DELT 2 8))(write-line DELTSTR DELTFILE
(setq POINTER(1- POINTER))))))(setq ENTNUM(1+ ENTNUM)))(close DELTFILE)
(princ"\nMOVING ENTITIES...PLEASE WAIT...\n")(setq FRAME 1)
(while( FRAME FRAMENUM)(setq FRAMENAM(strcat PREF(ITOA FRAMEN)))

(if(equal SAVESLD "Y")(progn(if(equal HID "Y")
(progn(princ(strcat"\nHIDING SLIDE: " FRAMENAM))(command "HIDE")))
(princ(strcat"\nMAKING SLIDE: " FRAMENAM))
(command "MSLIDE" FRAMENAM)))
(if(equal SAVEDWG "Y")(progn(princ(strcat "\nSAVING DRAWING: " FRAMENAM))
(command "SAVE" FRAMENAM)))
(if(equal SAVESLD "Y")(write-line(strcat "VSLIDE " FRAMENAM)SCRPT))
(if( <FRAME FRAMENUM)(progn
(setq ENTNUM 0)(setq DELTFILE(open "DELTAXXX.XXX" "r"))
(while( <ENTNUM COUNT)
(princ(strcat"\nMOVING ENTITY #"(itoa(1+ ENTNUM)) " OF " (itoa COUNT)
   " FRAME #" (itoa(1+ FRAMEN))))
(foreach A '(10 11 12 13)
(if(and(setq AS1(assoc A(entget(ssname SSET1 ENTNUM))))
(setq AS2(assoc A(entget(ssname SSET2 ENTNUM)))))
(progn(setq POINTER(1-(length AS1)))(setq TEMPLIST nil)
(while( >POINTER 0)(setq DELTSTR(read-line DELTFILE))(setq DELT(atof
  DELTSTR))
(setq TEMPLIST(cons(+(nth POINTER AS1)DELT)TEMPLIST))
(setq POINTER(1- POINTER)))(setq ASNEW(cons A TEMPLIST))
(entmod(subst ASNEW AS1(entget(ssname SSET1 ENTNUM))))))))
(setq ENTNUM(1+ ENTNUM)))
(close DELTFILE)))
(setq FRAME(1+ FRAME)FRAMEN(1+ FRAMEN))))
(setq FRAMENAM(strcat PREF(ITOA FRAMEN)))
(princ(strcat "\nFRAME NUMBER: "(itoa FRAMEN)))
(if(equal SAVESLD "Y")(progn
(if(equal HIDE "Y")(progn(princ(strcat"\nHIDING SLIDE: " FRAMENAM))
(command "HIDE")))
(princ(strcat"\nMAKING SLIDE: " FRAMENAM)(command "MSLIDE" FRAMENAM))
(if(equal SAVEDWG "Y")(progn(princ(strcat "\nSAVING DRAWING: " FRAMENAM))
(command "SAVE" FRAMENAM)))
(if(equal SAVESLD "Y")(write-line(strcat "VSLIDE " FRAMENAM)SCRPT))
(close LAYFILE)(close FRAMEFILE)
(if(equal SAVESLD "Y")(close SCRPT))
(command "del" "DELTAXXX.XXX")(command "del" "LAYERS.XXX")
(command "del" "FRAMES.XXX")(princ "\n\nFINISHED!\n\n")
```

```
(if(equal SAVESLD "Y")(princ(strcat "\nTO ANIMATE, TYPE:\n"
(chr 34) "SCRIPT <return> " SCRNAM " <return> " (chr 34) "\n")))
(setvar "HIGHLIGHT" 1)(setvar "CMDECHO" 1)(terpri))
```

TO INVOKE: Create this macro as an AutoLISP file (**.lsp**).

LET'S TRY IT: Let's begin by making two simple 3D forms on two different layers. For **TWEENIT**, it's necessary that the two forms have the same number of **3DFACES**, created in the same relative X-Y direction. The two models can be duplicates in new positions (creating a sliding model animation), new rotations or scales, or entirely different. First, type:

LAYER N 1,2 C W 1 C R 2 S 1 <RETURN>

This creates two layers, numbered one and two, and sets your current layer to one. For clarity, layer one is set to white and layer two to red. Now let's create a "profile drawing" on layer one.

Type: LINE 0,0 .5,.5 1,1 <RETURN>.

This creates a 45-degree line (split into two sections). Now type **SURFTAB1 8**, then **SURFTAB2 8**. This will create an 8 x 8 surface patch. To create a simple figure of revolution, an inverted cone, you must have a line of revolution.

Type: LINE 0,0 0,1 <RETURN>.

Now type **REVSURF**. At the prompt, pick the bottom segment of the 45 degree line, then the vertical line as center of revolution. Select 360 degrees of revolution. A partial 3D cone will be formed. Now type **REVSURF**, pick the top segment of the 45 degree line and repeat the steps to finish the 3D cone.
Now we'll create another 3D "keyframe."

Type: LAYER S 2 <RETURN> (to go to the second layer.)

Type: LINE 0,0 1,1 .5,0 <RETURN> (to make another set of 2D lines.)

Use **REVSURF** to revolve both of these sections. Be sure to select the first section drafted (the leftmost or "bottom" section) first.

Now erase all lines, leaving four 3D surfaces of revolution on two layers. Explode the first (inside) surface on layer 1, then the outside. Repeat with layer 2 in the same order.

Now load **MACRO26 (Load "MACRO26")**. AutoCAD Responds: **TWEENIT**. Type **TWEENIT**. The program prompts: "Do you wish to save slides? <Y/N>". Slides can be saved, in either hidden-line-removed or wire frame style, and viewed with a self-written .SCR file. Answer **Y**. TWEENIT prompts, "Do you wish to save drawings?" Drawings can be saved for further rendering with AutoSHADE. For now, respond **N**.

The program prompts: "What is the prefix name for your slides/drawings?" Provide a short prefix, such as TEST, or even a drive and path such as C:\TEST\TEST, which will be used to create slide and drawing names, such as TEST1.SLD, TEST2.SLD, etc. You'll now be prompted, "Do you wish to Hide slides? <Y/N>". Answer **N**. You may hide them if you wish, but this can greatly affect rendering times. You'll now be prompted: "What is the name for the script-file?" If you were just saving drawings, you wouldn't be prompted for HIDE or script-file. This .SCR will contain **VSLIDE** commands for each image you create.

Type:　TEST <RETURN>

The program now prompts you for the names of each layer, followed by an extra carriage return to end. Type **1 2 <RETURN>** in response to each prompt. There's one interval between the key model on layer 1 and the model on layer 2, and so on, as necessary. For each interval, you'll be prompted for the number of frames BETWEEN (not counting) each model. Type a low number as an example. Try five frames.

Now the program will prompt as it sorts entities by layer, freezes and thaws layers, calculates "motion vectors" to move each **3DFACE** a bit closer to its new position. Basically, the 3D model will "metamorphose" or change from the condition on layer 1 to the condition on layer 2, in seven steps. Each step will involve the separate movement of 128 **3DFACES** a bit at a time, from their position in the first model to their new position in the second model. During the transformation, TWEENIT will keep you apprised of its progress.

During this demo, you'll create a "metamorphosis" in seven steps, saving the slides and creating a script file to view them. When finished, TWEENIT will prompt you:

FINISHED!

To animate, type:

```
"SCRIPT  <RETURN> TEST <RETURN>
```

EXTENSIONS: You can create your models using any surface patch, **3DFACE** or technique, as long as the keyframe models contain the same total number of faces, created in the same STRICT directional order, so you can control the direction of animation of the "skin."

It's possible to extend this routine to create **.FLM** files and **.RND**'s for AutoSHADE, and ultimately to create a rendering script file for AutoSHADE to paint each model. If you're clever, you could use WTC to walk around the model while it's changing shape—you might save each version as **.DWG**, then write a script around WTC that inserts a new model for each step of the path. The model and path can even change at different rates! More programs of this sort can be found in popular magazines, in future editions of this text, or in the imagination of a good AutoLISP programmer. I can also recommend ATK, the Animation Tool Kit from Autodesk, and Autodesk 3DStudio.

SYSTEM VARIABLES QUICK REFERENCE

A number of system variables are available with Releases 10 and 11. Here's a list of them and how they're used.

ACADPREFIX   A read-only system variable. It contains a string value that indicates the directory name set by the **ACAD** environment variable. By using **SET ACAD=** you can specify an additional path for drawing files, LISP programs, etc.

ACADVER   A read-only system variable. It contains a string that tells you the AutoCAD version being used.

AFLAGS   Controls the status of the attributes in effect for the **ATTDEF** command. It uses an integer code as follows:

1	Invisible
2	Constant
4	Verify
8	Preset

Any time the *AutoCAD Reference Manual* indicates that a system variable is (**sum of the following**), as it does for this variable, you can have more than one code in effect. Therefore, if you wanted **Invisible** and **Constant**, you'd use their sum (**3**).

ATTDIA

Causes the **INSERT** command to use either a dialog box or regular command prompts. If it's set to 1, it uses the dialog box. If it's set to 0, it uses the prompts.

ATTREQ

When set to 0, this always uses the defaults for the values of all attributes during block insertion. If it's set to 1, it uses prompts or the dialog box, depending on how **ATTDIA** is set.

BACKZ

A read-only system variable that has meaning only if back clipping in **VIEWMODE** is on. It measures the back clipping plane offset for the current viewport, using the current drawing units. If you need to know the distance of the back clipping plane from the camera point, subtract **BACKZ** from the camera-to-target distance.

CVPORT

The identification number for the current viewport.

FLATLAND

This system variable guarantees compatibility with Release 9. If it's set to 1, then **OBJECT SNAP**, **DXF** and **AutoLISP** operate as they did in Release 9. If it's set to 0, then all the functions of Releases 10 and 11 are available. This is a temporary variable that will be removed on the next major update.

FRONTZ

A read-only system variable that has meaning only if front clipping in **VIEWMODE** is on and "Front clip not at eye" is on. This is similar to the **BACKZ** system variable. It measures the front clipping plane offset for the current viewport using the current drawing units. To find the distance of the front clipping plane from the camera point, subtract **FRONTZ** from the camera-to-target distance.

LENSLENGTH   A read-only system variable that measures the length of the lens in millimeters. It's used when **PERSPECTIVE** is **ON**.

MENUNAME   A read-only system variable that contains the name of the current menu.

POPUPS   A read-only system variable that indicates whether the display driver supports pull-down menus. If it's set to 1, then the driver supports pull-down menus. If it's set to 0, then the driver doesn't support pull-down menus.

SPLFRAME   This system variable controls whether the following will be displayed. If it's set to 1, then:

1. The control polygon for spline-fitted polylines is displayed.

2. The defining mesh of a surface-fitted polygon is displayed and not the fitted surface.

3. Invisible edges of **3DFACES** are displayed.

If it's set to 0, then:

1. The control polygon for spine-fitted polylines isn't displayed.

2. The defining mesh of a surface-fitted polygon isn't displayed and the fitted surface is.

3. Invisible edges of **3DFACES** aren't displayed.

SPLINESEGS   Determines the number of line segments to be generated for each **SPLINE** patch.

SPLINETYPE   Determines the type of **SPLINE** curve to be generated. 5=aquadratic **B-spline** and 6=acubic **B-spline**.

SURFTAB1   Controls the mesh density in the **M** direction. This is used by **TABSURF** and **RULESURF** for their primary density. **REVSURF** and **EDGESURF** also use this variable for one of the directions of the mesh.

SURFTAB2   Controls the mesh density in the **N** direction. This is used only by **REVSURF** and **EDGESURF**.

TARGET   A read-only system variable that contains the **UCS** coordinates for the target point for the current viewport.

TEMPPREFIX   A read-only system variable that contains the directory name for placement of temporary files.

TEXTEVAL   If its value is 0, then all text and attributes are taken literally. If it's set to 1, then text that begins with "!" or "(" is interpreted as an AutoLISP expression.

TEXTSTYLE   A read-only system variable that contains the name of the current **TEXT** style in effect.

TILEMODE   A system variable that toggles you from Paper Space to Model Space and vice versa.

UCSFOLLOW   If this is set to 1, then any change in **UCS** causes an automatic change to the plan view of the current **UCS**. If it's set to 0, then plan view doesn't change.

UCSICON   This system variable positions the **UCS** icon or turns it off and on.

0 = Off

1 = Place in lower left-hand corner

2 = Off

3 = Place at point of origin

Any number larger than 3 is converted to 1 and will place the icon in the lower left-hand corner.

UCSNAME   A read-only system variable that gives the name of the current **UCS**.

UCSORG   A read-only system variable that gives the coordinates of the point of origin, always in the **WCS**.

UCSXDIR   A read-only system variable that gives the X-direction of the current **UCS**.

UCSYDIR   A read-only system variable that gives the Y-direction of the current **UCS**.

VIEWDIR   A read-only system variable that provides the current viewport's viewing direction. This defines the camera point as an offset from the target point expressed in **WCS**.

VIEWMODE   A read-only system variable that displays a variety of modes. It uses (**sum of the following**), which means that you can establish multiple modes by adding them and using the sum as the code number.

1	Perspective is active
2	Front clipping is on
4	Back clipping is on
8	UCS FOLLOW mode is on
16	Front clip "not at eye" is on. If this is on, **FRONTZ** determines the front clipping plane. If it's off, **FRONTZ** is ignored.

VIEWTWIST   A read-only system variable that provides the view twist angle for the current viewport.

VSMAX   A read-only system variable that provides the upper right corner of the current viewport's virtual screen expressed in **UCS**.

VSMIN   A read-only system variable that provides the
                   lower left corner of the current viewport's virtual
                   screen expressed in **UCS**.

WORLDUCS   This is a read-only system variable. If it's 1, then
                   the current **UCS** is the same as the **WCS**. If it's 0,
                   then it's not.

WORLDVIEW   Since the **DVIEW** and **VPOINT** commands are rel-
                   ative to the current **UCS**, this variable will change
                   the current **UCS** equal to the **WCS** for the duration
                   of a **DVIEW** or **VPOINT** command. If it's set to 1,
                   then the change will occur. If it's set to 0, the
                   default, then it won't change.

DIMENSION VARIABLES QUICK REFERENCE

The following are dimension variables new to Releases 10 and 11:

DIMTOFL   If this variable is on, then a dimension line is drawn between the extension lines, even if the text is forced outside them.

DIMTIX   If this variable is on, then the text is forced between the extension lines even if AutoCAD would normally place it outside.

DIMSOXD   This variable keeps AutoCAD from drawing lines outside the extension lines. If **DIMTIX** is on and AutoCAD would normally draw the dimension lines outside the extension lines, you can suppress the dimension line by setting **DIMSOXD** to **ON**. If **DIMTIX** is **OFF** there's no effect.

DIMSAH   If this variable is on, then **DIMBLK1** and **DIMBLK2** are used as the arrowheads for each end of the dimension line. If it's off, then **DIMBLK** is used for both ends.

DIMTVP   Controls where text is placed, relative to the dimension line. **DIMTAD** must be set to **OFF**. **DIMTVP** uses positive or negative numbers. The distance from the dimension line is **DIMTVP * DIMTXT**. If it's positive, it's placed above the line. If negative, it's placed below.

DIMBLK1   Define the blocks used as the arrowheads at each
DIMBLK2   end of the dimension line. These are active only if **DIMSAH** is **ON**. If either is unspecified, then **DIMBLK** is used for that end.

Index

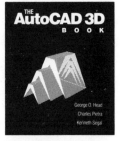

TO ORDER additional copies of *AutoCAD 3D Book* or any of the other books in our AutoCAD Reference Library, please fill out this order form and return it to us for quick shipment.

	Quantity		Price		Total
The AutoCAD 3D Book	_____	×	$24.95	=	$_____
The AutoCAD 3D Book Diskette	_____	×	$49.95	=	$_____
AutoCAD: A Concise Guide	_____	×	$19.95	=	$_____
AutoCAD: A Concise Guide Diskette	_____	×	$19.95	=	$_____
1,000 AutoCAD Tips and Tricks	_____	×	$24.95	=	$_____
1,000 AutoCAD Tips and Tricks Diskette	_____	×	$49.95	=	$_____
AutoLISP In Plain English	_____	×	$19.95	=	$_____
AutoLISP In Plain English Diskette	_____	×	$19.95	=	$_____
The AutoCAD Productivity Book	_____	×	$24.95	=	$_____
The AutoCAD Productivity Book Diskette	_____	×	$49.95	=	$_____
The AutoCAD Database Book	_____	×	$24.95	=	$_____
The AutoCAD Database Book Diskette	_____	×	$49.95	=	$_____
All six books & six diskettes (37% off!)	_____	×	$249.90	=	$_____

Shipping: Please add $4.10/first book for standard UPS, $1.35/book thereafter; $7.50/book UPS two-day air, $1.35/book thereafter.
For Canada, add $8.10/book.   = $_____

Send C.O.D. (add $3.75 to shipping charges)   = $_____

North Carolina residents add 5% sales tax   = $_____

                                                                 Total = $_____

Name _____

Company _____

Address (No P.O. Box) _____

City_____ State_____Zip _____

Daytime Phone _____

_____ Payment enclosed (check or money order; no cash please)

_____VISA _____ MC   Acc't # _____ - _____ - _____ - _____

Expiration date_____ Signature _____

Please mail or fax to:
Ventana Press, P.O. Box 2468, Chapel Hill, NC 27515
919/942-0220, FAX: 919/942-1140

TO ORDER additional copies of *AutoCAD 3D Book* or any of the other books in our AutoCAD Reference Library, please fill out this order form and return it to us for quick shipment.

	Quantity		Price		Total
The AutoCAD 3D Book	_____	×	$24.95	=	$_____
The AutoCAD 3D Book Diskette	_____	×	$49.95	=	$_____
AutoCAD: A Concise Guide	_____	×	$19.95	=	$_____
AutoCAD: A Concise Guide Diskette	_____	×	$19.95	=	$_____
1,000 AutoCAD Tips and Tricks	_____	×	$24.95	=	$_____
1,000 AutoCAD Tips and Tricks Diskette	_____	×	$49.95	=	$_____
AutoLISP In Plain English	_____	×	$19.95	=	$_____
AutoLISP In Plain English Diskette	_____	×	$19.95	=	$_____
The AutoCAD Productivity Book	_____	×	$24.95	=	$_____
The AutoCAD Productivity Book Diskette	_____	×	$49.95	=	$_____
The AutoCAD Database Book	_____	×	$24.95	=	$_____
The AutoCAD Database Book Diskette	_____	×	$49.95	=	$_____
All six books & six diskettes (37% off!)	_____	×	$249.90	=	$_____

Shipping: Please add $4.10/first book for standard UPS, $1.35/book thereafter; $7.50/book UPS two-day air, $1.35/book thereafter. For Canada, add $8.10/book. = $_____

Send C.O.D. (add $3.75 to shipping charges) = $_____

North Carolina residents add 5% sales tax = $_____

Total = $_____

Name _____

Company _____

Address (No P.O. Box) _____

City_____ State_____Zip _____

Daytime Phone _____

_____ Payment enclosed (check or money order; no cash please)

_____VISA _____ MC   Acc't # _____ - _____ - _____ - _____

Expiration date_____   Signature _____

Please mail or fax to:

Ventana Press, P.O. Box 2468, Chapel Hill, NC 27515

919/942-0220, FAX: 919/942-1140

BECOME EVEN MORE PRODUCTIVE...

... by ordering *The AutoCAD 3D Diskette*, which allows you to enter the AutoLISP programs and drawings featured throughout the book directly into your computer.

Each floppy diskette includes the tutorial drawings featured in Chapters 1-8, plus all the macros and AutoLISP programs from *The AutoCAD 3D Library*.

Your *AutoCAD 3D Diskette* will run on any 360K IBM-standard format computer and will save hours of tedious, error-prone typing. To order your copy, please complete the form below, detach and mail the postage-paid card.

MAIL TO: Ventana Press, P.O. Box 2468, Chapel Hill, NC 27515
Or, if you'd like it even sooner, call 919/942-0220.

- -

Yes, please send_____copies of *The AutoCAD 3D Diskette, Second Edition,* at $49.95 per diskette. Normal shipping charges $3. Add $6/diskette for UPS "two-day air." North Carolina Residents add 5% sales tax. Immediate shipment guaranteed.

Circle disk size: 5¼" or 3½"

Name _____Co. _____

Address (no P.O. Box)_____

City _____State _____ZIP _____

Telephone _____

                Payment enclosed (check or money order; no cash please)

                Charge my: VISA/MC Acct.#

                Exp. Date _____Interbank # _____

Signature _____

BECOME EVEN MORE PRODUCTIVE...

... by ordering *The AutoCAD 3D Diskette*, which allows you to enter the AutoLISP programs and drawings featured throughout the book directly into your computer.

Each floppy diskette includes the tutorial drawings featured in Chapters 1-8, plus all the macros and AutoLISP programs from *The AutoCAD 3D Library*.

Your *AutoCAD 3D Diskette* will run on any 360K IBM-standard format computer and will save hours of tedious, error-prone typing. To order your copy, please complete the form below, detach and mail the postage-paid card.

MAIL TO: Ventana Press, P.O. Box 2468, Chapel Hill, NC 27515
Or, if you'd like it even sooner, call 919/942-0220.

Yes, please send_____copies of *The AutoCAD 3D Diskette, Second Edition,* at $49.95 per diskette. Normal shipping charges $3. Add $6/diskette for UPS "two-day air." North Carolina Residents add 5% sales tax. Immediate shipment guaranteed.

Circle disk size: 5¼"   or   3½"

Name _____Co. _____

Address (no P.O. Box) _____

City _____State _____ZIP _____

Telephone _____

      Payment enclosed (check or money order; no cash please)

      Charge my: VISA/MC Acct.#

      Exp. Date _____Interbank # _____

Signature _____